OLAF TY...
SELECTED RECORDINGS 2000-2010

Selected Recordings 2000–2010

by OLAF TYARANSEN

HOT PRESS BOOKS

First published in 2010 by Hot Press Books, 13 Trinity Street, Dublin 2.
Copyright © Olaf Tyaransen 2010
The right of Olaf Tyaransen to be identified as the author of this work has been asserted by him in accordance with the Copyright, Design and Patent Act 1988.
British Library Cataloguing-in-Publication Data is available for this book.

ISBN NO: 0-9553419-4-9

Design: David Keane
Production Manager: Máirín Sheehy
Typesetting: Maeve Heslin
Studio Manager: Graham Keogh
Front & back cover photos: Mick Quinn

Printed by Colour Books, Dublin

All rights reserved. No part of this publication may be reproduced or transmitted in any form or by any means electronic or mechanical, including photocopying, recording or any information retrieval system without the prior permission of the publisher, in writing.

Olaf Paul Tyaransen was born in Dublin in 1971, but spent his formative years in Galway. This is his fifth book.

For Jack, Layla and Leigh
&
In memoriam Sebastian Horsley [1962-2010]

{MAL}CONTENTS:

011 INTRODUCTION
016 ACKNOWLEDGEMENTS
017 JOHNNY ADAIR
031 PETER BUCK
037 JOHN COOPER CLARKE
049 JP DONLEAVY
057 LARRY FLYNT
069 LADY GAGA
077 LARRY HARVEY
085 HUGH HEFNER
097 RON JEREMY
107 STEVE JONES
113 COURTNEY LOVE
125 MARTIN McDONAGH
131 SINÉAD O'CONNOR & SHANE MacGOWAN
147 CHUCK PALAHNIUK
159 DOLLY PARTON
167 JONATHAN RHYS-MYERS
175 MIKE SCOTT
187 DAMIEN RICE
201 TOMMY TIERNAN
211 U2

INTRODUCTION:

D *ia dhuit!* If you're reading these words while standing in a bookstore, then you're probably considering buying, or possibly even shoplifting, these *Selected Recordings: 2000-2010*. But why purchase – or steal – this book rather than any of those other fantastically enticing titles on display? Will it change your life, open your mind, piss off your parents, improve your social status, or get you laid?
Well, readers, all I can tell you is it definitely worked for me. To some extent...

If anybody had told me fifteen years ago that I'd still be toiling away as a journalist in the year 2010, at the no-longer-so-young age of 39, I'd have contemptuously laughed at their failure to recognise my literary genius. The masterplan was to be on my third or fourth novel by now, having also published a couple of acclaimed collections of poetry, and maybe thrown off the occasional stage play or film script along the way. Naturally, I'd also expected to be filthy rich.

So much for youthful presumptuousness. Blame drink, drugs, women, laziness, life, or whatever the hell you want, but the road took a different fork. And then repeatedly stabbed me with it. I blame my editor Niall Stokes. It's a lot easier than accepting any personal responsibility.

Seriously, there are times when my *Hot Press* gig feels less like a job, than being a serial competition winner. Once, twice or thrice a month, I get these pulse-raising phone calls: "Congratulations! You've just won a free advance copy of Muse's new album. This weekend you're flying to sunny Lisbon, all expenses paid, to see the band live in concert and meet them afterwards for a chat." (Hmmm... might I be able to wangle an extra night or two under the Portuguese moon?).

Or: "We've just couriered you a proof copy of DBC Pierre's latest novel. You're meeting him in the Groucho on Tuesday afternoon." (Better have a few quid on me for drinks. Actually, given Pierre's prodigious appetites, better make that a few hundred quid!)

Okay, the circumstances aren't always as propitious. Niall's assistant Roisin, who handles commissioning duties at *Hot Press*, can be a bit of a, well, a tyrant. I can hear her voice as I type; I'm not sure if she's acting stern or if she really would wield the whip if it came to it.

"You've got an hour with The Eagles in Chicago on Friday. It's for this issue so we need 5,000 words for Saturday lunchtime. Don't get pissed and screw it up. And don't even *think* about leaving the country without sending the Grinderman review in first!"

Yes, Roisin. Sorry, Roisin. Straightaway, Roisin. Now can I get up off my knees? Please?

Needless to say, not all of these competitions are worth winning: "We've got time backstage with Westlife in Wembley." Generally, though, the better ones come along frequently enough to keep you in the game. And, truth be told, Westlife have interesting things to say, if you know how to listen.

As you might intuit, the interviews collected between these covers are the cumulative result of those competitions I was happy to win. Very happy. It was a genuine privilege to spend time in the company of such fascinating characters as Dolly Parton, Hugh Hefner, Lady Gaga, Chuck Palahniuk, Bono and JP Donleavy. In some cases it was even a pleasure. I would've gladly met them all for free (but don't quote me on that).

There's little need for me to make any great claims for this book, mainly because it's already full of people making great claims for themselves. And justifiably so. For the most part, the interviewees featured here are genuine meritocrats: "celebrities" in the rightful sense of the word. That is, they're celebrated for their talent and their achievements rather than for having – or indeed for being – a large penis. Except for, in the former instance, hirsute porn star Ron Jeremy. And then there's the somewhat more follically challenged Johnny Adair, the exiled Loyalist paramilitary. Ahem!

A few words about interviewing. If you're looking for professional tips, I'd rather refer you to the widely acclaimed *How To Interview Celebrities* by Mr. Smug Tit. He is, after-all, an award-winning journalist. I'm just a curious guy from Galway with a digital recorder, twenty Benson & Hedges, and a bunch of questions.

The truth is that when you're meeting a celebrity – author, actor, musician or whatever – it's usually because they're selling something. If it's not a new book, movie or album, then it's just, well, themselves. The trick, if you can manage it, is to get beyond the sales pitch, and take the conversation somewhere more interesting – preferably into areas that the subject hasn't a prefabricated line on. Often an unexpected question like "when was the last time you cried/threw a punch/had a wank?" will prove revelatory. Sometimes it won't. You just can't be up to the fuckers! Or not all the time anyway…

Occasionally, the interviewee has already decided to spill the beans before meeting you. The Damien Rice interview is a good example. I'd fully expected the notoriously private musician to bat away any enquiries about his relationship with Lisa Hannigan. Instead, he opened his heart in the most extraordinary manner. Even now, it makes for riveting reading.

Painfully, one of the biggest lessons I've learnt over the years is to shut the hell up. The clock is often ticking, and much as my anecdote or opinion might entertain or enlighten my interviewee, we're not having a conversation in a bar. Actually, scratch that – we might well be having the conversation in a bar. But the interview isn't about me. Or it isn't supposed to be.

More than once in my star-crossed career, I've winced listening back to a recording that went something along these lines:

INTERVIEWEE: "Actually, I've never admitted this to anybody before, but back in the days when I really needed the cash, I worked for a time as a pros..."

ME [*interrupting*]: "Ha! That reminds me of the time when I worked in a nightclub and ... [*Two minutes of irrelevant waffle later*]... Anyway, what were you asking me?

INTERVIEWEE: "Oh... nothing."

I don't need to tell an intelligent and observant reader like you this, but – as I have to keep reminding myself – it's important not to be overly seduced. Especially by women. As Rivers Cuomo once so eloquently put it: "Goddam you half-Japanese girls – do it to me every time." Half-Japanese girls! Fortunately, I've never had to interview one. But Dolly Parton played me like a battered old fiddle.

Friendly as some people might seem, the celebrity interview is often essentially a business meeting disguised as an open and honest discussion about art or music or literature. More experienced media manipulators will sometimes have a go at convincing you that you're their new best friend. At least for the duration of the interview. I remember bumping into a famously troubled musician in the elevator of a trendy London hotel. Less than two hours earlier, he had been earnestly telling me about his suicide attempts, preferred method of drug ingestion, and bizarre sexual fetishes. When I greeted him in the mirrored confines of the lift, he shot me the disdainfully wary look of an oft-bothered rock star. His personal assistant whispered gently: "This is the guy from *Hot Press*. You were talking to him earlier." Suddenly a light flicked behind the shades, and he was full of charm. Or maybe it was something else. I didn't particularly care. The interview was in the bag.

Many of these interviews made headlines when first published. It's a feature of articles published in magazines. They'll tend to have generated headlines by the time they appear on the newsstands. Amazing how it happens. You send them in, free and innocent, with not a headline or subhead or strapline – or indeed anything else – to cloud their sweet purity. But by the time they're printed the subeditors have got to work and, hey, the whole tackle has been added. And then, before you can even say "Wow, that was a great headline you came up with" to the sub in question, something somebody said to you is being reported all over the world. Or at least in the *Evening Herald*.

You never know what's around the corner. Often it's just another corner – but sometimes it's something else entirely. Most recently, when I left Hole's Glasgow dressing room early in 2010, I suspected that Courtney Love's indiscreet confessions of a lesbian fling with supermodel Kate Moss just might be of some wider interest. Within 24 hours of the issue hitting the newsstands, the story had appeared on the front page of *The Sun*, and prominently in more than 200 other newspapers around the planet. I don't know if Hole shifted any more albums as a result, but that particular issue of *Hot Press* sold out in double quick time. How Moss felt about being so publicly celebrated as a bisexual lover is anyone's guess. Should the opportunity ever arise, I'll be sure to ask her.

Other controversies took me – and indeed everyone else – completely by surprise. The Tommy Tiernan interview happened in front of a live audience in the *Hot Press* Chatroom at the alternative Irish festival, Electric Picnic. The tent was absolutely stuffed, Tiernan was in particularly hilarious form, and everybody walked away tickled pink. Afterwards he confessed to me, "that was probably better than tonight's show is gonna be."

It wasn't until a fortnight later, when a prominent Sunday broadsheet ran the front page headline, *'Comedian's Startling Attack on Jews'*, that the excrement hit the revolving metal blades (the interview had been filmed and uploaded to the Net). Tiernan is one of the great Irish comedians, smart, funny, highly caffeinated, and utterly irreverent. He should be an international star, and may well be soon. But the way the media lit on it, this interview did his cause no good at all. His holocaust rant was admittedly 'tasteless', but in the context of all that he'd said before, it would've rather defeated the point if it had been otherwise. He was satirising the attitudes of people who slip into anti-Semitic mode at the drop of a Nazi military hat. But, in terms of the language he used, he took absolutely no prisoners and, as ever, if there is a possibility of feeble-minded people misinterpreting something, the iron law is that they will.

The whole debacle ultimately resulted in him having his American and Canadian tours cancelled. The fact that his inflammatory quote was reported as something he'd said in an *interview* implied that he was stating a personal opinion, when quite clearly he wasn't. In truth, our conversation was more of an unscripted comedic performance (with me, on occasion at least, as the fall guy) and – as it appears in these pages – should most definitely be read as such.

People are always asking me who's the most interesting person I've ever interviewed. It's a tough one to answer, and hopefully the reason why will be obvious from this book. It's impossible to compare Larry Flynt's account of the day he was shot, with Peter Buck's version of his infamous 'air-rage' incident. Or Lady Gaga's recollections of the chaos of 9/11, with former Sex Pistol Steve Jones's memories of his struggle with heroin addiction. They're all equally interesting in their own different ways. Nobody within these pages will bore you. If they do, trust me, it's entirely your own fault.

The interviews are arranged alphabetically, but can be approached in any random order you choose. If you want to laugh, head straight for my encounter with the motor-mouthed, attention-seeking Ron Jeremy. If you want to cry, try stealing this book: if you've read this far while still standing in the bookstore, the security guards are definitely watching you. It's entirely your call. I'll probably get my royalties either way.

Unlike my last collection, *Palace of Wisdom*, which focused on themes of decadence, substance abuse and general excess, there's no unifying subject this time round. These 20 interviews, in all their diversity, are basically offered as entertainment, plain and simple. Though you'll hopefully learn a few things, too. I most certainly did.

One thing's for sure: if ever I do get around to writing those novels, I won't be short of material. *Ha det!*
Olaf Tyaransen

{GALWAY, OCTOBER 2010}

SELECTED RECORDINGS: 2000-2010

ACKNOWLEDGEMENTS

As always, there are numerous people to thank. I'm particularly grateful to all at *Hot Press* magazine, under whose auspices this book was written, most especially its editor Niall Stokes. I've been trying to leave for the last decade or so, but he keeps those damned competition prizes rolling in...

Big thanks are also due to Mairin Sheehy, Stuart Clark, Roisin Dwyer, Jackie Hayden, Duan Stokes, Graham Keogh, David Keane, Mark Hogan, Maeve Heslin, Brett Walker, and all the crew.

The following individuals have all aided and abetted along the way (sometimes unknowingly): My parents Olaf and Margaret Tyaransen, my sisters Emma, Kate, Jennifer and Naomi Tyaransen, Leigh McCann, Jack and Moya McCann, Frank Ryder, Sharon Walsh, Dara Foley, Pat Ingoldsby, Niall Stanage, Jessie Lendennie, Mick Quinn, Eileen Hughes, Dan Oggly, BP Fallon, Brian Boyd, Peter Matthews, Liam Mackey, Cathal Dawson, Dave Diebold, Kevin Herraty, Des Free, Pi, Tony Fraher, Dara Lambe, Alanna Gallagher, Vinnie Browne, Barry McCann, Tory Irvine, Eoin McCann, Cian McNamara, Ian O'Doherty, Delia Clarke, Marty Mulligan, Naoise Nunn, Kieran Gorman, Graham Knuttel, Tom Mathews, Maurice and Andrea Culligan, Hazel Hendy, Justin McCarthy, Mark Kennedy, Peter Finlay, Kevin Whelan, Geoff Canavan, Howard Marks, Liam Coade, Aoife Nic Fhearghusa, Aiden Lambert, Paul Butler, Anthony O'Keeffe, Elaine Battle, Andrew Meehan, Seamus Sheridan, Gerry Flynn, Keith Newman, Greg Flanagan, Johnny Ferguson, Derry McGloughlin, Natasha Lohan, Michelle Mearns, Mette Borgstrom, Sheila Convery, Liz Headon, Irvine Welsh, Jason O'Toole, Kevin Healy, Paul Cotter, Cian Campbell, John Donnellan and, last but certainly not least, Conor 'Monty' Montague.

Even if that seems a lot, I guarantee I've forgotten somebody important. So extra special thanks to them.

CHAPTER ONE:
Johnny Adair

Johnny Adair is waiting for *Hot Press* in the Arrivals Hall of Glasgow Airport. There's no need for him to hold up a sign: from countless news bulletins and press shots, I already know what the infamous former UDA brigadier looks like.

Given his own serious security concerns, there's a good chance that he already knows what I look like too. Okay, maybe not. But these are the paranoid thoughts that run through your mind when you're meeting a man allegedly responsible for 43 deaths and nicknamed 'Mad Dog'...

It's 10am on a wet Monday morning, and he's the only person waiting. Short but well-built, he's wearing a military jacket and baseball cap, and looking twitchy and uncomfortable (or is that just me?). He shakes hands with myself and photographer Graham Keogh, and quickly escorts us to the exit.

"We'll drive to Troon and do the interview there," he says. There's a silver Vauxhall parked outside. Adair recently lost his license – for drink-driving - so his trusted lieutenant Ian Truesdale is sitting behind the wheel. Balding and craggy-faced, I reckon he's in his late 40s or early 50s.

Back in the bad old days in Belfast, Truesdale ran a taxi firm. The RUC used to call it 'Murder Cabs', because so many of its cars were 'hijacked' for UDA hits. Mad Dog once infamously joked that the only Catholics who travelled in Truesdale's cabs were "dead ones".

Like his former leader, Truesdale can't go back to Belfast. He's recently been released from a UK prison for selling heroin and crack with Adair's 22-year-old son Jonathan (aka Mad Pup) Adair. In 2003, Truesdale was charged with killing his daughter's fiancé in a UDA feud. His own brother gave evidence against him, but the charges were ultimately dropped. He currently lives in Bolton, but plans to join Adair in Scotland when his prison license expires.

Mad Dog sits in the front, sparks up a menthol cigarette, and commands, "Let's go!"

As the car pulls off it occurs to me that Special Branch probably now know what I look like as well. I ask is Adair currently under surveillance?

"I dunno, but I could well be," he answers in his thick Belfast brogue. "If I am, it's a total fuckin' waste of their time, and taxpayers' money, because I'm not doing anything these days. Nathin'! If they're watching me, they'll know that. I found some hidden surveillance cameras outside my old house in Bolton a while back, but I don't know if they're watching me up here.

"Back in Belfast, I was watched 24-hours-a-day. I'd say Johnny Adair was the most watched person in Northern Ireland. They must have spent hundreds of thousands of pounds watching me." He blows out a stream of smoke. "Maybe even a million."

The seaside town of Troon is about an hour's drive from Glasgow and, throughout the journey, Adair bombards me with questions. Where did I get a name like Olaf? Where do I live? Who's the most famous person I've ever interviewed? Have I met Bono? What was he like? Is he a bit of a dickhead or is he alright?

Truesdale wants to know if I've ever met Bob Geldof. "*Tell me why I don't like Mon-days*," he sings, badly, tapping an irregular rhythm on the steering wheel. "I fuckin' loved that one!"

Have I ever met Oasis? I say that I've met Liam. What was he like? Where did I meet him? Was he a mad fucker? Was he snorting Charlie?

Adair turns to Truesdale. "I actually had a dream about me and the lads from Oasis the other night. Mad, it was."

He turns back to me. Where have I travelled to? Do *Hot Press* pay for my flights? What countries have I lived in? "Thailand? What was that like? I've heard it's mad!"

We've both been to Jamaica. Adair loved it. Then again, he was just out of prison. I tell him that I wasn't too keen on the way they always tried to keep you within the tourist compounds, totally segregated from the local population.

"Ah yeah, but fuck that shite!" he says. "I went out and met all the Jamaican lads. I know they've a rep for hating white people but, one thing I've found is that, wherever you go, everybody always loves the Irish. They love us!"

It's something of an Ali-G moment. "Em ... but I thought you were British, Johnny."

He bursts out laughing. "I am! I am! But I'm Northern Irish too! Ach, you know what I mean, like. Ha, ha! Johnny Adair saying he's Irish? Fuck off!"

Once upon a troubled time, Johnny Adair was one of the most wanted men in Belfast. Nowadays, he's probably the least wanted.

The IRA are reputedly out of the revenge business, but his former UDA comrades have vowed to kill him should he ever return. In turn, Adair has vowed to come back (and indeed, made a fleeting secret visit there for a documentary about a year ago). But for the moment he's exiled in Scotland, like a character in a Shakespearean drama.

He lived in Bolton with his wife Gina immediately after his release, but they split violently when he discovered she had taken a young lover. Mad Dog now lives in Troon with his son.

"I like it here in Troon," he tells me. "The people here warm to me and respect me. It's 70 percent Prod here. It used to be famous for its golf courses. Now it's famous for golf – and Johnny Adair!"

Why not go somewhere warmer? Like Jamaica?

"The reason why I came to Scotland is because it's not a million miles away from home, and I feel at home when I'm here. Scotland is just like home back home, minus the bullyboys and thugs."

There's something uncharmingly oblivious about him. The bullyboys and thugs on the streets of Belfast were mostly his friends and comrades – at least in the Protestant areas. Besides, not everybody in Troon has warmed to him. In Belfast, he had problems with republicans. Here, it's with publicans. He's been barred from almost every bar in town.

"Not because of anything I did," he explains. "The cops brought my photo into every pub and told them to bar me. But there's one place that still serves me."

We find a restaurant, cheap and cheerful looking. The waitress obligingly turns down the music to facilitate the recording of the interview. Graham and Truesdale sit at the adjoining table. Adair orders a steak and a shandy. He removes his jacket, revealing heavily tattooed arms, and his cap, revealing a shaven head. His arms are strong, but not quite as beefy looking as they were when he was taking steroids and flexing his pecs on the evening news.

The tattoos are amateurish, mostly done in green ink... Mickey Mouse, 'UFF', 'Gina Forever', 'Mum & Dad', etc. Were they done in prison?

"Ach, these are all just silly wee tattoos that I got done when I was 13 or 14," he explains. "The age of consent for tattoos was 18, so there was a tattooist in Coleraine who used to do underage tattoos for kids of 13 and 14, and we thought it was a macho thing to do. They're all pathetic. I'll have to get them covered."

We're meeting to talk about his autobiography, *Mad Dog*. Although the book came out six weeks ago, this is only his second interview with a journalist from the Republic (the *Sunday Tribune*'s Suzanne Breen met him – in exactly the same circumstances and location – a few weeks back).

He wishes he'd done more. He was supposed to do *The Late Late Show*, and they insisted on a press embargo before cancelling him – twice.

He's not happy with them. It's caused him a lot of unnecessary hassle. "For me to get over there to Dublin, it had to be a whole military operation. With hired cars and safe houses and minders. So we organised all that, and then they pulled the plug. Then they raised it again so we put a new plan in place – and then they pulled it again. So fuck them! They shouldn't have fucking asked me to do something, and then pulled the plug at the last minute."

Even so, he'd be happy to do it if they asked him again. After all, he has a book to sell. Ghost written by journalist Graham McKendry, you could argue that *Mad Dog* has more holes in it than Troon's golf courses. In fairness, this is out of legal necessity. As commander of the UDA's C-Company, Adair was allegedly responsible for the murders of 43 Catholics. Needless to say, he doesn't admit to one of them anywhere in the book's 257 pages. Claiming credit whilst denying responsibility is a tough one to pull off. *Mad Dog* doesn't quite do it.

Adair was born and raised on the Shankill Road. He was fighting Catholics on the streets from his early teens. As he grew older, he graduated to a higher level of confrontation. Eventually, he was sentenced to 16 years for directing terrorism. Shortly after he got out of prison, he was run out of town. *C'est tout*!

What prompted you to write this book?

"Well, the main reason being that there's been a number of books written about me, but not by me. By ex-lovers, retired police officers, or whoever. And indeed many books written about the past conflict in Northern Ireland have featured me prominently in them. So obviously people were exploiting my name and, in doing so, making money at my expense.

"I've been pestered for years by publishers to do my own autobiography and I always declined, but since I'm now living a normal life, and there's peace in Northern Ireland, and the fact that people have continued to exploit my name, I thought, 'Why not write my own book in my own words?' You know, a book by me and in my own words, and not other people's half-lies and truths, which has happened in the past."

But your own book is full of half-truths!

He shrugs: "This is my autobiography, which is as close to the truth as I legally can go. Although it's a rather watered-down version of my life, I think it's a good-enough book. Most of the people that has read it have said that it's a good read. I'm happy with it. It's my words and people can judge for themselves."

Is there not a law against people like you making money from their criminal pasts?

He smirks: "Well, they're trying to bring in a law to prevent people like myself making money from their memoirs. But obviously it hasn't come in yet."

It's rumoured he received £100,000 from John Blake Publishers. What kind of advance did you get?

"I don't really wanna talk about that. That's personal. That's private. Do you know what I mean? I don't think it's the right thing for me to do – to discuss my finances with journalists."

Is your new life a bit of a comedown?

"Financially? Well, first, I was never a rich person. Had I wanted to be rich back home, I could've been. But money was never my motivation. Military was. And when you look back at some of the loyalist paramilitary leaders – or so-called leaders – they're all rich people because they were money-motivated. Johnny Adair was never money-motivated. Johnny Adair spent his time on the battlefield, directing the activities of his company against the enemies of Ulster."

He tells me that he was always a natural born leader, even when he was a kid. "I was always a person that stood out. I was always charismatic. I was always up for a laugh and humorous. I was always diving in at the deep end."

As a teenager, he was a proud skinhead, and fronted a four-piece band called Offensive Weapon. However, although he was a card-carrying member of the National Front, he insists he was never a racist.

"I became a skinhead and got involved in everything that surrounded that. The politics of it was National Front, but it meant nothing to me. There was no blacks in Belfast at that time so, because the National Front weren't into the IRA, it was just another way of me attacking the IRA, through the skinhead movement.

"We formed a four-piece punk band. We mainly played Skrewdriver covers, but we had a few original songs like 'Gestapo RUC' and 'We Killed Your Kid With A

Plastic Bullet'. Hundreds of skinheads used to come to hear us play. We were totally crap but it was always a buzz playing gigs. It made us feel important and popular. We loved it, while it lasted."

Who are you listening to these days?

"I'm not really into music these days, but I was passionate about it years ago. I used to always read *Hot Press*, back when it was like a newspaper. Nowadays I'd buy the odd Snow Patrol or Oasis album, but I'm not as passionate about music now."

His relationship with the music industry has been fraught. Legend has it that Tina Turner's record company got in touch back in the 1990s to ask him would he please stop using her song 'Simply The Best' to advertise his murderous brigade.

He laughs as he tells the story. "What used to happen when UFF C-Company did a show of strength – that means hooded men coming out reading statements – before they'd come out, we'd have a function. And prior to them coming out, we'd blast Tina Turner's 'Simply The Best' for about a minute-and-a-half, and the next thing the hooded men would come out and the crowd would just be in uproar.

"So the music industry must have heard about this, because somebody from Tina Turner's record company rang our offices – which at that time was the UDP offices on the Shankill – and asked would C-Company, and especially that man Mad Dog Adair, kindly refrain from using Tina's song as their anthem for displaying guns and what have you. Ha, ha!"

It wasn't just the music industry that wasn't happy to be associated with Adair. Clothing companies would almost pay him not to endorse their products.

"Nike phoned up one time," he recalls. "Because I was always in the public domain and after training I'd have been wearing my Nike training gear. And again they phoned up the UDP offices and asked would Mad Dog Adair stop wearing their clothes. I said, 'Fuck 'em – phone them back and tell them they should be paying me for wearing them!'

"But even now, if I wear anything, it has an effect. I like the Replay brand of clothes. And when I'm doing interviews and getting photos taken, sometimes I'll be wearing Replay. And in that documentary I did, I'm wearing Replay too. And the guy who owns the Replay shop in Belfast was saying to a pal of mine, 'Fuck's sake! The documentary was good and bad for us. After the documentary, most of the Prods are coming in and they're buying Replay. But the Catholics won't come in and buy the stuff because that bastard Johnny Adair wears them!' It's funny.

"But that's just the way Belfast is – it's sick, it's stupid and crazy, where people think, 'Johnny Mad Dog Adair wears Replay', and the Catholics go, 'fuck – I'm not wearing that so!' But the Prods go, 'I'm wearing it because Johnny's wearing it!'"

Does he have any regrets about the way his life has turned out?

"Well, to be honest, I regret the fact that a conflict ever took place, and I regret the fact that it lasted for 29 years and almost 4,000 people lost their lives. But it did happen. It was a conflict. It's just a pity that Mr. Adams and Mr. Paisley didn't do what they're about to do now in 1969. Had they done that, there wouldn't have been all the blood and guts spilt everywhere.

"But for me to say I regret stuff ... To be honest with you, I was over 21, I knew what I was doing and I took the oath – I swore an oath to the organisation – and for me to sit here now and say I regret it would make me a hypocrite. I regret the fact that my own people – my old so-called friends and comrades – put me out, and it wasn't the IRA that put me out. Well, they didn't actually put me out – I was in prison – but they put me family out. I hate the fact that my own people, that I would've died for, actually backstabbed me for 30 pieces of silver."

Are you not worried that they'll send someone to kill you now?

"I never did worry," he shrugs. "I never worried about the IRA. And the IRA was the most dedicated and ruthless fucking guerrilla organisation in the world. There's no doubt about that. I didn't fear anybody. At one time I was top of their hit list, and I didn't fear them. I never ran to Scotland or England or some other part of the world because they tried to kill me. I never feared death then, and I don't fear it now.

"I live normally now, but obviously when I lived in Belfast, I had to wear body armour, I had to have minders, and I had to live in a virtual fortress because the IRA was constantly targeting me. But here – the IRA aren't gonna target me. And the loyalist paramilitaries who say they're gonna kill me, I don't believe they're gonna come here and try. So I don't feel that I have to live in fear."

It's been four years since he was forced to leave Belfast. He's still confident that he'll be able to return someday. Indeed, his autobiography ends with the Terminator-esque line, "Make no mistake: I will be back."

There have been 15 attempts on his life over the years, and he's somehow survived them all. He proudly shows me the scar from a bullet in the back of his head. In April, 1999, he was on overnight release from the Maze Prison, and went to a UB40 concert. Someone shot him at point blank range. Amazingly, he lived.

"I believe in God, but I don't practice it," he says. "The reason I believe that there is a God is because of the person I've been and the many times I've been saved. And the things that have happened in my life. People say that God works in mysterious ways. I believe you can be lucky once or twice, but I've survived 15 attempts on my life – and that's just publicly, the ones that we know of, there could have been more. I've survived every one of them. Shot at point blank range to my head, and I survived."

What do you think you've done to deserve that?

"To deserve getting shot?"

No, to deserve surviving getting shot.

"Well, my time's not up," he shrugs. "Maybe I'm here for a reason. Maybe He's got something for me to do."

Time for the yawnsome million dollar question – has Johnny Adair ever pulled the trigger on someone himself?

"Well, ask a silly question, you'll get a silly answer," he smiles. "Have I ever killed anyone? No. I have been arrested and questioned at length back home in Northern Ireland about countless murders. Obviously there was no evidence and obviously I denied them. So for you to sit and ask me... there was never any evidence."

How did you wind up commanding C-Company then? Surely you can't lead killers without being one yourself?

"I was directing terrorism."

Surely that means you were killing people?

"No, I was directing my men at terrorists – going after terrorists and chasing them."

And then killing them?

"No, chasing them. Nine times out of 10 you couldn't get into these IRA men's houses because they'd got steel grills."

Did you ever kill any of them personally?

"No, I didn't kill anybody."

Did your men kill them?

"Well, I never sent anyone to kill anyone."

So what do you mean by directing terrorism?

"I just meant doing what the British Army and American soldiers are doing now in Iraq. Defending and protecting the community and the people from the enemies of Ulster."

He seems proud of his achievements as a leader. "I adopted the tactics of the IRA. Taking over houses. Getting sophisticated weaponry like AK47s. They were Northern Irish people with the same education as us. They weren't smarter than us. The only difference was what it said on our birth certs. Theirs said 'RC', ours said 'Presbyterian'. But I done what they were doing to us – and it worked."

Have you ever read Sun Tzu's *The Art of War*?

He looks at me blankly. "No, I just learned from the street."

But, to clarify, you haven't ever killed anyone?

"No!"

Yet you're posing with a gun on the cover of your book ...

"It's only a replica," he laughs. "I'll decommission it if you want."

He's been interrogated many times before, by interviewers far tougher than me. "The toughest ones would have been in the early days in Castlereagh when I was about 18. They would've physically assaulted me. Nathin' serious – a slap on the mouth, hair pulled, shook with a chair, and yelled and bawled at. But in more recent times, once I became toughened from the place, it was just easy. Mickey Mouse! Cops would try and be aggressive and I'd go, 'Fuck off, you dickhead, I'm not speaking to you!' And I'd embarrass them."

You mentioned Iraq earlier. Do you agree with the invasion?

"Ah, it's crazy, it's just gone too far. It's probably a mirror image of what happened back home in Belfast in 1969, when the soldiers came in. They thought they were there for a short time and 29 years later they were still there. And thousands of people were killed. Obviously Iraq is on a far greater scale. Just recently there was 140 people killed in one day. That's pathetic and it's sad – and it'll continue to go on. I don't know what the solution is. Pull out or stay on another five, 10, 15, 20 years. Could be a million people dead. I don't know. It's politics – and it's up to the politicians to sort it out."

We both go outside for a smoke, not really saying much, like prizefighters taking a break between rounds. He mentions that he's happy enough with the way the interview is going. I don't know if this is a good thing or a bad thing. Five minutes later, we're back sitting at the table.

Recently it was reported that you'd travelled over to Uganda to help build an orphanage that's going to be named after C-Company. What's the story there?

"This German guy, Nick, had written a book and he got paid €40,000 for the rights to it by some TV company in Germany. And he promised that he would build an orphanage for underprivileged children in Uganda, and he said he would name it after C-Company."

He's a Neo-Nazi, isn't he?

"No, he's reformed. He's a one-time Neo-Nazi. He was what he was and then obviously he realised that what he was doing was wrong. And what he's done is he's married a black girl out there.

"It's good that people like him who was what he was – at one time he was a Neo-Nazi and against blacks, and now he's out there helping the poor. They're all blacks, and he's paying for them to have a better future and a better education."

Such philanthropic activities might seem a little at odds with Adair's public image, but he sees himself as something of a Robin Hood figure.

"Well, I was a good man to my own community," he shrugs. "I gave money to old dolls and poor families and the handicapped and stuff. That's why I got support and respect."

Is it true that you were making that money from selling Class-A drugs to the local kids?

He scowls darkly at the suggestion. "I've never been arrested for drugs in my life, never had my home searched for drugs in my life in all my time and all my career as a paramilitary directing terrorism. However, there's been countless stories written about me that I was a drug dealer. I never took drugs."

You took steroids...

"Did I take steroids? Yes, I did. But nathin' else."

What about ecstasy?

"I took ecstasy in the early '90s, but have I taken drugs since that? No, absolutely not. I took steroids when I was bodybuilding, but the only drug I ever took was ecstasy in the early '90s, when it was a big thing."

What about acid?

"I took acid, but that's what actually put me off drugs because I'd a bad trip. And that was actually in the Maze. I took a microdot, and I had all these posters of Cindy Crawford in my cell, and I thought she was attacking me. I was fuckin' fightin' Cindy Crawford going 'Fuck off!' Ha, ha! So that put me off acid."

In fairness, you must have a lot of demons.

"If you're talking about demons and asking has your past ever caught up on ye, I've never ever had a sleepless night. I've had the odd bad dream, but not about anything like that. Not about anything that I've... not about anything that you might think I've done that was wrong and cruel. Never. But that might be because I believed in what I was doing. If you accept in your heart and your head what you're doing, and you believe in it, well, then, it's not like you're going out to rob an old doll or going out to rape someone. That's wrong. But if you feel that you're a soldier and you're doing the actions of a soldier, it won't affect you mentally."

Your former lover Jackie 'Legs' Robinson's book *In Love With A Mad Dog* is full of stories about wild drug parties that you and your men used to throw...

"She's a fucking header, that girl!" he guffaws. "Jackie was a lunatic. Jackie was a fatal attraction. I shagged her a couple of times, that was it. All of this shit about going out with me for nine years and mad parties in her house, she's a liar. She's just a total liar. A maniac, who could never get her way. But don't get me wrong. She did fall in love with me. But I was with my wife and kids. And she felt that because she fell in love with me that I had to love her. I never loved her. She was just another groupie."

Does Johnny Adair get a lot of groupies?

"I've shagged over 1,000 women in my whole life, and I'm only 43. And that's a fact. Isn't it, Ian?"

Sitting across the table, Truesdale agrees. "I could tell you some stories about Johnny," he laughs. "Oh Johnny and the women…"

Have you shagged many Catholic women?

"I have indeed," Adair beams.

Was that not sleeping with the enemy?

"Ach, but the war's over. I actually slept with the enemy during the conflict – some of my enemy's wives. And that's where a lot of the information would have come from. But we don't wanna go down that road."

Ach, we do…

"No. I don't want to get somebody in trouble. But I've shagged a lot of women."

This may well be true. However, fellow loyalist terrorist Michael Stone calls Adair "the pink paramilitary" and alleges he's actually having a homosexual affair with former C-Company volunteer Skelly McCrory (who also lives in Scotland).

There's no easy way to put this to Mad Dog. So I just say it out straight: "Michael Stone reckons you're gay as Christmas …"

Adair laughs loudly. "Stoner? Ha! Let me tell you about him. He was my hero, obviously, and when I got locked up I got to know his personality. Stoner thought he was better than everybody. He thought he was the only loyalist prisoner worth anything. There was better men than him there! And he condemned a comrade of mine, who was in for a minor offence – he was only doing five years. But this guy had done the business umpteen times. Unknown to Michael Stone, but I knew. And Stone thought that because he was only serving five years for a minor offence that he was a prick.

"He tried to humiliate the guy, so I got Stone in the yard and I walked him around and said, 'Michael, see that guy there. He may be only in for five years. But if what he's done had been caught on camera, it'd make you look like a fucking tea-boy! The only reason you looked so good, Michael, is because it was caught on camera.' [Stone carried out an infamous attack on an IRA funeral – OT].

"No disrespect. He admitted six murders – he done three of them in the graveyard, but the other three he didn't. I dunno what that was all about."

You're still not answering the question, Johnny. Are you gay?

"Look, me and him were still pals when I got out of the Maze in 2000. Obviously there's Johnny Adair groupies and people who want to shag me just because I'm Johnny Adair. And there was this wee pole dancer. She didn't go out with Stone or nathin', but I shagged her a couple of times. And then a couple of months after me sleeping with her, she fell for Stoner and they became partners. So she told him she'd slept with Johnny Adair. And he's a jealous person so obviously that hurt him.

"He was so jealous that I'd slept with the wee girl that he came up with this story that Johnny Adair was gay to ruin my credibility. That's where all that shit came from."

What about all that time you spent in jail with no female company?

"We did have women!" he insists. "We had anything in that jail. I had girls coming up to visit all the time. One girl in particular, a good big girl – Big Lily. She'd come in wearing a big coat, and look like she was fully dressed, but once I'd get her in the cubicle she'd open it and she'd only have suspenders on. We used to shag every visit. We used to have box cubicles that the screws couldn't actually see into. So we had proper sex, took our clothes off and all. It wasn't just quick sex."

So you've never had a gay experience?

"Well, Skelly was gay, my best friend, and that was no big secret that he was gay. But because he's my best friend, Stoner said we were lovers."

And, just to set the record straight, you're saying that you're not?

"No, no, no, no."

Truesdale vouches for him across the table. "I've known Johnny for 30 years and there's no way he's gay. No way!"

Mad Dog looks a little flustered now: "I don't really want to say this on tape because I don't want people thinking I'm big-headed, but anybody close to me will tell you that there's no one individual – outside a porn star – that has shagged as many women as me."

The late David Ervine said that when he went into jail, he chose to spend his time learning Irish rather than engage in the usual loyalist prisoner antics – basically, taking drugs and shagging the arses off each other.

"We weren't shagging each other!" he insists "Well, he's right to an extent. They weren't like the republicans. The republicans educated themselves. Once you're in jail, you can choose to educate yourself mentally or physically. I chose physically. I went in there 10-and-a-half stone and came out 13-and-a-half stone of solid muscle after four or five years. But a lot of the loyalists took drugs, had parties and spent their time just having fun. The way I looked at it, these were guys who gave up their freedom for a fucking cause. So they're stuck in jail, and maybe some of them are losing their wives or their girlfriends. So, so what? If they wanna have a ball, let them have a ball.

"When I was in charge in the Maze, I just let them do what they wanted to do. Though, I'd draw the line if things got out of hand."

He was still considered a leader in prison, influential enough for the government to talk to him. He tells me he met Mo Mowlam twice. "She was just like one of the lads, we respected her."

Amazingly, despite the fact that Belfast's a relatively small city, Adair has never actually laid eyes on Gerry Adams. "I've never seen him," he admits. "But I targeted him a few times, like."

A few years back, Gerry Adams told me that he'd been "blessed with very bad assassins."

Adair looks a bit miffed at this: "Well, the UFF tried to kill him in 1983. They failed, but fair play to them for trying. And then C-Company attacked his house in the early '90s. And he wasn't there. But we still got to where he lived."

He tells me that a lot of work used to go into targeting someone of Adam's stature. "There'd be weeks and weeks of careful planning, gathering information, following, watching. Sometimes it would take months.

"The men are only as good as their leader and the leader's only as good as his men. If I'd become weak then they'd have become weak. I was a great leader."

And behind every great man there's a great woman.

"Gina was a good woman, absolutely. But obviously we're not together now. We've split and there's another man involved [Wayne Dowie, a former associate of Adair's] and that's why I ended up leaving her. She was a good woman. I was with her for 25 years, and had four lovely kids with her. But obviously I was not a one-woman man and she wasn't a one-man woman either. You couldn't blame her, because of what I'd been doing and how many times I'd been caught. And it was never-ending with me because of who I was. Just groupie after groupie after groupie. You couldn't hide them all."

Did you ever catch an STD?

"I've never caught a sexual disease in my life, and I've shagged over a thousand women. Never in my life."

Ah come on, Johnny! You must have! I've only shagged about 800 and I've caught everything going!

He looks blankly for a moment and then bursts out laughing when he realises I'm winding him up. "Ha, ha! No, seriously, I've never caught anything. Even when I was a teenager, I always had more girls than anyone else."

What age were you when you lost your virginity?

"Fuck, about 15 or 16. Even from them early years, because I was always the centre of attention, girls were always throwing themselves at me. Right up until the present time now. More so now."

Do you have a girlfriend at the moment?

"Fuck, about twenty. I had a semi-relationship there, but I'm not seeing her now, so I'm young, free and single. Or old, free and single. Ha, ha! No, I just shag all around. That's what my life's about – just shagging. Isn't it, Ian?"

"Oh aye," Truesdale nods enthusiastically.

"I went to Africa last week for seven days," Adair continues, "and in those seven days, I shagged eight women. Eight black girls, and they were all beautiful. They were all honeys. People can't believe it, but, you see, when you have charisma ... [snaps fingers]."

Did you use protection?

"Oh, every time. Oh fuck! Over there? Absolutely! But they took me to a rugby game on the Saturday afternoon and I just... [snaps fingers]. You see, if you have it ... [snaps fingers]! We were just standing there and these two birds were beside us. I turned around to them. Within two minutes, I was away with the two girls. Fuck the rugby match!"

For some reason, all this talk of rampant sex brings Kevin Myers to mind. I ask has he read Myers' book [*Watching the Door*] about his own time reporting on the conflict.

"Ach, I don't really read books," he says. "I've never heard of him."

Well, Myers' book reflected a little on the connection between sex and death in Northern Ireland ...

"I dunno about that," he shrugs. "I hate death, but I love fucking sex. So that's my opinion of it."

According to Adair's own book, there was a lot of collusion between the security forces and C-Company. Does he think there could have been collusion in the 1974 Dublin bombings?

"I wouldn't have been aware at that time. I was only a kid then."

But would you be surprised if you heard that there was?

"I can't comment on that, because I don't know the facts surrounding it. But what I do know is, was there collusion in certain murders in Belfast? Well, take, for instance, Pat Finucane. To date, five of the people involved have been publicly named as agents and also by the UDA. So was it happening? Of course it was. Did I have friendly police officers sympathising with me, let's say? Yes, there was. So I wouldn't be surprised if there had been collusion in 1974. But that's war for you. It was a dirty war."

And dirty wars call for dirty deeds. In all sorts of ways. A few years back, Adair's son was shot in the legs in Belfast for alleged drug-dealing. Rumour has it that it was done on his father's orders.

Is it true that you had Jonathan shot?

"Absolutely not!"

Well, that was the word on the street ...

He looks annoyed now: "Where's the proof of that? You're a journalist, right? And many journalists has writ this, right? I'm saying to you, I didn't. And I'm sure if you asked my son, he'll tell you what he told the police."

What did he tell the police?

"The story goes that he was shot by hooded men or something. They pulled him in and he got shot."

Did you not find the guys who'd shot him?

"I made enquiries as to find out who done it and why they done it. But I couldn't really get to the bottom of it."

But I thought you ruled the streets. Surely you could've found out?

Mad Dog glares at me. Gulp!

So it wasn't that you wanted to demonstrate to your volunteers that even your own son wasn't immune to your law.

"No."

You know, it's very strange interviewing you, Johnny, because we both know that you're playing around with the truth a lot.

"If you ask me a question, I'll give you an answer," he says. "If you don't like my answer, there's nathin' I can do about that. I'm not gonna lie, I'm not gonna turn and around and say …"

Well, I just don't believe a lot of what you're telling me!

"Well, if you don't believe it then you just have to write that. I'm trying to be as honest as possible."

What's the worst thing that's ever been written about you?

"I don't like the fact that they called me a tout. Two things I most definitely amn't – one is gay and the second one is a tout. They called me a tout in the *Sunday World*."

And Jackie called you a tout in her book.

"She called me a tout?"

Well, she hinted at it, saying that she felt that sometimes you protested about them a little too much …

Now, he's really pissed: "I hated touts. One thing, hand on my heart, they tried to put me under pressure, they tried to put people around me under pressure, but I'd never take 30 pieces of silver. Never. I was always rooting touts out. I hated them. They were my biggest enemy – the threat from within."

He's not called Mad Dog for no reason. It's said that you have an explosive temper...

"I would have, but you'd have to have one to be a leader. You can't be a softie. You have to have balls and brains. It's no use having balls and no brains, and it's no use having brains and no balls. It won't work. You have to have both. I'd both. I wasn't scared to get involved directly. And I've got brains. Do you understand what I mean?"

I thought you weren't involved directly?

"I was involved directly... in the past... directing terrorism. I'm saying I was directly involved in military operations. That's not saying I killed anybody."

When's the last time you threw a punch?

He looks over at Truesdale and grins. "Bolton – Fat Bollix. About a year-and-a-half ago."

Who's Fat Bollix?

"Ach, just some bastard."

Not your wife, then?

"What?"

You got done for assaulting Gina in Bolton, didn't you?

"Oh sorry, yeah. Well, that wasn't a punch. That was a scuffle. She attacked me and obviously I defended myself."

Did you have that kind of relationship over the years?

"Ach, Gina was like myself. She's a tough nut – a tough, tough woman. She was taunting me about this other guy. And obviously I didn't bite, because it was something that I suspected but I couldn't prove. And she was drunk and I was drunk. And when she saw I wasn't biting, she just laid into me. And I was the one that was assaulted, I was the one that had marks. There wasn't a mark on Gina. And because of who I was…"

I thought her hair had been pulled out of her head?

"No!"

It was in your book!

"It was not in my book [actually, checking later, his book says that the arresting officers made that claim – OT]. She didn't have her hair pulled out. That was written in the media. The police came. I was drunk, Gina was drunk. Boom! The police automatically arrested me, took me, and charged me with assault. There was eight lacerations and scrapes and scratches all around my face. There wasn't one on Gina. All this stuff about me dragging her up a fucking park and kicking the fuck out of her, all that's nonsense. She'll tell you herself. But because of who I was, I couldn't stand up in court and say, 'Here – this is wrong, it was Gina!'"

Do you hope to live to an old age, Johnny?

"If I thought about that, it would worry me. It would probably frighten me. But I can't think like that. I just think, well, I'm alive now, I'm 43 and I look good for it and I feel good for it, and I'm still shagging 17-, 18- and 19-year-old wee girls. So not bad for a man of 43. I don't have a double chin, I don't have a big fat belly, I'm fit for my age. I can go four or five hours in bed with a wee girl of 20. So I put most of the fucking ones my age to shame. I just have a ball. Live life to the full. And keep those 20-year-olds coming! Ha, ha!"

Time's up, thank be to fuck. The waitress brings over the bill, and Adair insists on paying. He's reported to be living on the dole at the moment. He tells me that he's actually living on his wits (later we'll pay Truesdale £100 for his taxi services, and he'll give us a handwritten receipt for 'security').

Graham needs to take some shots. He suggests the seafront. We all troop out to the Vauxhall and Truesdale drives us round to the prom. It's a wet, foggy, miserable day.

Adair is extremely comfortable in front of the camera, and already knows all his best angles. "Ach, I've been doing this for years," he laughs, as Graham directs him. "From the early '90s, I was doing this kind of shite everyday. I'm well used to it."

We walk down onto the rocky beach, getting soaked in the process. Watching him proudly pose, it strikes me that Johnny Adair's really a bit of a dinosaur. The war's over and he's certainly not needed anymore. He's an anachronism, a foot soldier well past his date of usefulness.

Does he realise this? Probably not. As he stands on the rocks in front of the dark, frothing sea, I ask him to hold up a peace sign. He raises two fingers in a V. Graham takes the shot, but asks him to do it again.

Recalcitrant to the last, Johnny Adair closes them together, points them like a gun, laughs like a mad dog, and shoots back: "Bang!"

Freeze frame.

{MAY, 2007}

CHAPTER TWO:
Peter Buck

Surrounded by an armour-plated aura, Michael Stipe is not the most approachable guy on the planet. At least, not today he's not. The skeletal and scraggily dressed REM singer is sitting just a few feet away from me in the quaintly Victorian tea-rooms of London's Milestone Hotel, mumbling lowly to his media minder, perusing a menu, and fending off the outside world by keeping his tightly shaved head strategically covered with his hand. He looks like a hungover Yul Brenner. Everything about him says 'Do Not Disturb'.

Hot Press has flown to London on the understanding that, in tandem with Today FM, there'll be some face-to-face time with Stipe but, now that we're here the word comes down from the Warners International department that the plan has changed and now I'll just be talking to guitarist Peter Buck. In the UK primarily for a low-key launch gig in two nights time, the band have apparently agreed to do a total of just twelve-hours of European press to promote their new album *Around The Sun* (they might have been paid an estimated $80 million to stay with Warners, but they're obviously not expected to bust their promotional asses for it), and the media schedule's tighter than a post-election finance minister. All of my protests fall on deaf ears. This is unfortunate because both Buck and bassist Mike Mills are famously as confused as everyone else about the meanings behind many of their eccentric frontman's lyrics.

Awarded a deserved 9/10 by Niall Crumlish in the last issue, *Around The Sun* is the band's thirteenth studio album and if you're an REM fan you'll certainly get your money's worth. Stipe could inject passion and pathos into singing a train timetable, and so it is here. With a couple of up-tempo exceptions (album opener and first cut 'Leaving New York' in particular), the thirteen tracks are generally slow and mournful, and the songs as lyrically oblique as ever. Stipe could be singing about the state of the world. Or he could be singing about the state of his world. I consider chancing my arm and approaching him anyway but, just as I'm working up the nerve, the record company girl reappears to tell me that Buck is waiting for me in the suite upstairs and the clock is already ticking. When I meet him, the fortysomething guitarist looks tired and pasty-faced. Tall and bulky, he's wearing requisite shades, a black leather jacket, black trousers and a shirt so garish only a rock star or native Hawaiian could get away with it. As he politely pours *Hot Press* a glass of mineral water, he barely suppresses a loud yawn.

OLAF TYARANSEN: Hi Peter! Em, if you don't mind me saying, you're not looking madly enthusiastic about this ...

PETER BUCK: Ha, ha! No, I'm just really jet-lagged. Need to sleep. But it's cool.

Do you enjoy the interview process?

I love writing songs, I love playing in public, I like a little bit of the recordings – you know, the beginning: but talking about 'em, I could probably do without it. But, you know, it's what you do. I'm proud of the work and I want people to hear it. I suppose I feel like I don't do them justice. People ask me questions and I'm always going, 'Umm ... I don't know!' Ha, ha!

Have you figured *Around The Sun* out yet?

Well, that's the thing. Until the first interview I never really think about why you do this or what it means. And then after the first couple of days of interviews, people are asking you and you have to really think about what does it mean, why did we do this: I mean, I never go consciously into doing a record thinking, 'Oh, it's gonna be this kinda record or that kinda record'. It just ... *appears*.

I read somewhere that you never knew that 'Get Up' was written about you until Michael announced it onstage one night. Do you talk to him much about the meanings behind his lyrics?

Actually, I always thought it was about Mike *(Oops! – O.T)*. Ha, ha! But I really like Michael's work, and I'm kind of a fan. I just kind of like to listen to him go, and then tell him what I think about it. You know, a song like 'Leaving New York', to me, it's literally about what we do all the time – leaving someone behind and going somewhere else. But for me, I have trouble hearing the word 'New York', because I'm thinking about the Trade Centre and what the city went through and all that. And I don't really know if that was an intention of Michael's or not.

Were you in New York on 9/11?

No. I was in Seattle and I'm so out of touch with things – like I don't listen to the news or the radio or even read the newspaper really that much. I got up that morning, drove my kids to school, dropped 'em off and went home and went back to bed. And about 10 or 11 – which is about 2 o'clock in New York – my wife woke me up screaming. I was like, 'What?' I thought something had happened to my kids. So yeah, I was just blithely driving around, blasting the stereo, dropping the kids off to school going, *(scrunches face and puts on cute daddy voice)* 'Have a nice day!' I guess I should have realised that everyone else in the world was totally freaked out, but I didn't notice.

Do you think that the subsequent actions of President Bush and the neo-cons have made the world a safer or more dangerous place?

Hmm ... *(sighs heavily)*. Well, you know, I'm of two minds. One part of me is going, well, you know what? – I'm an older, rich, white guy, so this does not affect me at all. You know. It's the sense of empathy. But you want to see your country as the good guys, and I'm increasingly having a hard time feeling that way. When every single person that I talk to over here asks me about the war and what I think about it... It just seems like a huge disastrous error. Forget about the moral aspect to it – it's immoral I think – but, God, what a mistake! And it just goes on. My mom works with disadvantaged kids and she was just saying how much this whole thing with Iraq upsets her because she just knows that this is gonna ruin that whole generation of kids' lives. I mean, if you're lucky enough not to get killed or maimed, just the bombings, the terror, the … You know, it's not gonna end when this ends. This is gonna go on, just like it goes on in Vietnam right now.

What's going on in Vietnam right now?

There's a legacy still of the violence of Vietnam, whether it's landmines going off, whether it's having a huge amount of beggars – you know, maimed people – on the streets. Twenty years from now the repercussions from what's going on right now will still be happening. And every time some innocent person gets killed, there's another potential terrorist going to revenge that person.

Going back to music for a second…

Sure!! Ha, ha!!

This is REM's third album since Bill departed. Is it getting easier to operate as a three-piece? And do you still seek his advice or opinion?

Bill Berry? The last thing he wants to do is give opinions on things. I mean, he left the music business for good reasons – he didn't wanna have anything to do with it. Bill is still one of my best friends, but I don't really see him much because he's a real homebody. We always send him a copy of the record and he always says very complimentary things. I think he's just so relieved that it's not him doing it! But as far as feeling comfortable as a three-piece – we feel good in this arrangement but, to me, it's also a six-piece, because we've got these three guys working with us. Though they're not exactly proper members of the band they've been with us for a long time and they have input in the way things sound.

Pat McCarthy worked on this record. He's from Dublin, isn't he?

Yeah, I think his first session work, when he was about 15, was engineering *The Unforgettable Fire*. I don't know how he got the job but he kinda picked up from there. He worked on *Monster* with us. He was, for a little while, kind of a protégé of Scott Litt's – or at least they worked together. And I can remember an experience mixing, em, I can't remember what song, but it was on *Monster*, and no-one could really get it. Everyone was mixing for about three days and it still wasn't right. Then Pat and I went into the room with the song for about three hours and mixed it, and it was just like, 'Oh, that's perfect!' So when Scott and us parted ways – Scott went off to form his own record company – I remember thinking, 'Oh that Pat guy, he was really good'. But yeah, he led to the Irish connection. We recorded a lot of the last record [*Reveal*] in Dalkey. Pat had told us it's a great little town and we could go and hang out in Dublin.

Has settling down and having a family changed your attitude to life?

Well, I can't tell if it's just me getting older, or if it's having a family, but you certainly think of the world in a different way. I never thought about my future a whole lot – I mean, to me it was always, 'I'll live till I die'. Then you start to realise that these kids depend on you, so maybe I go to the doctor a little bit more, brush my teeth a little better. As far as the travelling goes, it makes it harder for me to be away. But then they understand that I have to do this. And when I'm at home I don't have a job, so I'm pretty much a 24-hours a day on-call parent.

There's a very folksy, fireside feel to a couple of the tracks on the album...
This time around, I didn't have any fixed plans when we went into studio. I had written a bunch of stuff. And my first demos were all really dark and gloomy – kind of like 'High Speed Train' and 'Electron Blue'. Those were actually recorded in my house. So there's a lot of stuff that kinda sounded like that. I started hearing the lyrics and feeling where the album was going, and I just felt that it wasn't feeling like a heavy record. It was still maybe a little dark – but the acoustic guitar I wanted to be kind of light, and have room for the songs to breathe. And I do play a lot of folk music and listen to it, so that kind of gets in there.

What's your favourite track on the album?
You know, one of my favourite songs that we've done in years and years and years – maybe in the last fifteen years – is 'I Wanted To Be Wrong'. I just like that song because I love Michael's lyrics (*"I threw it into reverse/ made a motion to appeal / you kicked my legs from under me/ and tried to take the wheel"*), it always provokes an emotional response when I'm listening to it or playing it. I don't know why – it just hits with me in a way that sometimes other songs don't.

Do you ever find yourself moved to tears on stage or in the studio?
Yeah, it happens. This last tour we had a thing where people would email in requests. And they started emailing in telling life stories and, as the wheel turns, telling a few death stories too. And we were in New Orleans and this woman emailed a letter to us. Her and her husband's favourite song was 'Strange Currencies'. And he had been in a car wreck and he had brain damage and he died – I don't know how but it wasn't a good thing. And she was crippled and she really wished we'd play it. And we started playing it and I looked over and I could see her – she was in a wheelchair. I just started sobbing. I had to turn around, I just couldn't deal with it – because she had started crying. I just turned around and went, (*softly*) 'Fuck!' It really hit home.

What's the biggest downside of being in REM?
Boy, you know, it sure beats working for a living so, whenever anything negative happens, I just always go, 'You know, if I had some job I hated, I'd probably be dead'.

Ever get any weird stalkers or strange mail or anything like that?
Ha, ha! All of the above – yeah. I guess, for me, it's not even a downside so much as it's something I've got to get used to, but I'm not really good with meeting new people. I'm not a very social person. But it just so happens that a big part of my job is meeting people all the time. And to me, that's just a nightmare. It's not like I don't like people, I just never learned how to do it. I went from being shy to being famous. Ha, ha!

It took quite a few albums – up until 1991's breakthrough *Out Of Time* – before REM became seriously famous.
Yeah, but even at that level, when people come up and start talking to you, they have something to say to you. Even now, when I get dragged to a cocktail party or something, to me it's just like I don't know how people do this. So I just become another person. I try to be an extrovert and talk and tell stories. But really I just

wanna get outta there. It really wears me out.

Are you into studio technology in a big way?

I use the modern technology. I'm kind of fascinated by it. Obviously, we occasionally use Pro-tools, we record digitally, and I use all kinds of effects and things. But I still think the best way to do it is to go in and record something live. Get the band to perform. Like 'Boy In The Well' is a really great feeling track on the new album, and that's us playing it live, with a minimal amount of overdubs.

Are you worried about people downloading your music free from the internet?

That never really bothered me. I mean, I know that everyone in the band has a different opinion on it, but we're lucky enough that we made our money back in the 20th century. And at this point, wherever we are in our career, assuming we're gonna sell, say, a million records, I'd rather have ten million people hear it and only a million people buy it, than a million people buy it and only a million people hear it.

That's an unusual position for a professional musician to take.

While there's something to be said for actually being paid for your work, for me if there's an opportunity for us to be heard or to touch people's lives… I'm thinking of the kids who live in Idaho or something that may not have a really good record store nearby, or they're living in a small town, but if they've got the internet then that's cool – that's fine with me.

Do you have any other business or artistic interests outside of REM?

Not really. Business doesn't really interest me all that much. If you make money, obviously you do have investments and stuff, but I'm not a particularly hands-on guy in that regard. You know, for me it's music. I don't have any interest in film. I don't wanna act. I can write, but I don't have a novel in me. Although every now and again, I think 'OK, when I've got a year off, I'm just gonna go up to the attic and write for two hours a day to see what happens'. And maybe I'll do that but, you know, I'm lazy and that seems an awful lot like work. If I could be guaranteed to get a great novel out of it then maybe I'd do it, but I have a feeling that I'd go up to the attic for two hours a day and end up with a bunch of scribbled pages that I'd hate.

What are you reading at the moment?

I'm rereading *Something Happened* by Joseph Heller. I read that in like '73 or '74 when it first came out. It's about middle-aged angst and hating your job and loveless marriage and alcoholism and family dynamics. I thought it was a real strong book but I don't think I really understood all of that stuff. So, going back and reading it now, it makes a lot more sense. Ha, ha! Although, thank God, it's not my life.

Have you been back in Britain since your 'air rage' incident on British Airways?

Oh yeah. That was in 2001 so I've been back a couple of times since then.

Wow – was it that long ago?

Yeah. Almost three years.

Sorry to bring it up so.

That's OK. Everyone else does! Ha, ha!

What are your feelings on it now?
Well, you know, it's part of my life and if I can live with it, I guess everyone else is gonna have to. Was it the hardest moment of my life? No, but you know ... *[shrugs]*.

It was a sleeping pill you'd taken, wasn't it?
Yeah – mixed it with wine. I blacked out, I don't remember anything. I mean, in a way, it's good. I'm sure I'd be much more mortified if I actually remembered. I don't know what went on because I couldn't tell from the testimonies. It didn't make any sense. I think that generally the large percentage of what went on that night was a misunderstanding. But I fly BA all the time and they don't hold anything against me and I don't hold anything against them.

For the most part, REM seem to have managed to avoid the usual rock & roll pitfalls of drink and drugs…
Yeah. You know, when we were younger, I did pretty much all the stuff you'd expect a guy in a rock band in the 80's to do. Ha, ha! On the other hand, we put out pretty much a record a year for six years and toured 150 – 200 shows a year for ten years. You know, I just have more important things to do than get wasted all the time. I always say about these people that just get so fucked up on drugs that they can't function are pathetic. And I've always felt that way.

So you don't approve?
I'm not saying that they're bad people but to me it just seems like what a fucking waste. I could see if your life was awful but if you've got something going for you – I just think those people who blow it are just stupid. And I feel sorry for 'em. And probably it is an illness of some type. For me, I've got the band, I've got my family. I just don't have time for that.

Do you have a motto in life?
Em… 'Let's panic later'. Ha, ha! I seem to use that a lot. Because everyone around me is always panicking. I live at a kind of high anxiety level, but I don't worry about stuff that much. I just feel that, you know, you can worry about this shit now or you can just deal with it when the time comes, and it'll probably be fine.

{OCTOBER, 2004}

CHAPTER THREE:
John Cooper Clarke

A wet windy weekend afternoon in the west of Ireland, and legendary performance poet John Cooper Clarke and your *Hot Press* correspondent are getting soaked to our skins as we sway exposed to the elements on Galway's Wolfe Tone Bridge, deep in demented discussion with one of the city's more genial winos.

We're both hungover from last night's restaurant wine, and also somewhat stoned from a more recent spliff, but when the guy staggered over asking for the price of "a cup of cider," we stopped to give him some change.

Taking in Clarke's distinctive stick-insect stylings - electrified bouffant hairstyle, long Mafia coat, dark shades and drainpipe trousers – the drunk performed an exaggerated double take.

"Jesus Christ almighty!" he cried. "Is it... *John Cooper Clarke?*" When Clarke confirmed his identity, he grabbed his hand to enthusiastically shake it. "I used to work the sites over in London. I remember seeing you in Brixton back in the day. What was that one again? 'Beasley Street'! You were fuckin' brilliant, man!"

Holding tightly onto John's hand, as though for dear life, he began to tell us his story, reciting an occasional mantra of, *"God bless you, Johnny ... God bless you, Johnny ... God bless you, Johnny..."* whenever losing his thread of thought.

After a few excruciating minutes of this, we eventually manage to get away only to discover that there's a couple of soaked but smiling fans waiting nearby waving tickets for tonight's show in the Roisin Dubh that they want signed. Ever the gentleman, Clarke (Cooper is his middle name) stops to oblige.

"What can you do?" he shrugs. "You get outta bed in the morning and ... it *begins*."

He certainly attracts a lot of attention. Everywhere we go, slack-jawed locals tend to stop and stare. Some even take snaps on their mobile phones. Mostly this is because they're mistaking the 60-year-old poet for one of the Rolling Stones. Clarke's well used to it.

"I was all cramped up with me bag at the back of a bus the other day," he tells me. "And this middle-aged woman kept staring at me. Like, really intensely! Eventually she worked up the courage to come over and say, 'Excuse me, I'm really sorry to bother you – but are you Ron Wood?' I told her, 'Yes, love, I just decided to give me stretch limo driver the day off and take the bus instead'."

Has he ever met his wealthier doppelganger?

"No – I've never met Woody. But I reckon he should give us a job as his decoy."

He might not be a millionaire rock star, but John Cooper Clarke has been famous in his own right for more than three decades now. Dubbed the 'Bard of Salford', he first came to public attention in the late 1970s opening for seminal punk acts including Buzzcocks, The Fall, Sex Pistols, Elvis Costello and Joy Division (he played a younger version of himself in Anton Corbijn's 2007 Joy Division biopic *Control*).

A bestselling debut poetry collection, *Ten Years in an Open-Necked Shirt*, and a series of albums – most notably 1980's *Snap, Crackle & Bop* and 1982's *Zip Style Method* – brought him to a wider audience in the early Eighties. Unfortunately, a debilitating heroin habit mostly put paid to the live work, but a series of lucrative TV adverts for Sugar Puffs cereal, which saw the Bard in constant battle with the Honey Monster, paid some of the bills.

Although he disappeared from public view for most of the Nineties, Clarke – who now resides in Essex with his wife and teenage daughter - has enjoyed something of a career resurgence in the Noughties. His snatch from the jaws of obscurity was largely enabled by bands such as Arctic Monkeys and Reverend & the Makers regularly namechecking him as a major influence in their interviews. The *Control* appearance has helped, too, and it certainly did no reputational harm when his poem 'Evidently Chickentown' was used to play out a memorable episode in Season 5 of *The Sopranos*. In recent times, he's been averaging around 200 live performances per year.

As we veer off Quay Street in search of a suitable location to record an interview, Clarke asks me, "What were we taking about before all that stuff 'appened?"

"I think it was something to do with banana skins," I reply.

"Oh yeah," he says. *"Baa-naa-na skins!* Do you know the way in comics and cartoons people are always slipping on banana skins? It might lead one to the conclusion that they're actually slippery. But they're not. I put two of them under me feet in the kitchen and tried to slide across the floor. I got totally stuck. It was like wearing mountain climbing boots. Fuckin' *useless!"*

Such surreal conversations are par for the course with the constantly entertaining Bard of Salford. Even on those rare occasions when he's being serious, that strongly unaffected Manchester enunciation renders almost everything he says a touch comical (something he uses to great effect in his live performances). He laughs constantly.

Eventually we wind up in Sheridan's Wine Bar (when we walk in somebody casually calls over, *"Ah sure, how's it goin', Ronnie,"* before studiously ignoring us for the next hour). Clarke orders a coffee while your correspondent opts for a refreshing glass of Raudi. The poet reminds me of a line from his as-yet-unpublished poem, 'The List of Shit That Don't Exist': *"An onanist without a wrist/ A journalist who isn't pissed…"*

OLAF TYARANSEN: What's your earliest memory, John?

JOHN COOPER CLARKE: Earliest memory? It's a long time ago. Hmmm… that's a tough one, isn't it? My early childhood was really weird 'cos there was a lot of deaths in the family at the same time. I got TB when I was a young kid. I don't remember anything before that, actually. When I think about my early childhood, it's in hospital.

Did you start reading books then?

No, I don't think I could read then. You know, it was very early and I missed a lot of school. So I just listened to the radio all the time.

Do you have brothers and sisters?

I've got a brother; he's twelve years younger than me. He's still living in Salford, works for the GPO. He ain't flavour of the month at the moment 'cos they're out – they're taking strikes, you know, so everybody hates him! I gave him some stick. We don't see each other a lot, to be honest. Twelve years is a big gap; he's got his mates, I've got mine. He's a funny kid, actually, my brother.

What were you like at school?

I fucked around and basically wasted loads of my time and everybody else's.

What age did you leave school?

Fifteen. It was Catholic Secondary modern, in Salford, and it was a crap school, but nobody left there unable to read. Even the dumbest kids read stuff. But that was quite a thing. wasn't it? Everybody read, didn't they, the same paperback with the torn cover. There was not so much TV because it was only on for four hours a night or something.

When did you first realise that you were going to be a poet?

I didn't know that until I was a teenager. At school we had this really good English teacher for a while. We had this guy, John Malone. "Mr Malone." He had a glass eye, a bit of a limp. He was always injuring himself on the summer holidays on some outdoor, red-blooded pursuit. You know, he fell 300 feet down a mountain-face in Snowdonia one year. You never knew whether you were going to see him next term or not, he was always doing waterskiing, climbing mountains. So he was this rugged type, but he had a poetic side, which he conveyed to everybody in the class, not just me. Writing that struck a chord, all the usual stuff: 'Charge of the Light-Brigade', a bit of Shelley, you know, all the old-school stuff. He used to read from what they used to call *Palgrave's Golden Treasury*. Yeah, and *Palgrave's Golden Treasury* was kind of the recommended… I wonder if you can still get it. I think it was made for schools. But a great mix of stuff in there. Probably the most modern stuff you would have got would have been Louis MacNeice and T.S. Eliot.

And you were into those guys?

Yeah, especially obviously 'Prufrock' (*Eliot's 'The Love Song of J. Alfred Prufrock'*). You know, that's so bleedin' mysterious even now, innit? What *is* that about? So, it's kind of about growing old, if you had to pin one aspect of it down, but the language of it is so mysterious, innit? Great number. Great poem. But he was two guys, wasn't he? I hated all that pussycat stuff he did. 'Macavity – The Mystery Cat'? I hated all that.

I would've thought that 'Macavity' would have been fairly close in humour and

tone to the sort of stuff you perform now.

Yeah, yeah. But I liked his more... He did 'The Waste Land' as well, didn't he? I love all that.

What kind of jobs did you do when you left school?

My first job was an apprentice motor mechanic. Didn't last very long. I had loads of jobs. I had a window cleaning round with my cousin, Sid, for a while, which was a pretty good earner – but we kept on running into trouble with rivals. It was like the ice-cream turf wars. So we pulled out of that. Then I got a job in the garment industry, working for this Jewish firm, cutting out linings for women's coats. Then I was a fire-watcher when I lived in Plymouth, on the docks.

You just sat there and watched out for fires?

Yeah. I just sat in an observatory with a pair of binoculars, you know, and if I saw any smoke from anywhere I got on the phone to the relevant people. It was one of them jobs where you don't have to *do* anything, but you have to *be* there all the time. So I did a lot of writing.

Did you ever actually spot one?

No. It never happened. But I was there for about two years. I did loads of writing.

What age were you when you wrote your first poem?

Oh, quite early. About fourteen.

Can you remember it?

No, I don't. It was an exercise we had at school. I can't even remember what it was about.

What's the first poem you do remember writing?

The first poem I remember writing? Ah, Jesus... it was so long ago! I used to write a lot about, sort of, Manchester at first. Very area-specific, kind of parochial stuff. And I used to make up football chants.

Can you remember one?

No. It's terrible, innit, not being able to remember any. But they were all totally obscene, and derogatory about the opposing team. They say folk music's dead, but that's where it lives – on the terraces. It responds to something instantly – and then 60,000 people suddenly know the words! Completely organic process. But my favourite's that one –United are playing Liverpool tomorrow – and there's a great song to the tune of *Topcat*. 'Kop-twats,' it's called. The song goes, *"Kop-twats, you thieving bastards!/ Kop-twats, you thieving bastards!/ We know you all sign on the dole/ And you live in a fucking shit-hole!"*

Some tabloid newspaper headlines are almost poetry in themselves.

Absolutely. Especially *The Sun*. They've got the best headline writing in the world. There was a blinder, the best ever, you know when Elton (John) and David Furnish had a civil ceremony back in the day – they've been married years now, haven't they? But the headline in *The Sun* was: *'ELTON TAKES DAVID UP THE AISLE'*. In a *family newspaper*?

When did you first start performing?

Oh, that would have been in the late '60s. There were several kinds of community newspapers starting up back in the hippie days, in the wake of *International*

Times and *Oz*. They used to run events as well. And, you know what it was like in the hippie days: they'd put up with anything, them hippies. After that I started performing at this club in Manchester called Mister Smith's. It was like a cabaret club, and it was aimed at kind of thirty-year-old newlyweds and they'd have people like Matt Monroe. Even Shirley Bassey played there. So I got a job kind of MC-ing. I'd do a few poems about places they knew and Manchester people. And it was kind of a [*adopts BBC voice*] 'fractured take on modern life'. So I'd do about twenty minutes and then bring on the main act.

What age were you then?

I'd have been 25 or 26. After the '60s I left it alone for a bit, and then I got married, moved to Dorset, got a job in printing. So I was in rural south-west of England, where I had a job as a printer, because in the meantime I had become a qualified compositor, in the days of lead type, you know. And so I left the poetry. I kept writing it, but I wasn't doing gigs or anything. And then we went back to Manchester and I got the residency at Mister Smith's, and I didn't have to do anything else, it was really good money. It was great, but, because I was trying to make it in that world of cabaret, I kind of dressed the part. I wore a suit, you know, Perry Como haircut. So, by the time punk took up, I already looked a bit… well, I didn't look like everybody else. I sort of fit in with the punk look: short hair, parallel trousers, skinny suit, in that Paul Weller/The Jam kind of punk look, rather than the Vivienne Westwood end of it. So I already looked the part, and that's when I started doing gigs with The Buzzcocks and The Fall, and that sort of got us out of Manchester. They were doing gigs all over the place. So I started moving around with them. And then I was seen as part of that punk phenomenon, and it got written up in the *NME* and all the rest of it.

How did punk audiences respond to performance poetry?

They were all like, 'What, are you going to do that in front of punks, are you? You're going to read *poetry* to *punks*?' And all that. But at the time I figured even if I die on my arse, it will get remembered and it will get written up.

Did you die on your arse?

Occasionally. In the beginning it was pretty bad. But it sort of worked because pretty soon everybody thought, 'Oh, he's got some bottle, doing it in Kirby Workingman's Club, you know?' You see, it all worked in my favour anyway. I'm glad I did it that way. Otherwise, I can't imagine what sort of life I would've had. Young people who write poetry now, and a lot of them are fantastic, they say, 'What would you do now, if you were starting out now?' I couldn't tell you, you know, it was all very serendipitous for me, the whole punk thing. Because people were interested in song lyrics in the first place. They were lyrically important, the punk rockers. But God knows what I would have done if that hadn't have happened. There wasn't any scene for poetry or anything like that – whereas now, there is a bit. There is a bit in London, and the main towns. You know, so I just say to anybody who asks me about it, all I can say really is, 'Do gigs!' And then get it out. Get a name and then sell books with it. What can you say?

Although you've recorded several albums, your first and only poetry collection was published in 1981.

Yeah. *Ten Years in an Open-Necked Shirt.*
Did it do well at the time?
It did, really. It sold-out. Yeah, I don't know why it ever went out of print. Really, it never stopped selling.
Would you consider printing some up and selling them at gigs?
For a while I did, but I had my mate selling them, and it was like, whatever I made selling books went on *entertainments*. In the end, it wasn't worth the arse-ache of carrying a box of books everywhere. It just all got spent. And my mate was, to be fair – God rest his soul, he was my best mate, you know, and died a couple of years ago – he was a hell of a drinker. He totally drank the proceeds, and he also used to complain about having to stay in the same place. 'You know that's why you're here, Steve. That's your job!' Steven is the guy who illustrated the book. There's a load of pencil illustrations, and he did the cover. He was a great painter. A fantastic painter, but he was a terrible drinker. So I never made anything. We're working like dogs, carrying books everywhere, you know what I mean, not having dollar one extra. 'Leave it to the shops, Steve. I'm going out solo 'cos I can't afford ya!'
Have you any plans to publish another collection?
Definitely. I've got loads of new stuff. I think I've got enough for more than one book. And I also started doing a book of Limericks in order to cash in on the lucrative yuletide stocking-filler market. It was aimed at kids but there's something about Limericks that invites the expression of off-colour sentiments. People feel cheated if there isn't an obscene pay-off. But this one was aimed at children so I thought, 'Keep it clean'.
Can I hear one?
There was one like this in it: *"I knew a fella called Ken/ He climbed up the hands of Big Ben/ Ascended at noon/ He fell to his doom/ At precisely six-thirty pm."* You can see how it would happen like that. It's aimed at kids, but the more I did it, the more obscene they became. But it's a lot of fun, innit, writing the old Limericks. Nice and clean family entertainment.
Who was your favourite out of all the various rock acts you've supported or performed with?
Impossible to say, but I always enjoyed working with The Fall. Well, 'enjoy' might not be the right word, but I've been on tour with them in recent years, and they're better than ever now. They're the only ones that I would watch every night.
Given Mark E. Smith's tendency to fire musicians, they'd have a different line-up every night.
Yeah, yeah. Possibly a different band every night! But punch-ups all the time. All the time. Terrible. I don't know how he survived. I mean, have you seen Smithy lately? He's totally fragile, he stood there every day getting a pasting – he never comes off best, you know. Paul Morley did a Radio 4 show about us, it was sort of like an obituary. It was kind of weird listening to it, it was like I had died. I felt like Glen Ford at the end of *The Fastest Gun Alive*, you know when he fakes his death in the end. You know Glen Ford, fastest draw. And when him and his missus are looking at his grave at the end. It was like that, that sort of weird experience. But the weirdest of all was that Mark was on saying all nice things about me. How

many people can say that?

How were the Sex Pistols to deal with?

Oh, gentlemen. Total gents.

Despite all the gigging, you really shot to fame in the UK as the face of Sugar Puffs cereal.

Yeah. That was sort of mid-Eighties, wasn't it? Fantastic. I really enjoyed that period. I had some albums out at the time as well. No, it was great, inspired, I love them ads. Actually, you can get them on YouTube. Me daughter got 'em up. She was really surprised when she come across them. Because they got better and better, you know, the ads, they got more slick. They were more kind of state-of-the-art. It got to be like a *Tom and Jerry* cartoon at the end. There one where the Honey Monster flattens me with a garden roller, you know, and they used this mat of me 'cos I'm totally flattened.

The ads didn't threaten your punk credibility, did they?

Most people I spoke to laughed about it. They thought they were hilarious.

Was that back in the days when you still got a royalty every time the ad aired?

Yeah, that's right. They don't do that anymore. They got out of that market, they do what they call a 'buy-out' now. But you got a royalty every time it was shown. It was like, *ka-ching! Ka-ching!* It was unbelievable, the amount of money. And the way they looked after you, you lived like a king.

On free Sugar Puffs?

Seriously, them 30-second ads, they used to take, like, three days to do. It was unbelievable. Especially since they had kids involved. All them kids were all from some central casting drama school. And they were only allowed to work a certain amount of time each day: child exploitation and all that. So they could only use them for about three hours a day. But they'd never get it right. So, really because of that, you were there, like, a week in a top-dollar hotel, charging everything up. They'd set you up with dinners too. And then mega amounts of money on top. Smashing. Where did it go? Where did it all go? I don't know. Where and when?

At what point did the heroin kick in?

Well, it was already kicked in, to be honest. I wasn't really a suitable face for breakfast cereals. But they didn't know anything about it. I kept it a big secret.

And at what point did it get messy?

Oh, pretty early on, you know, it went messy. But touch wood, here we are. Still alive. All behind me now.

Did you stop writing at that point?

Oh yeah, yeah. You've always got other things to do, in that world.

When did your first marriage break up?

It lasted three years! No, but we was too young, you know. What was I? About twenty-one, she was seventeen.

Are you still in touch?

I see her from time to time, yeah. She's still in Manchester. She seems to have got over it!

You lived with Velvet Underground chanteuse Nico for a while in the '80s.

I gotta say it wasn't really a kind of a romantic situation at all. Not at all. I got married off in the *NME*. Somebody snapped us going in the house, and married us off. But it wasn't really like that. I was living in Brixton at the time, and I already knew Nico because she had been living in Manchester around the corner from us, and we used to see a lot of her. And she went on a tour of Italy, but she had neglected to pay her rent before she left. And when she got back all her stuff had been thrown out of the house, and she kind of got her ticket. So she technically didn't have anywhere to stay, so her manager said, 'Any room at your place?' I says, 'Yeah, sure'. I mean, there was bags of room there. And I already knew her. And she just stayed at mine for quite a while in Brixton. In fact, while she was living there she was making an album, and John Cale came over, her producer. So I had him staying there as well. So I was flavour-of-the-month for a while. There was two-fifths of the Velvet Underground staying at my flat. You couldn't make it up, could you? It was fantastic.

Do you ever drink before shows?

I have a nip. But nothing, you know… words are shit to remember sometimes, because I go off the point and then come back to it, you know, but you can't really do that with poetry. The way I'd put it is: it's another kind of show if you've had a bit too much to drink. If you're drunk you tell yourself it was better. You know, 'that was better then usual'. Clouded judgement and all that. Do you know, I don't really drink very much anyway. Last night, that was very uncharacteristic of me. I don't think I was out of order. Was I out of order at all?

You were grand, except for that bottle you put through the window of the restaurant.

Well, that bottle through the window, and trying to pull somebody's wife and …

You went quiet for a long period in the 1990s. What happened?

The '90s was really a good time for me, actually. I quit using class-A drugs, and, you know, it was optimistic, really.

When did you meet your second wife?

Evie? Well, we were seeing each other since about '87, a long time before we lived together. And I moved in to hers in the early '90s. We had always sort of talked about getting together, but I wanted to clean up before I moved in with her. Because you wouldn't want to force that kind of life on somebody who is unprepared for it. And then my life completely changed. Me daughter, Stella, was born in 1994. She's fifteen now. Late parenthood. I totally recommend late parenthood.

Did it change you?

If it wasn't for her, my life would just consist of hospital visits and funerals. So thank God for her – in every sense. They say they keep you young: actually they put years on you!

Were you working much during the '90s?

The '90s were kinder to me than the '80s, really. I was heading down the pan there, in the '80s. It was the decade immediately after punk and really anything that was tarred with that brush began to look quite stale. And then it went from one extreme to the other and everything became a surface gloss: Duran Duran and Wham! That was the total opposite end of the park to the punks, wasn't it? But even so, I liked some of it.

More recently, bands like Reverend and the Makers and the Arctic Monkeys have been dropping your name a lot.

Yeah, it's great!

Do you know the Monkeys well?

I do know them pretty well. Great guys, all of them. In fact, I met them about a fortnight before they went global. I'm really glad I was nice to them now! You're not always, are you? You know, if you've just done the gig. I think it was with The Fall in a place called The Boardwalk in Sheffield, and then at the end, we were just about to go home, and the club proprietor said, 'Would you mind just saying hello to these lads? They've hung around, they like your stuff, and they're in a band. We think they're going to be really mega'. I said, 'What are they called?' He said, 'The Arctic Monkeys'. There's some names you can really imagine in the charts, can't you? And names are important. I thought, 'That's a great name. 'The Arctic Monkeys". I said, 'I certainly will, yeah. I'd be pleased to meet them.' So, they came in, and they're all really like shy kids, you know, looking at their feet, and shuffling about. They're still like that. They're really sweet, sweet kids. He's always dropping my name in interviews, which has done me a hell of a lot. In fact, I've noticed since that I've got a whole new generation of fans, but I'll tell you how that came about, how Alex (Turner) came to know my stuff – it was at school, because I was on the English curriculum for the GCSEs.

What poem?

'I Wanna Be Yours.' It's that one, *"I wanna be your vacuum cleaner breathing in your dust ..."* It's a sort of fairly innocuous one. You can see why that would be picked, you know, no swearing or anything. And then he went home, Alex right, and mentioned this poem to his mum and dad, who obviously knew about us. Because Alex's parents, I think they're a bit bohemian. They might have even been punks. I guess at that point they got my records out, and Alex liked them.

I read somewhere that he's got your name tattooed on his arm.

Yeah, somebody told me about that. I didn't know it went *that* far. I think they're a fabulous band. And he's a great rhythm guitarist. Plays it high up, doesn't he, like The Beatles style.

You turned 60 recently.

It's a fucking miracle, innit? Who knew that'd ever happen?

How did you celebrate it?

There was a surprise party. Me wife and daughter blindfolded me and shoved us in the back of the car, drove me to this pub-stroke-restaurant just outside where I live. And it was great. Loads of people. And I was all, 'I don't want no party, not for my sixtieth'. In fact, that's the last birthday I'm going to fucking have. In fact, I'm even going to lie about that. There's no way I'm going to admit to being 60. I'll be 59 for the rest of my life.

You're widely known in music circles, but do you have many literary associates?

Yeah, I know all those people – mainly through Michael Horovitz. He did that thing at the Albert Hall back in the '60s with all the Beat poets. Through him I've met the late Adrian Mitchell, for instance. And I met all them Beat poets – Allen

Ginsberg, Lawrence Ferlinghetti, Michael McClure, Gregory Corso. Actually, I met Corso years ago. He moved in with Nico when she was living in Manchester. So, in Manchester, in our little area of Salford, you wouldn't believe the people who lived there in that little area. But that's nothing. I've got to tell you this – you know when Nico was living there, you had Mark Smith up the road, Nico in there, and then somehow, for some reason, Gregory Corso moved in with her. There was like a beat enclave in Salford. Unbelievable.

What's been the highest point of your career?

The highest point? Really, there's so many. People are so nice to me; it's a kind of charmed life. I tell you, meeting David Johansen was a blast. This was back in the '80s when I went to the States. I did a couple of gigs with the David Johansen Band, this was after the New York Dolls had split up, he had that band with Sylvain Sylvain and a few other guys – but it wasn't the New York Dolls. Remember they had that album out on Blue Sky Records. 'Cool Metro' and 'Frenchette' – they were great numbers, actually, as good as anything the Dolls ever did, to be honest. And he turned to me, and he says, (*thick New York accent*) 'Johnny, you're good. But they don't know who you are. I'm gonna MC for ya.' And he did, every gig he MC-ed for us. Fantastic. Really nice. What a thoughtful guy. But he was great company. I mean a really funny, funny guy.

When was the last time you were in the States?

1982. Yeah, yeah, too long ago. It was a different place then, New York. I mean, I've heard it's not as dangerous anymore.

I think you'd do really well over there.

I think so too, yeah. Like I say, whenever I run into Americans I'm always amazed that they've never heard of me. So, yeah, I've got to go out there again. I love America.

Given that *The Sopranos* used 'Evidently Chickentown', I'd imagine a lot more Americans will have heard of you now.

What a shock that was! What a surprise, yeah. Fantastic. I was very pleased about that.

Was it lucrative?

Not yet. I've yet to have the payment for it, but I've found this, that the world of movies pays very slowly. I've still not been paid for *Control* either. But it has done me a lot of good, I've gotta say. You know what I mean, people recognise me from that film. And from that *Sopranos* thing.

Surely that would be your ticket into a successful tour of the States?

There's only one thing that would have been better than that – a guest appearance on *The Simpsons*. I like to think Sideshow Bob is slightly modelled on me. He could be, couldn't he?

Is that the main ambition now?

Absolutely. That's my ambition, yeah, a guest appearance on *The Simpsons*. Then my living will not be in vain.

Do you have a motto or a guiding philosophy in life?
Yeah, from *Jailhouse Rock*, you know the advice that Mickey Shaughnessy gives to Elvis, 'Do unto others as you would have them do unto you. Only do it first!'

{NOVEMBER, 2009}

SELECTED RECORDINGS: 2000-2010

CHAPTER FOUR:
JP Donleavy

Sixty years ago or thereabouts, the then-struggling young Irish-American writer JP Donleavy returned home to his isolated Kilcoole cottage after a trip away to discover that somebody had broken in and been living there during his absence.

"I had been away in Wicklow, and I came back and saw this whole mess, every dish had been used, the place was really appalling," Donleavy recalls in his curiously hybrid Irish-English-American accent. "And I just thought, 'My God!'."

When he ventured into his study and found the manuscript of *Borstal Boy*, he realised that the intruder was one of his wildest Dublin drinking buddies. "I came out to my studio and found this manuscript. I saw the mention of 'Borstal' or something on it, and I thought, 'Oh – Behan!'"

During his uninvited stay, Brendan Behan had also chanced upon the manuscript of Donleavy's novel-in-progress, *Sebastian Dangerfield* (he later changed the title to *The Ginger Man*). Perhaps to compensate for the fact that he was about to nick a suitcase containing all of Donleavy's shoes, the famously alcoholic writer had scribbled editorial suggestions all over the pages.

"He even autographed the thing!" Donleavy laughs. "But his comments were good, and I wound up following every single suggestion. He left me a note that said, 'This book is going to go around the world'. At the time, I thought, 'Well, he's exaggerating, he wants to cheer me up in some way'.

"But he was one of the first people to read the manuscript. You know, as translations began to appear – it's now gone up to 25 or 26 languages – and I often thought back to Behan who made all these predictions. But I guess this is where it's got me, out to this house here and trying to struggle on."

Now aged 83, the writer – who's 'kindly eyed, but steely jawed' – lives in splendid isolation in a charmingly crumbly old gray stone mansion on his 200 acre Mullingar estate, Levington Park. Featuring 27 rooms, it's quite some pad – the books, artworks, antiques, arched ceilings, marble fireplaces, weird furniture and stains all have stories to tell. The Rolling Stones have partied here. "My second wife was very involved in that world," he says, "though I never had much interest."

Donleavy doesn't receive many visitors nowadays (there's a large and imposing *'No Trespassing'* sign at his locked front gate). "One evening I did hear someone trespassing at the back of this house, and I was standing there with a loaded shotgun, seeing these shadows. And I let off a couple of shells in the sky, and the man got the message. That wasn't a problem again."

Trim, white-haired and immaculately dressed, he looks good for his age – but the years have claimed their toll nonetheless. Nowadays, he often doesn't leave the grounds of his estate for weeks at a time. However, he does occasionally venture out into the wider world. Sometimes he even meets famous politicians. As he scans through his back pages, searching for the remnants of a story he might once have told with fierce clarity and wit, you can see that his memory isn't what it used to be...

"What's the name of that man who was Taoiseach recently?" he asks.

Bertie Ahern?

"Bertie Ahern! Yes, I think I might have been with Bertie Ahern once, in the same group in a room, and the two of us had to stand together because – we might have been giving some sort of talk, or we were being asked questions. And I was standing up there, and he was a respectful politician. I said, 'God, Mr Ahern, this is going to give you a terribly bad reputation being photographed with me – the two of us together'. And he said, 'Ah, I don't know about that. I think that my being up here with you is going to give you a worse reputation!'" he laughs.

Probably true ... Did he ever meet the late JD Salinger?

"No, never," he replies, shaking his head. "My publisher in America did try to call on him, and the stories were legion about how you couldn't get near Salinger, and so, this particular story often amused me.

"Salinger's house, where he lived in the country – pretty isolated out in the woods and everything – went on fire, and his neighbour thought, 'Well, my God, Salinger's house is going to burn down'. And so he grabbed his garden hose, put lengths on to it, and rushed with his hose to put out the fire, and Salinger threw him off the place! *'Get the hell off my property!'*"

Despite his own aversion to visitors, Donleavy enjoys meeting journalists. "I find interviews very valuable because I realise that anyone who wants to interview me at this stage has a genuine reason," he says.

One slight snag with the house: Donleavy's 40,000 gallon indoor swimming pool is full of snot green weeds. He hasn't used it in a couple of years. "One would easily bankrupt oneself heating that thing," he laughs.

Given that *The Ginger Man*, which remains his best-known work, has reportedly sold more than 45 million copies since its first publication in 1955, you'd imagine that Donleavy could easily afford to heat his pool if he wanted. But chasing around the fields after his herd of cattle keeps him trim and healthy – as do regular bouts of shadow-boxing. An amateur fighter in his youth, he's still able to throw five or six punches in under a second.

"How many was that?" he asks, following a furious volley that stops just short of my nose. "I'm probably faster now than in my early days!"

By all accounts, Donleavy was quite the hot-headed pugilist – regularly getting into scraps in Dublin bars. Many of these altercations began over his then-unfashionable facial hair.

"I was in the Navy, and in the U.S. you couldn't grow a beard," he explains, stroking his silver whiskers. "And I remember when I left the Navy I thought, 'My God, that's the first thing I'm going to do' – it takes up a half hour of your morning, you are cutting yourself with razors, and so I said, 'I'm going to let my beard grow'."

Which obviously didn't go down so well in 1940's Dublin.

"That's right. Then my reputation began to grow because any of the fights that did occur never lasted more than fifty seconds maybe, if they were lucky. The only thing I had to be careful about was not to hurt my fists, because when you're hitting a jaw you're hitting a hard substance. And so I had to be very careful, because all these bones here are broken from punches.

"So I had to instruct myself how to hit the opponent in the mid-section. I was as worried hitting people there, because you can perforate an organ inside the body, you know, with the smallness of the fist. And so you were always in that terrible situation of (risking) being up for murder.

"I think my last big fight was with, probably, someone like Behan. Though neither of us threw a punch in the end. We had a row in Davey Byrne's or somewhere and went out onto the street to sort it out. And Behan said to me, 'No-one's come out of the pub to watch us fight – so why the hell should we bother?' So we didn't! Behan was full of charm."

Legend has it that there was once talk of a televised bout with Norman Mailer in New York sometime in the mid-1960s.

"That's right!" he laughs, looking as though he's only just remembered. "We were meant to have a big fight. Mailer was a really tough guy. It wasn't just a pose. Someone told me that they'd gone up near his house, and in the garage were punching bags, and they could hear, at 6am, these fists landing on the punching bags. Norman, he was a tough son of a bitch.

"So, I remember when finally we did meet, we shook hands and just laughed. But I met a lot of fighters in the end because I could throw five or six or seven punches in one second. And that's a lot of punches. Not many of even the better fighters could do that."

It's not surprising that he's so useful with his fists. Born to poor Irish immigrant parents in Woodlawn, New York City, in 1926, James Patrick Donleavy – 'Mike' to his friends – grew up in the Bronx. He first discovered his literary talent as a young teenager.

"I began to write, even as a schoolboy," he says. "I went to a pretty good school called Fordham Preparatory School, which was part of Fordham University. And my work was recognised by a couple of the teachers, and when I was being kicked-out for being a bad influence on the student body that was what was said, pleading on my behalf. One of the teachers said, 'You're throwing a boy out of this school. He will, as an author, probably be one of the few pupils who will make this school famous'. And, of course, they didn't pay any… sort of notion to that."

Having served in the US Navy during WWII, he took advantage of the GI Bill and travelled to Ireland in 1946 to study science at Trinity. While still at university, he set himself up as a painter – though his debut exhibition wasn't held until 1950.

"I had been a painter, you see, and that put me in a position where I had an audience of some sort. And my first writings were published as forewords to the catalogues and the exhibitions. So that was the beginning of my published career

– self-publishing."

Which discipline gives you most satisfaction?

"Oh, I think both have an equal position. I might find myself making notes all the time throughout the day – on various matters – and I might also be, at the same time, drawing something."

He tells me that he wrote his first novel as a means of helping to sell his paintings.

"I had gone to London and I was trying to sell some pictures, and I remember the man saying to me, 'Well look, your paintings, we are very impressed by them. They're marvellous pictures – watercolours and all kinds of things – and we'd like to set up an exhibition or something, but you just aren't famous enough yet'. And I just thought, 'How does one ever get famous enough?' It seemed impossible to do much about it. Then the idea of writing a book came up."

Donleavy has previously stated that he'd already decided upon his main ambition in life while still in his teens: "To write a book that will make your mother and father drop dead with shame."

He almost succeeded with *The Ginger Man* (which was banned in Ireland for many years). Wild, lusty and bawdy, it follows the misadventures of Sebastian Balfe Dangerfield, a 27-year-old Irish-American ex-pat, with a weakness for women and booze, living in bohemian Dublin after the war. He began writing the picaresque novel while still at Trinity, basing the Sebastian character on his friend and fellow American student, Gainor Stephen Crist. However, it took several years to complete.

Even today the novel reads well, though Donleavy's wildly erratic prose style takes a little getting used to. "My big advantage is being practically uneducated," he laughs, "and my grammar being appalling." Packed with verb-less sentences, the narrative frequently switches tenses and swings vertiginously between first and third persons. In the following passage, a hungover Dangerfield returns home to find his wife has left him:

"*Sebastian went looking for aspirin. The house looks unusually empty. The closet. Marion's clothes are gone. Just my broken rubbers on the floor. The nursery. Cleaned out. Bare. Take that white cold hand off my heart.*"

The book was rejected by more than 30 publishers in the UK and US. Eventually, Behan advised him to submit it to Maurice Girodias of the Paris-based Olympia Press. "I couldn't get published because of the nature of the work," he recalls. "Publishers thought it was obscene and that they'd be prosecuted for publication."

While it specialised in literary erotica, Olympia had (almost accidentally) published some of the most leftfield authors of the time – including Burroughs, Trocchi, Miller and Nabokov. However, unbeknownst to Donleavy, they were about to move into more hardcore territory. Girodias happily accepted *The Ginger Man*, seemingly on its literary merits, but then published it as part of the pornographic Travellers Companion Series. Donleavy wasn't even credited as writer.

On receiving his first green-jacketed copies in the mail, the outraged author

– who'd been paid £250 by a middleman in a Soho bookshop – swore: "If it were the last thing I ever did, I would redeem and avenge this work. The book was treated as a piece of pornography. It wouldn't get any reviews. It was a total disaster. I never had what one would imagine would be the pleasure of becoming an author and getting an audience and all the rest of it."

Initially it was Girodias who sued Donleavy, after the author re-sold the rights to publish the novel to a small, now defunct, London publishing house called Neville Spearman. Girodias argued that Donleavy had no such entitlement under their terms of agreement, and took him to court. A long, torturous and bitter legal dispute ensued. It took more than 22 years of litigation, but, by the end of it, in a stunning coup de grace, Donleavy wound up owning Olympia. Having declared himself insolvent, Girodias was preparing to buy back the Olympia Press title at an auction in Paris. Donleavy heard of the sale and sent his new wife to France with a bagful of cash. Girodias ran out of funds at $8,000, Donleavy's wife (or "the mysterious woman," as the hapless French publisher saw her) made a final bid and – voila! – he was the new owner of Olympia.

Even today, Donleavy doesn't have a good word to say about his arch nemesis. "Clearly we were bitter enemies," he says.

For his part, in an interview shortly before his death in 1990, Girodias described the story of their battle for ownership of *The Ginger Man* as "fabulous. Much better than the book, actually."

Over the course of his legal marathon, fought in various courtrooms in London, Paris and New York, Donleavy had by necessity become something of an expert on international copyright law.

"I learned so much about the law. There was a British writer named Ian Fleming – a very well-known writer who wrote these sort of detective novels *(the James Bond series)* – and he got into a lot of difficulties and troubles, and his lawyers wrote to him in London: 'We advise you, that with all your problems in this regard that you are presently having with piracy, and all sorts of things, that you write to Mr J.P. Donleavy, who we regard as being a great authority in this area, and may help you more than we can, because we haven't the experience that he has'."

And did you help him?

"A little. I got to know him briefly. He was great company, and fascinating to have around. He spent a lot of time on some island *(Jamaica)*, I believe."

Although Donleavy has penned more than a dozen novels since *The Ginger Man* (including *A Singular Man, The Onion Eaters,* and *A Fairy Tale of New York*), he seems to be relatively at peace with the fact that he'll be best remembered for his infamous debut.

He still writes every day, working laboriously in longhand in his study and getting his secretary, who works in a different wing of the house, to type the pages up (on some days they don't even see each other). It is what you might call old school.

"Oh yes, my day is busy all the time," he insists. "You know, from the moment I wake up, and even when I sleep – my thoughts and stuff – so I'm making notes and doing things all the time. Observations. And literally, every day I might, say, get down at least 100 words on various matters. But if I'm working on a manuscript I have to sit to it, doing the work, and go through it. And my re-writing is… considerable. I might have 12 versions that I end up going through. And every little word I kind of fit it exactly, so that everything is perfection, in terms of that it is right in its rhythm nearly."

Nearly. But for all the drafting and re-drafting, he has never matched *The Ginger Man*, its impact stretching over the decades. The book was in the news again when it was reported that Johnny Depp wanted to make a movie version. The reason for his interest is obvious. A fellow Kentuckian, Depp was a very close friend of the late gonzo journalist Hunter S. Thompson. Always a big admirer of Donleavy's writing, Thompson once declared that "without *The Ginger Man*, there would have been no *Fear and Loathing in Las Vegas*."

Back in the 1970s, Thompson wrote Donleavy a letter to that effect. Does he remember receiving it?

"Vaguely," he replies. "That was always pleasant to hear that someone liked one's book. I think I might have sent back a kind of thing. I never seemed to have got into back-and-forth communications with people."

He met Johnny Depp to discuss the potential movie project.

"Good God, that Mr Depp, he certainly attracts a lot of attention," Donleavy chuckles. "We had a long talk together in New York, and he came around to where I was staying – I'm a member of this place, probably one of the only surviving ones over many years, called the New York Athletic Club – and he came up and we were talking in my room which overlooks Central Park, a very beautiful location. And I remember when he saw a manuscript on the floor he said, 'What's that? That looks very curious. I can read some of the title'. 'Yes,' I said, 'well, the full title is *The Dog on the Seventeenth Floor*'."

It's Donleavy's current work in progress.

"I've been working at it every day now. But it's a book about New York, and, I suppose, if one was summing it up, it's about the problems that arise with a man and a girl, and she turns out to be one of the richest girls in the world. And suddenly it's amazing the kind of things that crop up around this difficulty – a woman being so rich that it actually inhibits relationships. And the girl, who actually does exist, is very beautiful."

She's based on someone you know?

"Yes, this very charming and beautiful girl: she came on a couple of visits here. I remember we went down to the lake – we walked to the lake – and her boots, there was a hole in one of her boots, and it was ice cold, the water. She never complained and I was very much taken by that. 'My God, here is a woman who doesn't complain about anything'."

The expression that passes over his face suggests that maybe this is exactly what he needs in his life right now: a woman who doesn't complain. The moment passes. Would you, I ask, welcome a film version of *The Ginger Man*?

"Yes I would, with someone like Depp, who controls so much, and likes the role, and I've seen him play it, and I realise he could do something pretty striking with it. But it's a difficult role. I have watched it played by, well, Richard Harris being the first one to play it, and a few other people."

Harris played it for three days on the Dublin stage…

"And the Church stepped in and banned it," Donleavy says. "It was pretty scary because, you see, The Church could send out people – members of the religion – dressed in their gear, or not, and follow you all around town. We were followed everywhere we went. They closed down all access, the telephone company cut off lines …"

Are you religious at all?

"No, I sort of lost my religion at a pretty early age – from about 13 or 14 I sort of felt unsympathetic. And I was actually at Catholic schools – Jesuit schools – they were the most liberal and intelligent of the people, so it was never pushed down my throat, Catholicism. But they regarded me as a real threat.

"It gives people an imaginative situation," he adds, "which encourages and restores their, sort of, welfare, in the sense that they can relax a little bit about their problems. So I regard religion as being very important and beneficial."

A father of four adult children, Donleavy has been married and divorced twice – to Valerie Heron in 1946, and to Mary Wilson Price in 1970 (who later went on to marry a Guinness heir). Although currently single, he still very much enjoys female company. In his 1997 collection of essays, *An Author and His Image*, he even placed a lonely hearts-style ad at the end of his book.

"Did I?" he says, looking intrigued. "Really? What did I say?"

I pull the book from my bag, flick to the end, and read: *"Slightly reclusive, but anxious to get out more, gracefully older, fit man… still capable of eight-and-a-half successive deep knee-bends, nine sit-ups, and five-and-a-half push-ups, and with minor public status, requests pleasantly attractive younger lady of principle with a bent for flower-arranging and entertaining…"*

Donleavy laughs: "Let me see that book. That's always the danger of meeting people like yourself, you go right in."

He leafs excitedly through the book, as though seeing it for the first time. "Isn't this astonishing! I don't know if I can remember even seeing this cover, or anything to do with this. I don't remember this."

Well, there must be so many editions of your books out there at this point.

"Yeah, probably. God, if you could I'd love to be sent a copy of that, because I can't remember even having this book."

I tell him he can have my copy…

"Are you serious? Goodness. Well, maybe you could write something on the cover that you are giving this to me, because that's very much appreciated."

As I inscribe the message, it feels like our interview is coming to an end. He's tired and I don't want to push him, but a cheeky question seems in order: has he seen much sexual decadence over the years?

"Not a great deal," he shrugs, with just a hint of disappointment. "You know, I regarded myself as just a professional gentleman, and one tried to keep relationships alive. I generally had a girlfriend around. And this is one of the times in one's life which wouldn't be unusual, in one's age group, to not have that many ladies about – but I'm still in touch with various people that I have things in common with."

When was the last time you had a lady friend visit the estate?

"Well, they come here as visitors," he reflects. "One, say, two or three weeks ago. But it's tough at one's age to begin to get any long-term arrangements made with women. They figure, 'Well, how long are you going to hold out?'"

He throws a flurry of punches. "That's how many punches? I don't know, you can't even see them!"

The old machismo, it seems, is still alive, even if his powers have been waning...

"But I can't," he says, "go up and demonstrate this to women, and say, 'Hey look! I'm perfectly healthy'. You know, sometimes I used to scare the wits out of a couple of girlfriends because I would suddenly – knowing that they might see me walk down the hall there – I'd start to go like this down the hall *(he lurches across the room like Quasimodo)*. Ha! And they'd see this scary old figure. But women are very conscious of: how long has he got left to live?"

Not meaning to be rude, but I would have thought that could present itself as quite an attractive proposition for certain women...

"Yes!" Donleavy laughs. "Well, now they could figure, 'Will he leave any money?'"

He keeps the answer to himself.

{MAY, 2010}

CHAPTER FIVE:
Larry Flynt

According to his autobiography, *An Unseemly Man*, the very first time that Larry Claxton Flynt had sexual intercourse, he perpetrated premeditated rape. Once the dirty deed was done, he murdered his victim and disposed of the body.

Although the founder and publisher of *Hustler* magazine has served a certain amount of jail time over the course of his wild and eventful life (mostly for contempt of court), he's never been charged for that particular crime. Naturally, it's the first thing I mention when I'm introduced to the notorious 65-year-old pornographer.

"I'll never live down that story," Flynt sighs, speaking in a slow, raspy, Kentuckian drawl. "What a lot of people don't realise is that young boys raised on a farm mess around with the animals. It's part of growing up, you know? I must have been eight or nine years old at the time. It's just a silly thing. But most people move on in their life and they forget about it, or they're too embarrassed to bring it up. Me, I'm always able to talk about everything."

So you haven't been tempted to have sex with any chickens since? "Nah – I like girls much better," he guffaws.

It's a beautifully balmy afternoon in Beverly Hills, and we're meeting in a luxurious, glass-walled enclave on the tenth floor of the imposing Los Angeles HQ of Larry Flynt Publications (or "the skyscraper that porn built," as one local bartender put it). The panoramic view is spectacular – to the west, the modest city skyline gives way to the rolling Pacific, to the east you can see the San Gabriel Mountains, high above Pasadena.

While the bulk of Flynt's vast personal fortune (estimated to be in excess of $500 million) was amassed peddling smut of the lowest gynaecological order, you certainly wouldn't realise it from his place of work. His lavish personal office – which was used in the filming of Miles Forman's acclaimed biopic *The People Versus Larry Flynt* – is larger than your average hotel lobby, and is expensively decked out with oil paintings, rugs, statues, antiques and objects d'art. Truly, it's a room fit for a porn king. Flanked by two priceless Tiffany lamps, his impressive hand-carved desk is slightly bigger than a snooker table and must weigh at least a ton. Paralysed from the waist down following an assassination attempt in 1978, Flynt sits impassively in his customised, gold-plated wheelchair on one side, while I holler my questions over from the other.

He's a large, powerful-looking man, with a blotchy, medicated face and receding red hair. He's not especially friendly: he just sits there, expressionlessly, calmly taking me in. Occasionally he wraps one of his trembling and heavily bejewelled paws around a tumbler full of ice and throws a few cubes into his mouth, noisily crunching them to slush. Even when he's not chewing ice cubes, he can be quite hard to understand. Some years ago he suffered a stroke caused by an overdose of his painkiller medication; he's had mild pronunciation difficulties ever since. Sounding permanently out of breath, he also harrumphs quite regularly, like a horse.

I've been loosely granted 30 minutes for the interview, but they're not guaranteed. His PA has already informed me that, "Mr. Flynt prefers shorter interviews." He'll let me know when my time is up.

Ten years ago, Flynt's eldest daughter, Tonya Flynt-Vega, wrote a book entitled *Hustled* in which she claimed that he had sexually abused her as a child. I decide to postpone asking him about it for a while. Not that there's any shortage of questions. Writing about Flynt in the introduction to *An Unseemly Man*, Oliver Stone (who produced the biopic) described his rags-to-riches life as a minefield of contradictions:

> On one hand, Larry Flynt was raised dirt poor in a one-room shack in Kentucky. On the other, he knows what it is to have more money than he could ever spend. He has had sex both with a chicken and with some of the world's most beautiful women. He has been a fervent born-again Christian and a reckless atheist. He has lived a pagan, orgiastic lifestyle, but he has also had to contend with being paralyzed in the prime of his life. He has been railroaded and jailed by the justice system, but he has also had his most noble triumph in the halls of the Supreme Court, in one of the finest hours of recent American legal history. He is someone desperately trying to obtain a certain respect, but he is also hopelessly tethered by his crude roots and the derivation of his wealth. And finally, while he has known the great power of running an empire, he has also known the hopelessness of watching the true love of his life suffer from AIDS and eventually die of a drug overdose.

Stone wrote those words more than a decade ago. Since then, Flynt has opened a Hustler casino and a string of sex stores, fought even more contentious legal battles, and scandalised Washington by offering cash payments for information about politicians' sex lives – ending a few high profile political careers as a direct result...

So where to begin with this unseemly man? There are signed photographs of Larry and his (fifth) wife with President Jimmy Carter and Bill Clinton facing outwards on the desktop. I remark that I'm surprised they'd consent to meet him.

"They all love to meet me, but they don't wanna be associated with me."

Flynt once ran for President himself – standing briefly against Ronald Reagan in 1983. "Ah, I was just having fun," he smiles, nonchalantly waving his hand. "I didn't have any illusions of grandeur. I just wanted to muddy the waters a little bit."

More recently, he was a candidate in the 2003 California recall of Governor Gray Davis, styling himself as a "smut peddler who cares." He ultimately placed sixth in a field of 135 candidates.

"I did that for the same reason – I just took advantage of the platform. I'm in the casino business, too, and I think the State of California has been treating casino owners pretty shabbily. They're dealing primarily with the Indians and it's not really an equal playing field. I don't care what they give the Indians in terms of gaming, but they should make the same thing available to our casinos. That's the reason I got involved in the governor's race."

Does he know Arnold Schwarzenegger?

"Yeah, I know Arnold," he affirms. "Every time I see him I almost avoid shaking his hand, because he's got so much power in his hand. I've got rings on both hands, so when he shakes my hand, he just smiles and goes, 'Hello Larry! Hello Larry!' and he squeezes my fucking hand and I'm ready to fucking *die!* I've been trying to get him to change some of the gaming regulations, but I can't get nowhere with him."

Flynt opened the Hustler Casino in nearby Gardena in 2000. Reportedly it adds another $20million to his bank balance every year.

"I'm a gambler, that's how I spend all my spare time," he explains. "I'm primarily a poker player. Poker or blackjack. I love it. And besides, I don't do much water-skiing, mountain-climbing or any of that kind of stuff, you know, so I gotta find activities that I'm comfortable participating in. So cards is a very good choice."

We're meeting in the week that Hillary Clinton's been caught out lying about coming under sniper fire during a visit to Bosnia. Although Flynt's a Democrat, he's not impressed by any of the candidates in the race to replace George W. Bush.

"It's really depressing," he sighs, heavily. "I can't believe the way these candidates – all of 'em – are getting caught in lies. And then they're fessing up by saying, 'Oh well, I mis-spoke'. I dunno why they use this term 'mis-spoke'. I don't know why they just can't say they *lied*. When I see this going on in a presidential race, I think, 'Man, do you really want any of these people in the White House?' They tell a lie when the truth sounds better. It's just silly."

Do you give money to any candidates?

"I give money to some of the lesser candidates, some of the senate races and things like that. I didn't give it to any of the people that are leading the pack."

If you became President tomorrow, what's the first thing you'd do?

He stares off into space for a moment and then chuckles softly. "You see, I really have more visions of being a dictator than I do President. Because even though I'm staunchly against the death penalty, if it was in my power to do it, I would march Bush and Cheney out of their offices and onto the lawn under that big oak tree, and I'd *hang* them bastards! Because that's what they deserve! But they're gonna ride off into the sunset, they've already lined their pockets, and they're gonna live happily ever after. That's not right! And Americans aren't any better off because they spent eight years fucking up the country. So you look at dictators down through the centuries, I mean, they knew that the heads had to roll from time to time to keep... order."

Is that how you run your businesses?

"Yeah. I don't have to kill them. They just leave if I get mad enough."

Do you have a bad temper?

"I only lose my temper about twice a year. Someone has to make a really big mistake to get me mad, but I've got one. I keep it under control."

It suddenly occurs to me that perhaps it's not so strange that he knows Jimmy Carter. After all, back in 1977, Carter's evangelist sister, Ruth Carter Stapleton, briefly converted Flynt to Christianity. Although he continued to publish *Hustler* (vowing to "hustle for God"), he apparently took it seriously – even claiming that he'd had a vision of God on his private jet. But not any more. "I got over all that," he laughs when I mention it.

Do you still believe in a God?

"No way! To me, the hereafter is sort of like a fantasy-land for people who are afraid of the dark. The mind is a very complicated organ, and it puts people through a lot of spaces because we have numerous numbers of mental disorders and manic depressions, mania, psychosis, schizophrenia. They all come out of the brain. And in many ways, although we know a great deal about it, we only know about a tenth of what we could know in terms of how the brain functions.

"These people that have these born again experiences or these spiritual experiences... First of all, it's embarrassing so they're not gonna go see a shrink. They'll talk to a neighbour or a pastor of a church, and then they join the flock and they're set for the rest of their life to take in that fire and brimstone on a weekly basis. I'm very, very comfortable about my feelings about humanity and what's on the other side."

Flynt was an underage recruit in both the army and the navy before becoming involved in the bar and vending-machine businesses. Living in Dayton, Ohio, in the late 1960s, he opened a strip joint named the Hustler Club, the first in the State to feature fully nude dancers. Business was so good that within a couple of years, he owned and operated six Hustler Clubs in as many different cities.

In March 1972, he published a primitive four-page black & white brochure called the *Hustler Newsletter*, ostensibly to advertise his clubs and dancers. The monthly publication was well-received by his customers and soon began to expand – first to 16-pages, and then to 32.

In mid-1973, the US sank deep into recession, which had a catastrophic impact on his strip joints, as punters tightened their spending. Hit with a major tax bill and finding himself heavily in debt, Flynt had to find financing quickly. He decided to turn the *Hustler Newsletter* into a national sex magazine, financing it with strip club money that he should have used to pay his tax bill. *Hustler* had been in existence for less than four years when he and his lawyer, Gene Reeves Jr. were shot outside the Lawrenceville county courthouse in Georgia, where he was due to face charges of obscenity related to *Hustler* on March 6, 1978.

He tells me that he can still vividly recall the incident.

"You don't ever forget stuff like that. It happened to me when I was 36 and in the prime of my life. But I've always been someone who doesn't dwell on anything I can't change. I don't like spending my life feeling sorry for myself. I was already caught up in the fight for free speech at the time – so I continued to fight for free expression. I did it on all fronts. I had the money to do it, and I had the motivation to do it. So I probably would not have fought as diligently if I hadn't of got shot."

Although nobody was ever charged, both Flynt and the authorities believe that the shooter was a white supremacist serial killer named Joseph Paul Franklin.

"He's waiting on a death sentence on four other capital murders," he says. "He was a white supremacist. He supposedly shot me because he was upset about a photo feature of a black and white couple published in *Hustler*."

Flynt's sexual vision was unashamedly vulgar. Unimpressed with *Playboy's* idealised and soft focused 'girls next door', *Hustler* was deliberately tasteless, crude, scatological and gynaecologically explicit, presenting readers with 'sluts next door'. The debut issue of the magazine appeared in July 1974 and immediately caused major controversy by featuring 'pink shots' (i.e. up close and personal images of female vaginas). His distribution company threatened to have it removed from the market, sparking the first of many legal battles.

He persevered, though, and before long *Hustler* hit international infamy. Flynt was approached by a paparazzo who had nude photographs of former First Lady Jacqueline Kennedy Onassis relaxing by a pool. The shots had been taken four years previously, when she was 41-years-old. Flynt paid $18,000 for them and ran them in the August 1975 edition. It proved to be an excellent investment. The controversy brought him to international attention, and *Hustler* sold over a million copies within a couple of days.

As it happened, Jackie's late husband was the first US President that Flynt ever met. "Yeah, I met JFK briefly back when I was in the navy," he nods. "Just shook hands with him and said hello."

Funny how things turned out, eh? Nude shots of his wife later made you rich…

"Yeah," he grunts, chewing another mouthful of ice cubes.

He still pays big bucks for controversial shots. Just last month, he hit the headlines when he offered 22-year-old Ashley Alexandra Dupré – the call girl involved in the recent downfall of New York governor Eliot Spitzer – a cool million dollars to pose naked for *Hustler*. She turned him down.

Flynt insists that she made a mistake. "My advice to her attorney was that she should make as much money as fast as she can, because this story isn't gonna be around for very long. He's probably advising her, and she's probably got friends or associates advising her on book deals and potential movie deals and what have you, but, you know, people always make the mistake of not properly taking advantage of their 15 minutes of fame. So I think that's gonna be her problem."

It's also been rumoured that he paid some US soldiers $750,000 for a set of nude shots of Private Jessica Lynch (the supposed "POW" dramatically "rescued" from an Iraqi hospital). The photographs had apparently been taken in an army barracks. Ultimately, he decided not to publish them.

"That's the only time I ever bought pictures that I didn't run. I realised that she'd been a pawn in the war on Iraq. They had her in this hospital and the Iraqis wanted to give her back to the US Army and they told them no, they wanted them to hold onto her so they could put together this Hollywood-style rescue team – and try to deliver her as Bush's Joan of Ark, so to speak.

"When I realised how shabbily she'd been treated by the Bush administration,

I made a decision not to publish the photographs. They were taken in a more innocent time and no doubt she had many happy boyfriends along the trail, but that's no big deal. I just didn't want to exploit that particular angle when the government had screwed up so badly."

Speaking of governments screwing up, during the impeachment proceedings against Bill Clinton in 1998, Flynt offered a million dollars for evidence about the sexual affairs of Republican lawmakers, explaining that "desperate times require desperate measures." He published the results in a special magazine named *The Flynt Report*, an act which directly led to the resignation of incoming house speaker Bob Livingston. His muckraking investigations are far from over. In June of last year, he placed an ad in the *Washington Post* offering $1million for documented stories involving sex with current congressional members or high-ranking government officials.

"I don't expose these guys just for the sake of exposing their sex life. I expose them because of their hypocrisy. I see that as the biggest enemy facing democracy. It's their hypocrisy – if they lie to their wife and they lie to their mistress, how do I know that they can even be trusted? You've gotta understand that to become a politician, you've gotta have a massive ego, you've gotta have a strong sex drive. Most of those guys are located in Washington, which is away from their family. So they're like lab rats, you know? And it's not that difficult to catch them out. The only way I can have an influence on government is doing just what I'm doing. Very carefully and methodically bring 'em down, one by one."

You must have some powerful enemies...

"Yeah, well what they gonna do? They've dragged me through the courts, imprisoned me, I've been shot, you know. So what else can they do? So I'm just going for broke."

In the early years, Flynt fought a number of high profile courtroom battles regarding the regulation of pornography and free speech involving the First Amendment. His most infamous case began in 1983 when the Reverend Jerry Falwell sued him over an ad parody in *Hustler* that suggested Falwell had lost his virginity to his mother in an outhouse. After five years, the case wound up in the Supreme Court. The court ruled that public figures cannot recover damages for "intentional infliction of emotional distress" based on parodies. Apparently, he and Falwell developed a very civil relationship afterwards.

Also in 1983, he refused to disclose his source for a controversial surveillance tape of FBI agents deliberately entrapping car manufacturer John DeLorean and ended up in court again. Flynt turned up one day wearing an American flag as a diaper, and was found guilty of contempt of court. He had already been charged with contempt earlier that year during yet another trial – this one involving a 1976 libel against Kathy Keeton, the then-girlfriend of *Penthouse* publisher Bob Guccione. That case finally reached the Supreme Court in 1983. During proceedings, a heavily medicated Flynt repeatedly shouted *"FUCK THIS COURT!"* (and wore a T-shirt bearing the same sentiment). He also referred to the judges as, "Nothing but eight assholes and a token cunt!" (referring to Justice Sandra Day O'Connor). Although arrested for contempt, the charges were later dropped.

American justice doesn't come cheap. How much money has Flynt spent on lawyers over the years?

"You know, over the last 35 years probably about $50million. That's just for lawyers, that's not settlements or anything, just legal fees."

After all of his courtroom experiences, he could probably dispense with the attorneys and defend himself at this stage.

"I might not have a law degree," he says, "but when it comes to the question of obscenity and the First Amendment, I probably have more knowledge than anybody."

When's the last time you were in a courtroom?

"I've been staying pretty quiet on that front. But back when I was fighting with all of them over the release of the DeLorean tape, they jailed me for not giving up my sources, they threw me in for contempt of court. I was like living in a courtroom. I wouldn't recommend anybody behave the way I did, but it finally got to a point where the prosecutors told my lawyers, 'We don't wanna see your client any more! Don't bring him in here!' Because there was a circus every time. I took the attitude: if they're gonna treat me like a joke, I'll just act like one."

As a committed freedom of speech advocate, Flynt still bankrolls numerous legal battles.

"We're constantly putting out bushfires all over the country," he explains. "I just supported and paid to defend a woman in Texas who was charged for… you know, they're like Tupperware parties where the women get together in the neighbourhood, and they buy and exchange sex toys. They busted her for that and sex toys was made illegal in the State of Texas. But we got all that overturned.

"A few years back the Republicans tacked a rider to a big defence bill for the year and tried to make virtual porn obscene. Now virtual porn means that there's no actors or actresses, no children involved. Digitally, a company like Pixar here in California can create lifelike figures out of thin air – and that's what you call virtual porn. The question was raised if there's nobody being exploited in this – you know, it's just computer imagery – do they wanna interfere with your thought process? They wanna tell you that you can't handle seeing something even though it's not real.

"Senator Orrin Hatch got that thing through. My attorney, Lou Sirkin, took that to the United States Supreme Court and won the case. You see, if you don't fight these laws, they become the law of the land. And the reason I do it – and a couple of other people that I'm friends with, like the Freedom Coalition people – if we don't get together and fight 'em, the government will just keep steamrolling. They pass some of the stupidest laws. Some of the cities and the States do the same thing. It's impossible to fight all of them, so we've just gotta pick and choose."

Freedom of speech is obviously one of Flynt's major passions. While they're never going to stick his face on Mount Rushmore, some consider him an American hero. "It's one thing to study the First Amendment in class, and it's another thing being in the trenches and dealing with it. Like in 1977, I stood before a judge and he sentenced me to seven to 25 years in jail for publishing *Hustler*. Now, fortunately, that got reversed on appeal. But I think something like that has to happen to you before you realise that, hey, individual rights is something that can no longer be taken for granted. You can lose them as easily as you can gain them. You can go out and take a poll today – 98% of the people will tell you they believe in free speech. Go back to them and say, 'Well what about hate speech, flag-burning and pornography?' They'll say, 'Uh, I didn't know you were talking about that!'

"So all of a sudden a 98% favourability drops to 50% or below. So everyone has their own version of what free speech should be. They don't realise that, in order to defend free speech, you have to stand on a podium with somebody who, to the top of his lungs, advocates everything that you have fought against your entire life and makes your blood boil... Well, if you can defend his right to free speech, then you have earned your position to be a part of the rare few that can do it."

The Jackie O issue made Flynt a millionaire. In 1976, he created his privately held company Larry Flynt Publications (LFP) and began publishing and distributing other sex magazines – most notably *Barely Legal* and *Taboo*. A decade later, LFP began publishing more mainstream magazines as well. In 1996, LFP sold off the distribution business and most of its mainstream titles. Two years later, they began to produce pornographic movies. Today, LFP publishes just one mainstream magazine – *Tips & Tricks Video Game Codebook*. However, it still turns a more than healthy $150 million profit every year. Needless to say, the rise of the internet has irrevocably changed the face – and other bodily parts – of the porno business. But while newsstand sales are down, his online business is good.

"*Hustler* obviously sells less today, but back in the early '90s we realised the impact the internet was gonna have. It was inevitable that this was going to erode the circulation of not just men's magazines but of publications in general. And it's done that. Even newspapers are fighting to stay alive – they're losing 2 or 3% of their circulation a year."

How do you get on with Hugh Hefner?

"I've known Hefner for years. He kind of thinks he invented sex and he always wants to take the high ground. It's really difficult for me to have much of a relationship with him. He does deserve a lot of accolades for being in the forefront of the sexual revolution and the feminist movement back in the '60s, but he's still pretty much stuck in that period of time. He didn't grow. You've heard of that theory called the Peter Principle. You know, a guy grows so high in the company and he can't grow any higher. He's just peaked out. I think Hef fits that mould."

We've been talking for more than half-an-hour, and I'm concerned that he'll terminate the interview at any moment. Time to turn up the heat a little. Your daughter, Tonya, published a book in 1998 accusing you of molesting her as a child. You disowned her at the time. Have you patched things up since? Curiously, Larry seems to brighten up a little when I ask this question.

"I took a polygraph test and passed. And then she called and I'd instructed my secretary to tape any calls that she made. So she made some calls and she apologised for what she did, and said she didn't know why, and would I forgive her, and all that sort of thing."

And did you forgive her?

He shrugs: "She's got a host of mental problems and I don't need them on my

Johnny Adair

SELECTED RECORDINGS: 2000-2010

Johnny Adair and Olaf

Peter Buck

John Cooper Clarke and Olaf

SELECTED RECORDINGS: 2000-2010

JP Donleavy and Olaf

Larry Flynt

Lady Gaga

SELECTED RECORDINGS: 2000-2010

Larry Harvey

Hugh Hefner

Ron Jeremy and Olaf

Steve Jones

SELECTED RECORDINGS: 2000-2010

Courtney Love

plate now."

You've got four other children. Are you close to them?

"No. I'm close to one daughter that works for me here *(Theresa Flynt is VP of Development of Hustler Hollywood Stores)*. The rest of my kids spend the whole week discussing how I screwed up their lives. Ha, ha! That's how they spend their lives."

You're now onto your fifth marriage...

"Well, I'm with somebody," he says. "I've been married for a while. But the sparks don't fly like they used to."

I don't mean to be rude but, erm, is it all still working down there?

"Yeah. The bullet that sunk me didn't hit my spinal cord, it hit the base of my spinal cord. It hit my *cauda equina* – which is Latin for 'horse's tail', and it's a bundle of sensory nerves that come out of the base of your spine cord. So I just basically lost my motor nerves in my lower extremities. But the sensory nerves are still there."

Do you have any regrets?

"I wish I'd worn a bulletproof vest when I went on trial that day. Ha, ha!"

Hustler used to publish a regular cartoon called *Chester the Molester*, created by your cartoon editor, Dwaine Tinsley. However, Tinsley was imprisoned for molesting his own daughter in the 1980s, and you rehired him when he was released.

"Well, he's since passed away. What he was accused of was very much out of character. His conviction is no longer on the books. That was throwed out by the court. So it's difficult for me to talk about. Was he a child molester? I don't really know. He worked for me for about 25 years and I never had any inclination that he had any kind of sexual preference involving children."

Over the years, *Hustler* has frequently pushed the boundaries of taste, and published graphic photoshoots depicting everything from gang-rape to incest. One particularly infamous cover in 1978 depicted a naked woman being fed into a meat grinder (ironically, it appeared during his 'born-again' phase).

So is Larry Flynt a misogynist?

He shrugs his shoulders: "Well, I've had thousands of girls pose for my publications and I've never had one – not one – tell me that she was being exploited or that what she was being asked to do was demeaning to women. I can understand why you've got both the religious right and the feminists criticising pornography. But they're coming at you from two different directions." He crunches another ice cube. "There are two classes of people that oppose pornography – those who don't know what they're missing, and those who don't know what they're talking about.

"I've been blamed for every ill that society has embodied over the last 30 years. But I hope it will happen in my lifetime that people will begin to get over this sex question, you know? We know very little about human sexuality other than that people do it. But it's difficult to get an intelligent dialogue going on about human sexuality because the church feels threatened by it – and the feminists are the same. But the feminists attacks are dwindling because (Andrea) Dworkin and some of those other people have all passed away and they've gone, so the only 'patriarch' you have is Gloria Steinem. And she's lost a tremendous amount of her influence and will continue to lose it."

Flynt blames feminists for the controversial defeat of the Equal Rights Amendment back in the early 1970s.

"We'd got a constitutional amendment – they needed 38 States to ratify it and they fell one state short. Feminists felt that all the rhetoric regarding the women's movement should come out of New York. And they forgot about that woman in Topeka, Kansas, that's trying to get three kids and a husband off to school and work. Although she was proud to be a feminist, she didn't really have time to be part of the team. So the radicals turned off a lot of those people. The feminists shot themselves in the foot – they defeated themselves. Otherwise the Equal Rights Amendment would've passed. 1971 is light years away. A lot of the people in college graduating today weren't even born then, so they don't know the history of the Equal Rights Amendment, why it didn't pass. And they don't really understand why they have to work for 25% less than what men work for in the same job."

With that, he looks over at his PA and nods. My time's obviously up.

But not quite. Larry's PA invites me to a talk he's giving this evening to a media studies class in the University of Southern California. It's basically a screening of *The People Versus Larry Flynt*, followed by a Q&A session mediated by award-winning *San Francisco Chronicle* columnist Robert Scheer.

There's a full house. I sit with Larry's wife of 10 years, Liz, a softy spoken LA-native of Mexican extraction (apparently she used to be his part-time nurse), and we witness him charm a highly sceptical audience. Liz applauds his every joke. His armed bodyguard waits watchfully in the wings. Initially, the students want to know what he thought of Woody Harrelson's portrayal of him in the movie. "Woody played me better than I play myself," he laughs.

Many of the questions that follow are similar to the ones I asked him earlier – and often he gives exactly the same response, word for word. He gets a standing ovation at the end.

Afterwards, we head on to The Four Seasons for a late dinner. Larry's trembling hands make him quite a messy eater, but Liz is on hand to wipe his soup from his chin. She barely has time to touch her own. He's an entertaining and amiable host. He even offers some post interview analysis. "I'm always at my best when someone's really trying to nail me. When you asked that question about my daughter, I started to enjoy the interview."

He regularly talks at universities. "I've talked in over half the universities in the country. As well as overseas – I've spoken at Oxford, Cambridge. You get the message out to young people. Because they're really so sheltered – regardless of how open their family might be that they come from. They get to college or law school and they need somebody to give them a sense of the real world."

He tells me that he's been to Ireland twice, staying in Dromoland Castle. "I really liked it over there." When I mention that I've been trying to pin down an interview with Courtney Love (who played his fourth wife, Althea, in the movie), he offers to call her for me. "Courtney's been having a real tough time lately, but me and Mel

(Gibson) have been trying to help her out. She's a nice girl."

When I mildly chastise him for repeating the same quotes at the USC talk, he guffaws and says, "Before you go, one good line for you. When you ask me for a quote, I'll give you this. This is an original, okay? Keep it, you're free to use it. Two things you'll never know about a man – why he loves his dog or his woman. Because you always see a guy with two you wouldn't have neither one of!"

I don't quite get it, but laugh politely anyway. "Mr. Flynt's full of lines like that – just funny little words of wisdom," Liz tells me, smiling adoringly. Before his bodyguard wheels him off to his waiting Bentley, he offers me a final life philosophy: "Happiness is a way to travel, not a destination. You always hear people say, 'Well, if the mortgage is paid off, I'd be happy', or 'If the kids graduate from college, I'd be happy'. Everybody wants to be happy tomorrow. But when I get out of bed everyday, I think, 'What's gonna make me happy today?' That's why happiness really is a way to travel and not a destination."

"And are you happy at the moment?" I ask.

"Considering all the issues, yes, I think I'm very happy. A guy would be a little bit loony if he said he was 100% happy, but… you know."

With that, Larry Claxton Flynt laughs, harrumphs, and is wheeled off goldenly into the night. Maybe he was hustling me, but I couldn't help liking the guy.

{APRIL, 2008}

SELECTED RECORDINGS: 2000-2010

CHAPTER SIX:
Lady Gaga

Given that we're meeting to discuss an album entitled *The Fame*, the venue for *Hot Press*'s encounter with Lady Gaga couldn't be more appropriate. It's shortly after 9pm on a Dublin Saturday night, and we're sitting in a brightly-lit RTÉ dressing room backstage at *Tubridy Tonight*. There's a small crowd of paparazzi hanging around outside, and William Shatner and La Toya Jackson are occupying the adjoining rooms.

A star, star, burning bright, the 22-year-old New Yorker – real name Stefani Joanne Angelina Germanotta – is wearing a gold party frock, long black latex gloves, and some mad *thing* in her blonde hair (it's too big to be a ribbon and too small to be a hat). She's heavily plastered in make-up, and her fake lashes almost completely obscure her eyeballs.

She's pretty hot stuff – in more ways than one. Critics are already describing her as the next Madonna/Blondie. Cynics, on the other hand, are carping that she's more like Britney/Christina with intellectual pretensions.

Love her or laugh at her, right now *The Fame* – which features songs with titles such as 'Paparazzi', 'Money Honey' and 'I Like It Rough' – is doing exactly what it says on the tin, and making Lady Gaga one of the most ubiquitous stars in the world. Frothy and frocky, the music combines disco, electro-pop and rock with a splash of burlesque and more than a hint of sexual decadence. In less than an hour, she'll be performing her worldwide No.1 single 'Just Dance' on live television. Right now, though, Lady Gaga is all mine.

Actually, not quite. Her two female assistants decline my polite invitation to vacate the room. "We're going to stay," one of them firmly informs me. "Sorry, that's just the way it's gonna be!"

OLAF TYARANSEN: Hey Lady, how you doing?
LADY GAGA: Life is beautiful right now.
Do you know there's some paparazzi waiting outside?
There are? The Irish paparazzi? Oh my goodness! I thought they only existed in two cities in the world – London and Los Angeles. The magic Ls!
What!? There's none in New York?
You know, I haven't been to New York since we went No.1 so I do not know. For me, I can't judge that as of right now. But the paparazzi in New York, I think, are

busy working on politics and stuff. They don't bother with silly blonde pop stars.
You grew up in Yonkers, didn't you?
No – Manhattan.
Oh, your Wikipedia entry is wrong then.
Well, I certainly did not write that Wikipedia entry!
Apologies! I do know you went to quite an exclusive high school (*Convent of the Sacred Heart*). Was your background very privileged?
Uh… no. My school had some very high profile young women in it *(its alumni include the Hilton sisters, Caroline Kennedy, etc – OT)*. And I should say that I feel that I was quite privileged growing up, that I did get to go to an incredible school and had piano lessons and had a very good family. My mom and dad are Italian-Americans – first in their generation to go to college. Entrepreneurs who worked from the ground up and earned every dollar that they made. I'm very lucky to have such inspiring and hard-working parents.
Were they musical?
My father was in some cover bands – as a singer and musician – and used to go down the shore and obsess over Bruce Springsteen. He used to pretend to be John Belushi with his buddy, and they would do Blues Brothers at different bars. My mom did theatre when she was younger. So I come from a family that was in the arts – my dad painted as well – but they ended up doing more technology, telecommunications stuff. Like I said, they were the first to go to college, so I guess it was just kind of like the family's way to go out into the world and make a name for the family.
Were you in Manhattan on 9/11?
Yes *(puts hand to mouth in shock)*. Do you know that you are the very first out of hundreds *(of interviewers)* to ask me that? Unreal … *(shakes head)*.
Do you want to talk about it?
That morning, for whatever reason, gym class was suspended. So we had two free periods in the morning and me and my girlfriends were doing girlfriend things as usual – getting breakfast at Jackson Hole around the corner and eating in the comfy chairs outside the chapel. And we walked upstairs and someone said, "Orianne's mother called" – Orianne was my best friend – "and a plane has hit one of the towers." And I remember that we thought it was a helicopter. Because every once in a while something knocks into a skyscraper in New York because they're so damn tall. And I remember that all of a sudden the… ether of the whole building started to change, and we were called into the classrooms to watch the television. And I just remember walking in and watching both… The first tower had already gone down, and I watched the second go down – and it was just smoke. And then we all just ran to the roof as the teachers screamed down the hallways, "Don't go up there!" We ran to the roof to see if it was true.
You could see what was happening from the roof?
Yeah. From the roof of my school you could see clear downtown – and it was just black. And I remember I couldn't reach my mother for, like, four hours. She worked across the street from the World Trade Centre. And the lines were just a mess. Eventually my father called and told me, "I spoke to her – she's fine, she's

walking home." But it was very sad because we walked from the school, across the park through the 'Imagine John Lennon' memorial. I asked my dad, I remember, if we could go past there when it happened. I used to go there every morning. And as we were walking, there were these very young men in trade jackets covered in soot. Completely covered in soot but with streams of water demarcating tears in their clothing and on their faces. It was the most terrifying moment of my life, easily.

Has that experience fed into your music at all?

I have written music that was inspired by that day, but I wouldn't say that my current album is terribly focused on September 11th *(smiles)*. And to be perfectly fair, I think that one needs to earn that kind of... *permission* from the public to be able to speak about those kinds of things. John Lennon, for example, had earned and cemented his image as an icon in the world when he said, "Give peace a chance." It's like you have to earn the ability to talk about politics, and I don't think that someone in their underwear, covered in sequins and feather eyelashes, should sing about September 11th.

Could it not be argued that your upbeat party vibe is a reaction to that terrible event?

Well, the New York street revival is surely in full force now as I begin to tell the story of the neighbourhood that nobody knew about. I think that what my record speaks to more than September 11th – which, arguably, you could say is the mark of the beginning of this incredible depression that we're in now – is that I reckon with ideas about fame and money and how they make young people feel. And I offer a way to sort of make friends with all of these things as opposed to allowing them to poison us and rule our lives in the very ugly way that society says they do. The record's really fun.

And yet you seem so serious!

I'm quite serious about my record, but the record itself doesn't take itself too seriously. It's a good time. It's full of joy. It's a celebration. It's all of the things back in the '70s and the '80s that the party used to be. It was art and fashion and fun – and it was okay to be that way.

I'm just going to throw a couple of names at you...

Sure.

Grace Jones.

I just met her a few days ago. She is the most incredible, like, Aztec warrior of a woman. I washed her feet.

How did that come about?

She was bleeding. I said, "Grace, you're fucking bleeding!" and she was, like, "I know I'm fucking bleeding, darling!" And I said, "Just a minute ..." and I just began to *(mimes spitting into a hanky and rubbing feet)*. And I told her I felt like Mary Magdalene.

Madonna?

I haven't met Madonna.

There are lots of obvious comparisons between yourself and Madonna...

We certainly have a lot in common. She's somebody that I certainly danced around in my room to with my mother when I was growing up. And she's an inspirational Italian-American woman who was political and religious and all of those amazing things.

The Scissor Sisters... actually, you could be their cousin!

I love them! Thank you! I'm a big fan. I passed out at one of their concerts in Coney Island a few years ago.

Was that during your legendary drug period?

During my 'white' period? Yes. That was during my Bowie period that everybody so gracefully missed out on. Those moments of my life are quite fragmented so I couldn't even tell you. But I love the Scissor Sisters. I only wish that they had been more successful in America, because Americans could've used a little tits on the radio.

You went to the same school as Paris Hilton. I'm aware you didn't know her very well, but I'm just wondering what you think of her rise to fame?

(Lady Gaga visibly freezes and one of her assistants interrupts: "She doesn't answer questions like that regarding other artists. So could you ask another one? Sorry!").

But Paris Hilton isn't an artist... oh, alright. You've mentioned Donatella Versace in many of your interviews. Oh, I love her! We've been in contact with one another. I adore her and speak quite frequently about how I mirror her image in my fashion, and admire her. And we've been speaking about me putting in for some Versace clothes *(laughs)*.

Do you get a lot of free clothes in this gig?

We do, but I feel kind of bad because I'm a bit of a snob when it comes to what I wear. And as grateful as I am for all of the free things that I'm sent, I don't wear 79 per cent of it, because it just isn't my vision.

You studied briefly at the Tisch School – is that how you pronounce it – at NYU?

Yeah. The *Tits* School. That's where I was! *(laughs)*

Hot Press **actually has an association there. The students make music videos for Irish bands as part of a competition we run every year.**

Tisch has just a wonderful programme. It was actually my dream school that I wanted to get into. I got in when I was 17. I was so terribly excited, and I studied art history and writing and music and theatre and it's just amazing. But it wasn't the programme for me. But I don't know that any programme really would have been the programme for me, because I was sort of resolved to this idea and philosophy that you're better off learning about art on your own. And that you really can't pay for it. Like, the school is terribly expensive. And I told my father and mother, I'm like, "You're paying for me to learn about art: just let me go wait tables and learn about it on my own." And they were like…"Whatever!"

Have you ever actually waited tables?

Oh my gosh! I mean, talk about my 'white' period, that's all I did for, like, five years. I actually waited tables since I was 15.

What do you mean when you say "white period"?

I mean that in jest, because you had said Bowie. As in Bowie's *(thin)* white *(duke)* period. But I waited tables since I was 15. I worked as a hostess during high school; it was my way of making money so that I could go to dance clubs and go see music and stuff at night-time on the weekends without having to ask my father for money. Because, "Daddy, can I go to the movies?" "Well, the movie's only $6 so here you go!" You know, it's like I could never really get all the way downtown and grab a couple of drinks, so I decided to get my own job so that I could be a free independent woman. And I did the same thing in college. I worked three different jobs. I did an internship for a bit at Famous Music.

You were writing for Interscope when you were 20, weren't you?

Uh-uh. I was 21. I had gotten dropped from Def Jam and I began to write a lot. And I got approached by Interscope as an artist. And while the paperwork was still going on, they became also interested in me as a writer. And I had written some songs with *(Moroccan producer)* RedOne that were played for Akon. And he got very excited and hired me as a writer. So it sort of happened simultaneously. They were interested in me as an artist, but I began my initial relationship with them as a writer, and began to work on other projects. And I was sort of known as, like, the quirky girl from New York City who had a very strange light and sensibility about her – that Akon and Vincent Herbert and Jimmy Iovine thought could be a star.

Do you have a long-term plan? Are you looking a few years ahead or just riding out the moment?

I guess the plan is that I'm just never going to stop.

Is it all about the records or are there other things planned?

Certainly I want to direct music videos, and I want to have an art exhibit, and I want to make clothes, and all kinds of things. But it's always hard for me to talk about that, because I feel like it's sort of like very typical of artists to speak quite carelessly about their "empires." I don't look at myself like an empire. I wanna make real honest work. So if I do a clothing line, I'm not gonna do it on the side or while I'm on the road. I'm gonna stop, sit down and make a clothing line properly.

John Updike, who died earlier this week, once said that, "Celebrity is a mask that eats the face." Given the theme of *The Fame*, what are your thoughts on that?

He also said that a true New Yorker secretly believes that anyone living in any other part of the world is secretly joking. He also wrote that. Actually, tell me that quote again.

"Celebrity is a mask that eats the face."

Oh! *(gasps in astonishment).* Are you going to see my show tomorrow? I'm gonna cry right now *(eyes water up).* You have to see my show. There are three art films in my show. Gosh! I didn't even think of the Updike reference. This is when you know that you've got that intuition about culture. And he just died.

I'm not following you... .

I did these three art films. I call them *Crevette*. 'Crevette' means 'shrimp' in French. I named them that because – it might be quite silly of me – but shrimp are small and decadent and tasty. Which is what I intend for my little 57-second films to be. And in these particular films, which I show throughout the performance... it's called *Who Shot Candy Warhol?* And the first film is called *Pop Ate My Heart*. And the second film is called *Pop Ate My Brain*. And the third is called *Pop Ate My Face* – in which I am sitting helplessly in a white room with a strange man holding a yellow rubber gun with pink blood all over my heart, and a pantyhose that distorts the image of my true identity. And it's just so... it's just so fucking funny that you asked me that.

I was sent by the ghost of John Updike!

You were! You were! I mean, it's just so funny that you asked me that. And in the film I profusely am asked by this strange man, "What is your real name? Tell me your real name!" And I say, "I don't understand the question."

Sounds very Warholian.

Yes it is. I would've liked to have been his girl-muse.

What do you think of Damien Hirst?

I love Damien Hirst. Actually, I find his work to be incredibly mesmerising. Although a bit unhealthy at times. Someone asked me the other day of a likely British gentleman caller, and I said I really liked Damien Hirst, but I would prefer that my children not grow up surrounded by cows in formaldehyde. But I do love Damien Hirst. I like the 'death of God' nature of what he does. He asks us to look at quite organic and natural things, and once you measure the distance and the temporal reaction of the, "Oh my God, there's parasites eating away at a carcass!" there's a fear that grows and an intense genuine shock that breeds something that has nothing to do with feeling natural. And I appreciate that so very much.

Given your Italian background, I presume you're a Catholic?

Yes, very much. I believe in God.

Does Hirst's 'death of God' theme not offend your religious sensibilities?

No, not at all. What a scary world it would be if we didn't have people that challenged all of these institutions. I'm a religious woman, but I don't pretend for a minute to be necessarily enthralled in the institution of the Church. But I'm a decidedly spiritual and religious woman, yes. I don't think you need to follow the letter of the law in order to be religious. I respect a lot of Catholic traditions, but Damien Hirst is right. It's modern. And while Damien Hirst's school of thought will always continue to modernise – and ten years from now he will say, "I was wrong – no, this is what it is!" We have so many institutions that for thousands of years never modernised and never said, "Oh, we were wrong – no, this is what it is!" So I tend to respect the opinions of artists more than I would respect the opinions of religious authorities, governmental authorities, papers and things and tablets that have been unchanging since BC Anno Domini thousands of eons of centuries. Artists admit when they're wrong.

I should probably ask you about the election of President Obama.

Yes! How exciting! Can you believe what we've done? I don't think Americans even realise yet this tremendous thing that we've just accomplished.

Was that your first ever vote?

No, my second. I'm 22. I broke out into intense hives when John Kerry lost to Bush.

Did you play any awareness events or fundraisers for Obama?

No, I didn't. But just before the inauguration, I did something with Pepsi. Where I did this very sweet little 'Dear Mr. President' letter where I begged him to give me no reason to write a protest song, because I hate writing songs that aren't about dancing and singing and having a good time.

It strikes me that there's a lot more depth to you than you let on in your music.

Maybe you didn't listen to my record carefully enough *(laughs)*. The intention when it comes to pop art is for people to argue about whether or not it's valid. And if you really listen to the lyrics of *The Fame*, in my opinion it's an incredibly brilliant reckoning about what the commercial idea of fame does to us as young people, and what the young artist Warholian concept of fame can do to save them from that.

Warhol once proclaimed that in the future everybody will be famous for 15 minutes. Is that what you're talking about?

I'm talking about the idea that you can self-proclaim fame on your own. "I am famous!" "No, you're not!" "Yes, I am!"

What? Standing in front of a bedroom mirror singing into a hairbrush?

Did you just say that? *(Looks over at assistants)* Did he just say that? You have *got* to see my films!

(Assistant: "You've really freaked her out! He's from the future!")

You're from the future!! It's quite scary. In my second film, I'm brushing my hair in front of a mirror talking about how pop ate my heart and then he swallowed my brain and what's left for me to live for... but my fame.

And are you enjoying your newfound fame?

It's very funny the way that this all happened. I have been doing this forever, right? And I quite honestly go into those intense artistic creative caves, or I work for like weeks at a time and barely see a soul on the earth except for my assistant, my choreographer, the inside of a studio and a set. So I did these music videos where I was up for, like, 72 hours straight – you know, like James Bond being tortured in the middle of Vietnam – I mean just, like, crazy. And then I emerged in a hallucinatory state and they said, "You're No.1 all over the world!" And I'm like, "Oh... fabulous!" I'd been working so hard, I didn't even realise I was No.1.

Have people started to look at you funny?

On my way to the airport, the day my second video had been done, I was followed by paparazzi getting on the plane. Then in London it was like a massacre. So I just really don't know. Right now, London is... it's the apocalypse. I imagine that LA is not the same way. And in New York, like I said, the journalists just don't fucking care about pop music. But I know that because I've got a song called 'Paparazzi' on my record, that everybody must think that as I'm chased helplessly around the city by cameras that I must be beaming and doing backflips. But quite honestly I'm terrified of their ability to degrade and trample upon all of the most beautiful and artistic dreams that I've been working on my whole life. And unfortunately they are my subject matter so I have to be nice to them *(smiles)*. It doesn't frighten me on a physical level, but it frightens me on an intellectual level. Just their capability to destroy my work. Because they can – and you know they can.

There is this perception that once you've put your head over the parapet and into the public eye, people somehow own you and have a right to know everything about your life.

I don't know that it's the public's innate right to know everything about my life, but I do think that the nature of making music is being private in public. So

I could let you know as little or as much as I'd like in my actual work, but I am quite a spitfire when it comes to journalists asking me how I like to be made love to and things like that.

Damn! There goes my final question!

You know what I'm saying! Those sorts of questions to me are the very thing that shoot my art in the face. Because they immediately become paramount to the actual record, and because I am blond, and because I write about fame and money and pornography, and I perform it in my underwear, I'm already begging the world to fucking take what I do seriously. Whereas if it was thirty years ago, I would just be another one of Andy Warhol's muses. It wasn't so outrageous then to do what I do now. In fact, I wouldn't have been very controversial at all.

{FEBRUARY, 2009}

CHAPTER SEVEN:
Larry Harvey

Located deep in the sun-baked heart of Nevada's vast and inhospitable Black Rock Desert, it looks like the set of *Mad Max In Wonderland*. To a crazy, continuous, cacophonous soundtrack of literally hundreds of different sound systems, all pumping everything from Irish trad to German techno at full blast, thousands upon thousands of bizarrely costumed people wander around a post-apocalyptic landscape – a vast sand canvas, festooned with myriad large scale artworks.

Most of those who aren't attired in outlandish costumes are either naked or else have their bodies painted in bright *Braveheart* colours. Just about everyone, though, is wearing stoned and vaguely dreamlike expressions, as though they can't quite believe what's materialising before their eyes (understandably enough, given that typical artworks include a thirty-foot tall purple mushroom, a fake field of papier mache sunflowers, a full-sized wooden Oriental temple, and a graveyard with headstones marked 'Cheerios' and 'Duracell').

In *Dust Devils*, the highly impressive Dearbhla Glynn directed, Irish-made documentary about the annual and ever-growing Burning Man festival in Nevada, there are numerous scenes guaranteed to boggle the minds of even the most alternative-thinking and event-hardened of viewers. Are drugs involved? Undoubtedly. But out there, in the desert wastelands, LSD also stands for 'Lots of Sand and Dust'.

It would seem reasonable therefore to assume that the chief architect of this surreal spectacle would be some mad, peyote-munching, long-haired, guru type. But no, Larry Harvey – who founded Burning Man back in 1986 – is nothing like that. At all. A tanned 56-year-old American, in combats and sleeveless hunting jacket, he looks more like a successful rancher or oil man on vacation than a counter-cultural icon.

Take it from me, though, despite his outwardly straight appearance, in years to come Larry Harvey will be as respected an American counter-cultural figure as Jack Kerouac, Timothy Leary or Ken Kesey. Burning Man is much, much more than just your typical alternative festival. Now attracting upwards of 30,000 people annually, for one week only, Black Rock City – the festival site that's built, and ultimately burnt, by its temporary inhabitants – becomes the fifth largest city in the State of Nevada.

As founder and executive director of Burning Man, over the years Harvey has fought numerous legal and political battles with the Nevada authorities and federal government to keep the festival alive. He's a realist, not a dreamer. Or rather, he's a realist and a dreamer. And like another great visionary before him, he also started his career as a carpenter. Perhaps there's something in the wood.

Born in 1948, Harvey grew up on a small farm on the outskirts of Portland, Oregon. His family was poor, but he and his brother had an idyllic childhood nonetheless. Having graduated from high school, he attended university for a while, studying literature and history, but was bored by academia.

"I wasn't really a drop-out – more of a drift-out," he laughs. "After a while in college, I decided I could do a better job of educating myself. I didn't like the way the professors would take their subjects out of their pockets like a watch, dangle it, and then put it back into their little pocket again. So I just started reading courses on my own, and I'd go to university libraries wherever I was and find my way through bibliographies of whatever subjects excited my passion."

Although he was drafted into the army in the late '60s, he never made it to Vietnam, instead serving his time at a military base in Germany. Discharged with an honourable mention, he returned to the US. He travelled for a while, eventually settling in San Francisco. He was in his mid-twenties. While he knew a lot of hippies, he was never really all that convinced by flower-power. Even today, he's a much bigger fan of the Velvet Underground than The Grateful Dead.

"I believed in the hippie ethos for about thirty minutes one day in Golden Gate Park, under the influence of LSD," he chuckles. "But I was raised by very down-to-earth, rural people – peasants really – who were brought up in the dustbowl and forced to the west coast working as migrant labourers, so my background wasn't very middle-class, whereas the hippies around me were all middle-class.

"And I just didn't buy it. I didn't believe it. I didn't really believe that you could change the world by taking drugs, listening to rock & roll, and having a lot of sex. All pleasurable activities, doubtless, but not world-changing."

Larry paid the rent by doing carpentry jobs here and there, interspersed with spells of truck driving.

"I was hanging out with what I called the 'Latte Carpenters'," he recalls. "They were this group of crazy carpenters who were leading a fairly bohemian life – in between jobs they'd gather at a friend's house, drink wine, play flamenco guitars, talk about art and philosophise generally. It was an easy life on the sunny west coast."

One idle August afternoon in 1986, Larry was hanging around shooting the breeze with his carpenter chums when he had a brainwave. He suggested that they should all pool their talents (and spare lumber), build a big wooden effigy of a man, and then take it down to the beach and burn it.

"It might seem odd, but that wasn't a particularly remarkable thing to do," he smiles. "There seemed like a good human aesthetic to it – or at least there was in my head. Much of what we did was devoted to immediacy anyway."

They set to work, eight of them spending the afternoon carving and crafting an eight-foot tall Wooden Man. They loaded him into a truck, gathered some wine and weed, and drove down to a local beach. Initially, it was just the eight of them but by the time they burnt the Man at sunset, the party had grown to about thirty people. Such a good time was had by all, that they made a pact to return and do it again the following year.

Twelve months later they returned to the beach with a bigger Man and held an even bigger party. As it became obvious to all this should really be an annual thing, Harvey decided to christen his event.

"We could've named it Lumber Man but that would have lacked finesse, so I named it Burning Man."

He denies that his inspiration came from Robin Hardy's cult 1973 movie, *The Wicker Man*. "It's got nothing to do with *The Wicker Man*. People keep asking me about that. I assure you we do not burn earnest Methodists, chickens or goats. No, I'd never seen the film."

Over the next few years, they continued to illegally burn the Man on the beach as a guerrilla event. Inevitably though, with word spreading through the San Francisco alternative media, and both the Wooden Man and the party around his cremation growing larger each time, the authorities finally got wind of it.

In 1990, an official representative of the federal government showed up at the beach and told them that they couldn't burn anything there.

"At this point we were trying to secretly smuggle this giant 40-foot-high Wooden Man onto a beach," he laughs. "So we were carrying it down a cliff, with teams assigned to arms, legs, torso and head. It was pretty funny. He was looking at it. And the Man was nice-looking – these were all skilled carpenters and craftsmen so it was quite intricately designed. It *ached* with craft. And the government official was impressed. And he did a wonderful thing for a bureaucrat. He made a deal with us that we could raise it but not burn it – and then he ran away. In case we burned it! And my colleagues were all saying, '*Burn it! Burn it!*' But (a) I'd given my word, and my father had always taught me to keep my word, and (b) through political instinct I thought that maybe I should honour a political deal because it might be useful later."

By now Burning Man's reputation as a brilliant party event had spread and an awful lot of people had shown up. Having watched Harvey and his friends erect the four-storey high man, most of the crowd now demanded to see it burn.

"So suddenly, having raised the statue, it was time to lower it again – as per our deal. But we had no provision for dealing with an audience. We had no bullhorn. We didn't have a voice to address them with. And there occurred a mini-riot. They were disappointed that their sensational thrill wasn't going to happen. And the crowd turned ugly. We got it down by diverting them with a fire-breathing performance from a friend of mine who was an old carnival performer. So we created this little side show, which was enough to divert the beast's attention long enough for us to be able to lower it and put it out of harm's way."

Harvey was pissed off that his party was being gate-crashed by freeloaders who'd had nothing to do with the building of the Man, and who understood none of the philosophy behind it.

"I was shaken because we'd ignored the fact that we'd acquired all these spectators, and it seemed to violate a certain sense of sanctity about it. It had been a unique extension of us, but it was nothing to them. It was just a show – a big fire on the beach."

His rather unique solution was to take Burning Man out to the middle of the desert. It was his party, and he'd fry if he wanted to. And if anybody wanted to join him, they'd have to fry too!

"Taking it out to the middle of nowhere really solved that essential audience problem," he explains. "Because in order to go to the Black Rock Desert, which is in the naked heart of the wild west, the trip itself is an initiation. Survival there is a struggle in the teeth of volatile natural forces. You were a forced participant. There was no margin for spectator-ship. Anyone who was willing to do that, and willing to survive under those conditions, was in the soup with all of us. We were together."

That first Burning Man in the desert in 1990 is now as legendary as U2's brief stint in the Dandelion Market, with everybody claiming to have been there.

"I've heard so many people claiming to have been there that it must've been about 4,000 people," he chuckles. "But in reality it was really more like 80. And we simply went there to burn the man, as we had on the beach."

As the '90s progressed, Burning Man's reputation continued to spread and, despite the harshness of the desert environment, more and more people began making the pilgrimage.

By the mid-1990s, Burning Man was attracting upwards of ten thousand people – most of whom were showing up in costume, and contributing by building and burning their own effigies and artistic creations. Harvey realised that he'd created a monster. His little village had grown to become a small city, and needed some kind of order.

"At first, we called it a 'city' ironically," he says. "But then it became apparent that we had responsibility – the responsibility of urban planners. For years in the early 1990's it was such a small thing, there was no gate and we hadn't thought of any way to enclose it and create boundaries. The trouble really was being found by those who were coming. It's literally like outer space out there. It's about 200 square miles of flat, Euclidean plain – not a bird, not a bush. Alkaline. Inimical to life, inimical to machinery, inimical to everything to do with man or what man makes. The fact of the matter is that, within a year or two of going out there, we became responsible for people's lives. It was so hard to find, and so easy to get lost in and around our little city, that we began to buy radios and a group formed to go rescue people. Because you could get mired in that desert and die of dehydration within hours. That kind of death is very common there. And anyone who strays from the flock, from the herd, nature might claim. Once we'd organised the safety crews, our civic identity strengthened further."

Of course, there were other civic responsibilities inherent in building – and burning – an entire city in the middle of nowhere. Real life concerns, like insurance, quickly became issues.

"We had no insurance to begin with," he admits. "We learned all our lessons the hard way. We now have insurance, we now have attorneys, we now have a city that has pretty much everything that a city has. A daily newspaper, two or three angry alt-weeklies that disrespect the daily – as it should be – and we have about forty or fifty radio stations, because you can self-broadcast.

"We also have some services that cities don't have – but might consider. We have greeters: when you come to our city you're personally greeted by someone. And we've learned how to instantly acclimatise strangers. It became clearer to me as it grew that there were more strangers than there were people who know one another, so we'd gone beyond a kind of communal village kind of experience – with all of its virtues and all of its vices."

In 1996, things hit financial crisis point. Burning Man had basically been a free event, with no advertising and no tickets sold. The Man itself was paid for by Harvey and his friends, and everyone coming out there had to bring enough food, water and supplies to survive. However, as the event mushroomed and morphed from small town to fledgling city, other costs were mounting.

"Originally we would just pass the hat," he laughs, touching the one on his head. "It was a communal sensibility. Usually we'd get a little dough that probably wouldn't quite cover the cost. But of course passing the hat amongst thousands of people doesn't work. So then we created a gate."

It wasn't a normal kind of gate…

"It was more of an art installation really because it was a gate without any walls attached to it – it was just a gate in the middle of nothing. And we depended on the fact that we were still so small that we wouldn't tell people where it was and people would get their secret instructions as to where to go, once they went to the gate.

"The only trouble was that half the people couldn't find the gate! So it was a non-viable economic model and, of course, at this point, we were trying to build a city and that well outstripped the resources of anybody's credit card. We eventually solved that problem. Interestingly enough, as we became more of a civilised entity and people respected the place more as a public sphere that everyone belonged to, we were able to put up a fence around our city. Now that fence is still there. It's about five square miles in the shape of a pentagon, but it's only three feet tall and made out of plastic – perforated so the wind can blow through it – and yet it works. One, because we are respected by most people. And two, because we use radar. Ha, ha. We use boat radar. We can see them coming from miles away."

Although they now charge for tickets to Burning Man, it still couldn't be accurately described as a commercial event. To Harvey's mind, it's all about community – and he's gone to great lengths to preserve that spirit.

"We preserved communal values on a civic scale in two ways. First to come and live there, the communal strategy is rather important – the lone person has a hard time in such high temperatures. There are dust storms that blot out your hand before your face and pluck up your tent and all your belongings and toss them ten miles into oblivion in an instant.

"But we did another thing once we became a city that helped create a kind of communal tie at the scale of a city – and that was to ban all commerce. Originally, of course, it was simply inappropriate. If we went to a picnic and you said, 'Oh, we need some olives', your friend wouldn't say, 'Oh, I've got some. I'll give you a deal. How about two bottles for five dollars? I'd charge you less but there aren't any other olives here, are there? – *friend*.' Ha, ha. Well, that would be a savage and inappropriate thing to do!.

"So at a certain point, since everyone was coming to plan to survive anyway, we just said there is no market here – nothing can be bought or sold. And in doing that, prohibiting market transactions, we did something that was beyond that negative, that prohibition. We created what we finally discovered was a gift economy. And we began to deepen that philosophy as time went on. You could almost say that we're Disneyland inside-out. In our Disneyland, the participants entertain one another with fantasy and creative works. But it's far more interesting because every one of those creative works comes with a biography attached to it. It hasn't been hatched in a lab somewhere."

Another advantage of banning commerce and running a gift economy is that people tend to be more respectful towards each other.

"People do find it hard to believe that you could have this festival of creative excess and this great Bacchanalian party – because it is that, as well as a ritual – and, at the same time, keep public order. What we discovered is that if everyone is creating the city they're in, and the medium of that creation is a gift that the margin for anti-social behaviour shrinks down to about that 2% of people who're trying to get even with their old man."

Having said that, Burning Man does have some crime – but, according to Harvey, it's not a serious problem.

"Bikes get stolen but most of that's due to confusion," he chuckles. "There are assaults but the percentage is minuscule. In 30,000 people it will occur, but it's nothing compared to the level in another city of the same size. And it's nothing compared to a Mardi-Gras where everyone is drunk, and pickpockets are everywhere, and fights are breaking out in every bar. It just doesn't happen in our city because everyone is invested in it."

If trouble does break out, they've got the means to deal with it. They pay three-quarters of a million dollars a year from the till to the Federal Government for police services ("Personally, I think they're overpaid!"). However, the police don't patrol inside the city. Burning Man have their own private rangers for that. "They're trained in non-confrontational mediation and they're very good at it. Their motto is, *'Making reasonable excuses for your behaviour since 1988'*."

A small number of people have died at Burning Man over the years. The most recent fatality was just last year, when a woman died following a fall from a vehicle out on the playa.

"Yeah, a woman died last year," he admits. "And another fella died recklessly driving his motorcycle outside of the event. But there's death everywhere. It's safer in Black Rock City than it is outside. But, you know, if somebody dies at the County Fair it doesn't make the same kind of headlines it does when it happens at our event."

Of course, being responsible for a (temporarily) thriving city of 30,000 people is a job not to be taken lightly. While there's undoubtedly a lot of drug-taking in Black Rock City, Harvey himself isn't really in a position to indulge in recreational substances any more. He learnt that lesson the hard way.

"Years ago, I took a drug that affected me quite strongly and then, of course, an official from the Bureau of Land Management showed up," he laughs. "I spent the next hour escorting her around and doing an inspired imitation of normality. But since that time, I've been entirely sober. When you're responsible for that many people, in a life or death environment, you have to be a serious person."

Serious indeed. Although Burning Man only turns a small profit (most of the money from ticket sales is reinvested in the artworks), they do have a corporate structure – though everything is decided by consensus. Larry Harvey is currently executive director of the project and also serves as chairman of Burning Man's senior staff and Black Rock LLC, its executive committee. He also co-chairs the organisation's Art Department and scripts and co-curates Burning Man's annual art theme. Also a political planner, he supervises the organisation's lobbying efforts and frequently attends meetings with state, county and federal agencies. It's pretty much a full time job for him (though he says he's far from rich from his efforts). He works 15-hour days for more than eight months of the year.

"If we were doing a more normal thing there would have been no problem," he says. "It's not a conspiracy, but it is almost an instinct of the established order to try and thwart us at every turn. And we've fought immense battles. People often ask if we're tempted to sell-out? That's an easy one. Who would buy our business model? Our 'customers' are actually citizens and community members. We haven't branded them, we've allowed them access to an identity that they've created themselves. How could we sell that? You couldn't! I mean, we're not against commerce – we sell tickets. But what we've created is a space and a realm and a ritual around which, and within which, the world is de-commodified."

Although some critics carp that the event isn't what it used to be, Harvey himself reckons that the Burning Man spirit is truer and stronger now than ever before.

"We're not just building a city anymore," he says. "Now it's becoming a social movement on a large scale. Just as we master what we have to do, we tend to double the task. Having doubled it recently, we'll double it again."

{AUGUST, 2004}

… SELECTED RECORDINGS: 2000-2010

CHAPTER EIGHT:
Hugh Hefner

"Quite frankly, I think I'm probably the luckiest guy in the world."

At the ripe young age of 81, Hugh Marston Hefner, founder and editor-in-chief of *Playboy* magazine, claims to be living the American dream. In actual fact, with a little help from Viagra, he's living the American wet dream.

World famous, stinking rich, and boasting a genius-level IQ of 152, Hefner (better known as 'Hef'; though apparently his closest friends call him 'Ner') lives, works, parties, and copulates in the Playboy Mansion West, a massive, 30-roomed, gothic-style castle on a beautifully manicured 5.7 acre estate in the most expensive part of Beverly Hills.

Rarely seen out of his trademark black silk pyjamas, Hef shares his humungous home with three young and pretty girlfriends, Bridget, Holly and Kendra (the stars of the hit reality-TV series *The Girls of the Playboy Mansion*) and an ever-changing chorus-line of buxom Playboy Bunnies. All of the centrefolds for his magazine are shot on the property. An army of 80 helpers – including butlers, security, chefs, zookeepers, landscapers and gardeners – cater to his every need, and ensures that pretty much everything in Hef's world is exactly as he would like it to be. Hef's estranged wife, Kimberly Conrad, and their two teenage sons live in the house next door. Christie Hefner, his daughter from his first marriage, is CEO of Playboy Enterprises, and looks after her father's vast business portfolio, leaving him free to pursue his own interests (sex, movies, sex, business, and more sex)…

The man's home is a castle. Michael Jackson had Neverland. A gentleman of rather different tastes, Hef exists in Alwaysland. If he doesn't have something, chances are that that's because he doesn't want it. Needless to say, he rarely leaves the house.

"No, no, I do get out," he assures me. "But it's worth noting that this is an indoor/outdoor property."

"If beauty is truth/ and surgery the fountain of youth/ What am I to do?/ Have I got the gift to get me through/ the gates of that Mansion?" – U2, 'The Playboy Mansion'.

Getting though the gates of The Playboy Mansion is no easy task. *Hot Press* first requested an audience with Hef – or 'Mr. Hefner', as his staff solemnly refer to him – many months ago. So began a long slow dance with his various PR departments.

First you talk to his people's people's people. When you've passed that audition, you talk to his people's people. Finally, you talk to his people – who want to know, again, what's your circulation, who the interviewer will be, and who else you've interviewed. They want to see samples of the work and copies of the magazine.

Eventually, if you pass all of the tests, you get to talk to his *rock*. Hef's rock is situated to the left of the massive gates to the Playboy Mansion. "State your business!" it barks, as my car purrs into its domain.

"I have a journalist here to interview Mr. Hefner," the driver says.

"Name?"

"Oh-laugh Tie-ran-something. Em… from Ireland."

"Please wait, sir," the rock crackles.

As we wait, I flick idly through the most recent issue of *Playboy*. Miss September is a large-breasted, Brazilian-waxed, 26-year-old African-American named Patrice Hollis (whose 'turn-offs' include "bad breath, short guys, a bad attitude, cockiness"). Patrice is photographed in a variety of poses, ranging from wholesome girl next door to seductive vixen. However, compared to what's out there today, there's nothing especially lewd or vulgar about the nude images. Of course, everybody reads this particular magazine for its – ahem – articles, and there's no shortage of those. In amongst the regular columns and features, there's a couple of lengthy pieces on college football and the adult voyeur website RedClouds, in-depth interviews with actors Clive Owen and Jaime Presley, and a new short story by Tobias Wolff. Not bad value for $5.99.

After a few minutes, the rock crackles again. "Alright driver, here's what's gonna happen. In 30 seconds the gates will open, admitting you to the property. You'll drive straight through to the front of the house. You'll be met by security. Discharge Miss Tyran… em… Olaf at that location. Then continue through the arch, straight down for 100 metres to the far gates. You will leave the property immediately. Are we clear?"

"Yes, sir," says the driver.

As the gates slide open, a panicky thought occurs: did I only get this interview because Hef thinks I'm a *girl?!*

I've deliberately arrived half-an-hour early in the hope that I'll either get more time with Hef, or at least a decent tour of the grounds. As things work out, I get both. A friendly PR girl named Teri Thomerson is waiting for me at the door of the house, and she happily takes me on a walkabout. There's lots to see. We visit the zoo (mostly monkeys and peacocks), the aviary, the tennis courts, the koi pond, Hef's Hollywood star (a replica, obviously), and the forest. We're in an adolescent fantasy land. The Game House is a small, musty-smelling building, housing Playboy pinball machines, a pool table, and an array of full-size arcade games (Pac-Man, Donkey Kong, Frogger and Centipede). The luxurious trampoline carpet is about three inches deep and there are small bedrooms – designed to resemble the cabins of a ship – at the back. For those guests who wish to relive their teenage years, there's even a small room modelled on the back of a van (complete with tacky mirrorball).

There's a mocked-up giant-sized five-dollar bill with Hef at its centre displayed prominently on the main Game House wall. It was a gift from his former employers at *Esquire* magazine. Back in the early 1950s, Hef requested a $5 raise from the editors there. When they refused, he left and started his own magazine. Within less than a year, sales of *Playboy* had outstripped *Esquire*. As one of the dismayed editors famously moaned at the time, "Hefner out-titted us."

The Grotto is probably the most famous area of the mansion. Four separate hot tubs, a waterfall, a flotilla of blue inflatable dolphins bobbing in the turquoise pool. You stand under the hot Californian sun, take it all in, and think, 'Yes, I could probably force myself to live like this.'

Once the tour is done, we go into the Mansion itself. Teri takes me through the screening room (a serious movie buff, Hef screens old films every weekend) and leaves me in the library with its leather couches, double backgammon table, large Renaissance-style portrait of Hef clutching a copy of *Playboy*, and numerous framed magazine covers from over the years. The bookshelves are lined with a complete *Encyclopaedia Britannica*, various *Playboy* publications, and an eclectic scattering of old hardbacks.

In the corner of the room, a beautiful young blonde in a tiny pair of white shorts is working away on a computer terminal. I make the mistake of politely asking her name, and she shoots me a truly filthy look. Oops! Too late, I realise that this is Holly Madison, Hef's 'number one girlfriend', and by now a bona fide celebrity in her own right. She's obviously miffed that I failed to recognise her (I blame the clothes). Within a couple of minutes, the man himself appears. In the flesh, Hef is a short, moderately handsome, grey-haired man, who doesn't look a day older than 69. Needless to say, he's wearing black silk pyjamas and a velvet smoking jacket. All that's missing is the bottle of Diet Pepsi (the pipe was abandoned years ago).

Hef is straight to business. He shakes my hand firmly, and then throws his arm around my shoulder. A photographer materialises and takes two quick pictures. "There you go," Hef says, patting me on the shoulder. *"Proof!"* (A week or so later, a Playboy representative rang to apologise, saying the pictures hadn't come out. I probably should have squatted down a bit).

We sit across from each other over the backgammon table and exchange pleasantries as I set up my recorder. Hef harrumphs a lot and makes various old man noises. I've been warned that he's slightly deaf. "Have I ever been to Hawaii?" he asks, looking puzzled. "Oh, *Ireland!* Sorry, I misheard you. Em… no, I have not. But I've been invited to speak a few times at one of the universities there. And I know it took a long time for *Playboy* to be legal in Ireland. I was very aware of that."

Apparently, on a per capita basis, Ireland is one of your biggest markets.

"Well, that's what you get with a little repression!" he laughs. "But I understand all that. My best buddies in both grade school and in high school were Catholic, and my first wife was Catholic. Repression comes in a lot of different bottles, but it's all essentially the same brew."

Born in Chicago in 1926, Hefner knows all about repression. "I was raised in a typical Midwestern Methodist home with a lot of Puritan repression," he explains. "There wasn't much love and affection at home."

An undistinguished student, more interested in socialising and drawing cartoons, he went to Sayre Elementary School and Steinmetz High School, and then served in the US Army during the closing months of WWII. Stationed by a typewriter, he served as an infantry clerk, and didn't see any combat. After service, he majored in psychology at the University of Illinois. There, he edited the college paper and also occasionally sold cartoons to magazines. In 1949, he took a course in women and gender studies, writing a paper examining US sex laws in light of the newly published Kinsey Institute research on male human sexuality (years later, he'd donate significant amounts of money to the Kinsey Institute). He says that the kernel of the idea for *Playboy* came to him around this time.

That same year, at the age of 23, he married fellow student Mildred Williams. Their marriage lasted a decade, and produced two children. Shortly before their wedding, Mildred admitted that she'd had an affair, something he described as "the most devastating moment of my life." In an attempt to save the relationship, she gave him free rein to have one too. Do you think that everything since then has been a reaction to that moment?

"Yes, yes I do," he nods, earnestly. "But I'm fascinated with that. The reason that I majored in psychology in college is because I have always been fascinated with why people behave the way they do. But I think that I am now doing what I was ideally suited to do, and I'm also doing what other guys would kill for! So I bless and am grateful for some of the conflicts and problems that actually took me in this particular direction. I mean, if my parents had not been very conservative and religious, and had given me a lot of love and affection, where would I be? I think that, sometimes, the problems take you to a better place."

But you've known heartache?

"Yeah, sure."

Good! Serves you right, you jammy bastard! He doesn't look amused.

"I don't make any joke about it. I wouldn't trade places with anybody in the world. I'm not a fatalist, but I do think that I'm doing what I was meant to do. There's certainly nothing else I would rather be doing."

In the early years of his marriage, Hefner supported his family by producing cartoons and working first in the subscription department and then as a copywriter for *Esquire*. Denied that infamous $5 raise, he decided to quit and start up his own men's magazine. He raised a bank loan of $600 (using his furniture as collateral) and managed to persuade 45 different investors to come up with another $7,400. His conservative and religious mother gave him $1,000.

"She never really fully understood the magazine," he says. "It's interesting, as a matter of fact, when I was looking for money to start the magazine in 1953, I went to my family and tried to get a loan or an investment – and my father said no because he didn't think it was a good investment. It was my mother who took me aside and said that she had some money of her own, and she gave me a cheque for $1,000. The company launched with a total investment of $8,000 – a thousand from her and a thousand from my brother were the largest investments that I got. So even though she didn't really believe in the magazine, she believed in her son.

"And later on my dad came to work for me – he was a certified public accountant, so he became the treasurer of the company. And when my father passed away, I learned to my very pleasant surprise that he had – because they'd wound up with a fair amount of money because they'd invested in *Playboy* – left the Playboy Foundation a third of his estate. Which was very nice."

The first issue of *Playboy* was put together on the kitchen table of Hef's cramped Chicago apartment. He'd originally planned on naming his new publication *Stag Party*, but he was forced to change it when *Stag* magazine objected. A friend suggested *Playboy* as a title and a bunny as a logo (because rabbits have a lot of sex). Unable to afford to pay anybody to take their clothes off, he instead bought some old shots of Marilyn Monroe ("with nothing on but the radio," as she later quipped) taken a few years before she became famous. Did he ever meet Monroe?

"No," he sighs. "My brother was actually in her acting class – Lee Strasberg's acting class – in New York. But sadly she died before I got a chance to meet her."

Maybe they'll meet in the afterlife. Somewhat eerily, Hef has already bought the crypt beside the LA grave of his first-ever centrefold star, and plans to be buried there at Pierce Bros Westwood Memorial Park. "We're going to spend eternity together," he smiles.

You wouldn't prefer to be buried in the grounds of the Mansion?

"Well, in addition to Marilyn, several other very dear friends are buried there, and the cemetery is very close by here."

The debut issue of *Playboy* was published in December 1953. He didn't put a date on the cover. "Because I literally only had enough money for the first issue, I figured I'd leave that out."

His so-called 'Playboy Philosophy' was explained in his first editorial. Although he was still married, it was basically a call to arms for independent young bachelors. "We like our apartment," he wrote. "We enjoy mixing up cocktails and an hors d'oeuvre or two, putting a little mood music on the phonograph and inviting in a female for a quiet discussion on Picasso, Nietzsche, jazz, sex."

A totally new kind of men's magazine at the time, *Playboy* was an instant success, selling more than 50,000 copies. "It far surpassed my wildest expectations," he says, happily. "I wouldn't be here today if that issue hadn't sold so well."

So the book *My Struggle* by Hugh Hefner would be short?

"Yes, yes," he chuckles, amusedly. "Volume one, issue one – end of story."

So it hasn't really been a roller-coaster, has it? You took off and simply kept going up!

"Well, I wouldn't say that," he laughs. "We're on a real ride again but, you know, there were periods. We have never really played on a level playing field. In other words, (*Playboy* in) America continues to be in some quarters controversial in ways that it isn't in much of the rest of the world. We don't get the same kind of newsstand display, or the same kind of advertising, that we enjoyed in the 1960s and 1970s. There was a backlash, and that backlash was particularly evident in the 1980s and much of the 1990s."

Was that AIDS-related?

"No, I don't think so. I think it simply had to do with the moral majority and the Christian Right connecting to some extent with the anti-sexual part of the women's movement. In other words, the fact that it arrived at the same time as AIDS in the 1980s is just a coincidence. AIDS didn't get Ronald Reagan elected. Reagan put in the Meese Commission at the Justice Department, and all of that happened because Reagan was elected by, in part, the moral majority and the Christian Right. And that was, politically, a conservative backlash to the freedom and the move to the left that occurred in the latter part of the 1960s and the 1970s. You get that conservative backlash. And from that point on, religion – or at least the right-wing portion of it – has been very organised in this country, and played a very real part in politics."

Are you religious yourself?

"No. Spiritual. But I think we live in a world that none of us really fully understands and we try to make as much sense of it as we can."

Do you believe in God?

"Not a Biblical God. But I don't think we know what this is all about. But you're asking am I an atheist? No. Because you look at all of this *(gestures out the window)*. Some of my most religious or spiritual moments, quite frankly, come from walking in the back gardens with the animals and the trees, etc. I mean, to just look at the very nature of Nature. It's all too awe-inspiring to not feel as if there's something. But then to codify it and turn it into children's stories to some extent diminishes the wonder of what it's all about. One hopes that at some time somewhere in the future we will know, but certainly at this point I don't think we do know."

Flush from the success of *Playboy's* first issue, Hef immediately hired staff and commissioned some original nude photographs. The second issue sold even better. The third sold better again. Within 12 months, he'd already made the first of the many millions to come.

However, he wanted to produce something better than just a mere wank mag. In 1956, looking to raise the tone, Hefner hired Auguste Comte Spectorsky, an East Coast sophisticate, as his editorial director. Spectorsky brought in fiction from the likes of Norman Mailer, Vladimir Nabokov, James Baldwin, Jack Kerouac and the like. *Playboy* quickly became far more than soft porn, even if the literary depth was likely lost on most readers. Indeed, if you took the girls out of the picture (which was, of course, unthinkable), it was essentially a literary magazine. Did you ever meet Kerouac?

"No. We published several pieces of his – both fiction and non-fiction – in the '50s. But I don't think our paths crossed."

How about Nabokov?

"We've corresponded, but I don't think I've ever met him. When you're talking about famous people, sometimes you're not quite sure whether you've really met 'em or not. But we've definitely corresponded. Nabokov wrote a number of pieces for us. He was a butterfly collector and he once, in a letter to me, drew a butterfly that looked like the *Playboy* rabbit at the end of one of his letters."

Hef tells me that F. Scott Fitzgerald was his hero growing up. Did he ever think of writing fiction himself?

"That's the road untravelled," he sighs. "When I was in high school, even in late grade school, I created a lot of comic books and wrote a lot of short stories

– most of them mystery stories and horror, etc. But it's the same thing as with the cartooning – at one point I wanted to be a cartoonist but I think that the magazine and the editing of the magazine supplied that need, and I am better as an editor than I would be as either a cartoonist or a writer."

Have you ever published any of your own cartoons in the magazine?

"At the very beginning. But then I stopped buying my stuff because it wasn't good enough," he laughs.

By the beginning of the 1960s, *Playboy* was growing at a phenomenal rate, selling more than a million issues per month. With very deep pockets, Hef quickly began to build up an empire – and, following his amicable divorce from Mildred, a very public image as the most envied bachelor in America. He hosted a popular syndicated TV show called *Playboy's Penthouse*, purchased the first Playboy Mansion in Chicago (he didn't move to California until 1975), and opened the first Playboy Club.

The '60s were extremely profitable for that decade's biggest swinger. By 1971, when Playboy Enterprises went public, the magazine was selling a phenomenal seven million copies a month. There were 23 Playboy Clubs, resorts, hotels and casinos, with more than 900,000 members worldwide. The company's assets included book publishing, merchandising, a modelling agency, a limousine service, a record label, and a TV and motion picture company. Hef acquired a jet – a black McDonnell Douglas DC-9-30, which he called *Big Bunny* – and used it to travel the world. Undoubtedly, he soon became a member of the Mile High Club. Reputed to be involved with an average of 11 of each year's centrefolds, he was having a lot of sex. While he has admitted to experimenting with bisexuality around this time, he slept mainly with women.

What's the longest period of celibacy you've had?

"My marriage, I guess," he smiles. "The only time that I wasn't getting a lot of sex was when I was married. An experience a lot of us could identify with."

As a fully qualified sexpert, what would be his recommendation for the most fulfilling kind of sex?

Hef straightens up in his seat, and smiles coyly. "Well, I think there are many roads to Mecca. I think that it depends on what your particular dreams are. Most of it comes from early childhood. You know, I think your love maps are drawn from very early experiences and fantasies. And then you play them out for the rest of your life."

And what are yours?

"Most of mine, quite frankly, being raised in a very typical conservative home with a lot of repression, I think that most of mine came from the movies. The movies and the music of my childhood. I was born in 1926 so I grew up during the Great Depression and the early part of World War II. It was a very romantic time. And I think that's essentially who I am. I'm a romantic at heart. Romance in terms of both boy meets girl, but also the adventure of the romance, like in those wonderful musicals."

Or boy meets *girls*...

"Yeah, that's right," he chuckles.

Have you ever tried cyber-sex?

"Nah. I think that cyber-sex is for people who don't have the real thing. But I think the variations on the theme are expanding, and that's a good thing. To some extent they've always been there in one form or another, but now it's not so hidden and I think that's positive."

Although he's now in his 80s, with three stunning girlfriends on call, and the help of a little blue pill, Hef claims to enjoy sex as much as ever. He probably just doesn't have it as much as he used to. Has your lifestyle slowed?

"Well, I'm down to three girlfriends – I had seven about four years ago. But I've slowed down naturally in terms of, you know, the passing of the years, but also I'm in a different place just in terms of my head now. During the '50s and '60s, it was workaholic time. Then I had a stroke in the 1980s."

Which you later called "a stroke of luck."

"It was, because I used it in a very positive way. Although I also think that that was the reason I got married again. The second marriage was prompted by, at that point, feeling my years and seeking a safe harbour."

By the 1970s, largely thanks to *Playboy*, the sexual floodgates had opened and numerous other 'one-handed' magazines started to appear, most notably Larry Flynt's *Hustler*. However, Hef refused to lower to the challenge by going pink (showing the girls' vaginas) and kept his publication reasonably decent. *Playboy's* Bunnies were naked, as ever, but their legs remained closed.

"That just wasn't the road I wanted to travel," he explains. "I was not trying to create a sex magazine. There had been lots of publications before *Playboy* that included sexual content. What I was trying to do was create a magazine that gave sex a good name and had something positive to say about sexuality. And simply making the magazine more explicit wasn't going to solve that. What surprised me, quite frankly, after more than half-a-century, is that even the nudity in *Playboy* is still as controversial in America as it used to be. And that is one of the things that limits us to some extent in terms of the advertising that we get and the distribution that we get."

Today, *Playboy* sells about three million copies a month – not bad when you consider the competition posed by the internet, and the vast array of other men's magazines out there. How involved is Hef now in the day-to-day running of the magazine?

"Well, we have offices in both Chicago and New York. But I'm still very much hands-on in terms of the general layout of the magazine."

Needless to say, Hef's hands are on more than just that ...

"I approve all the covers, approve all the Playmates, all the pictorials. I pick all the cartoons, do the party jokes, approve the letters. So I have a continuing influence. For the last couple of hours before you arrived, I've been in telephonic connection with my editors on various things for the magazine."

Is that what keeps you sharp?

"I think it helps, yeah. I think that one of the things that keeps me young and vital is the work – keeping your mind busy, and doing what you love."

Throughout the conversation, Hef regularly slips into corporate speak: "The magazine and the brand represent a certain kind of lifestyle that I think is the future, and something I think is very important."

Of course, not everybody was delighted with *Playboy's* phenomenal success. The feminist Gloria Steinem (who once went undercover as a Bunny and wrote a scathing report) has commented: "There are times when a woman reading *Playboy* feels like a Jew reading a Nazi manual."

It was a spectacularly stupid statement, and not one that Hef paid very much heed to. An unashamed libertarian, he's been attacked from all fronts numerous times over the years and has always given as good as he got.

"I was arrested once – over pictures of Jayne Mansfield," he says. "But that wasn't really what it was all about. What lay behind it was the fact that I was editorialising against the Chicago police and the Mayor's office because they had arrested Lenny Bruce. So I was giving them a bad time, so they decided to come around and give me a bad time. All the problems and the conflicts, etc., are also why I'm still in the centre of the storm after all these years. One would not expect, having had such success in the '50s and '60s, to still have it going in such a remarkable way – and for the brand to be so hot again after all these years."

Of course, while Hef has generally kept his nose clean, there have been various *Playboy*-related scandals and tragedies over the years. In the 1970s, his private secretary Bobbie Arnstein committed suicide after involving *Playboy* in a drug scandal. In 1980, the Playmate of the Year, Dorothy Stratten, was brutally murdered by her rejected husband. Most recently, former Playmate Anne Nicole Smith died following an overdose.

"I wouldn't say we were close, but obviously we cared about her," Hef sighs. "She was really a curiosity. A girl who came from a very ordinary Texas background, and caught the fancy of the media. It's very difficult to define what celebrity is about today. I mean, you can be a celebrity by simply showing up on television a few times and getting the fancy of the tabloids, etc. But she was definitely one of the Playmates who'll be remembered."

When was the last time Hef shed a tear?

"Shed a tear? The last time I saw a sentimental movie. I'm a very sentimental person. I wear my emotions on my sleeve – proudly so – and I think that's the way it oughta be."

Presumably, a few tears were shed when his second marriage broke up. In 1989, Hef got married again, having proposed to Kimberly Conrad (Playmate of the Year 1989) at the Mansion. This union produced two sons, but the couple separated in 1998. He says that the break-up initially got him out of the house a bit more.

"At the end of my marriage in '98, I did start simply going out to clubs, etc. In the last few months I've backed off a little bit from that, starting to take it a little bit easier, but it's easy to do because I'm busy doing the TV show and I've got the girlfriends here. Most of what I'm looking for is already here."

He tells me that he's been a Democrat for longer than he can remember. "My folks were Republican, so I was a Democrat from when I was a little kid and couldn't even vote."

What's Hef's take on President George W. Bush?

"He's not my President. This is a very sad period in American history. Again it's the moral majority and Christian Right thing – and we got it in spades with Bush. I mean, Bush is a more extreme version of his father, and of Reagan. By contrast, both Bush Sr. and Reagan were very good Presidents."

Have you met many Presidents?

"I've met a few," he shrugs. "Carter, and Hillary and her husband. Hillary isn't the President yet, but her husband."

Who do you support for the next Presidency?

"Well, I've given money to both Hillary and to Obama. So we'll support the Democratic ticket."

Do you support the troops in Iraq?

"I support the troops, but I don't support the fact that they're there."

What do you think of Arnold Schwarzenegger?

"He's a very good governor. He's a friend, too. In his early days here in Hollywood, he used to hang out in the Mansion."

Did you ever have any interest getting involved in politics yourself?

He erupts into laughter. "People have asked me that question and the reality is that I would never trade my life for that life! I mean, you'd just have to be doing a whole lot of things you wouldn't want to be doing, that's all. To spend all your time shaking hands with people you don't want to shake hands with – *no*. I get involved in politics in a second-hand way by trying to do what I can to get the right people elected, but I would never want to be a candidate."

In fairness, he has far better things to be doing. When he's not having sex or conducting important Playboy business, Hef spends a lot of his spare time watching movies. Movies are his first love and he's got a library of over 4,000 films to prove it. He's been involved in various movie productions over the years – including bankrolling Roman Polanski's *Macbeth* and Monty Python's first film, *And Now for Something Completely Different*. In 1980, he earned his Hollywood star on the Walk of Fame for his efforts in getting the iconic Hollywood sign repaired.

A few months ago, it was announced that director Brian Grazier is to make a film of Hef's life.

"I've suggested the possibility of Hugh Jackman to play me, but I don't know," he says. "I'm excited about it. I really love the movies – the old ones especially, but I watch the new stuff too. We watched a really hilarious film last Sunday, a surprise hit, an English film called *Death at a Funeral* – outrageous and very funny and I recommend it. But my own special favourites are the old classic films. *Casablanca* is my favourite film because it touches all the buttons. It has patriotism and unrequited love and humour and a great song."

At the age of 81, he may be slowing down but, following a sluggish '80s and '90s, his Playboy empire is beginning to expand again. Last year they opened a new casino in Las Vegas. Is Hef a gambler?

"No, because I see the advantage of being the house. There's a reason why Las Vegas has all those big luxurious hotels. They are built on the money of the people who are losing at the tables. We were in gambling with great success from 1965/66 on. We had a casino in London and then wound up with several more in London and around England throughout the latter '60s and '70s and into the early '80s.

"We had to get out of the business in England because things got really conservative there. But we're back into it again now with the Palms in Las Vegas and we've a few other things – including England – under negotiation."

What ambitions does he now have?

"To continue to live as long as I can, and continue doing what I'm doing now, and savour the enjoyment of it all. I'm in a wonderful personal relationship, the brand is hot again *(raps knuckle off table)*. My mother lived to 101. If you want to live a long time, the first thing you do is pick your parents well."

In terms of staying alive, does he keep an eye on genetic research or investigate new medical techniques?

"No, nothing special. Just take care of myself, get regular physical check-ups. I take blood pressure medicine and take care of myself."

What's been his proudest moment?

"Proudest? Well, the thing that I'm proudest of is that I feel as if I've had some positive impact on the changing social-sexual values of our time. That's certainly what I take the greatest pride in."

Any words of advice to young people?

"What I've always said is that I'm a dreamer. There are a lot of pressures as you're growing up – peer pressures, family, society – that urge compromise, and I think we're here for a just a short period of time, and whatever one's particular dreams and aspirations are, I think that's the route you've got to take. Because life is short."

As he shakes my hand and gets up to leave (presumably to go and have sex with Holly, Bridget or Kendra – or possibly Holly, Bridget *and* Kendra), he has one final thing to say: "I know I'm living out a lot of other guys' fantasies. But what you need to understand is that I'm living out my own as well. That's really what it's all about."

And with that, Hef is gone. Nice fellow. Fair fucks to him!

{OCTOBER, 2007}

SELECTED RECORDINGS: 2000-2010

CHAPTER NINE:
Ron Jeremy

For a guy who's verifiably had sex with more than 4,000 women, Ron Jeremy seems desperately eager to impress. Just not with his tardiness. After three days playing phone-tag across Los Angeles, the 55-year-old actor finally arrives at my oceanfront Santa Monica hotel almost two hours late for our breakfast appointment.

Short, portly, mustachioed, and scruffily-attired, the world's most unlikely porn star shoots the receptionist a filthy look as he ambles into the lobby to greet me. "Hey man, I'm so sorry I'm late," he apologises in a broad Jewish-New-Yorker accent, "but I rang here and *SOMEONE* – yeah, I'm lookin' at you, lady! – told me the address was in the highs not the lows. I was driving the wrong fuckin' direction for half an hour!"

I assure him it's no problem, though in fact it is. I'm flying back to Ireland this afternoon, and my California-based sister and her children are due to arrive in an hour for a quick family get-together. The photographer also has to go, so, with no time for a proper shoot, we hastily convene by the hotel pool for a quick snap. Ron has a photographic suggestion. I'm to hold my hands about ten inches apart (roughly indicating the length of his infamous penis), while he stands beside me, sympathetically holding his fingers much closer together. "I do this 'comparing sizes' picture with everybody," he tells me. "It's just a thing that I always do."

In case I don't believe him, he pulls a copy of his best-selling autobiography, *The Hardest (Working) Man In Showbiz*, out of the plastic bag he's carrying and opens it to the photo section, entitled 'Famous Friends'. "Look, here's me with Keith Richards... Samuel L. Jackson... Rick James... Brad Pitt." He turns the page over, pointing each picture out to me: "Johnny Depp... Chris Rock... Ice-T... Robin Williams... Axl Rose." He flips the page again: "Debbie Harry... Fred Durst... Robert Evans... Tommy Lee... that was taken at the Playboy Mansion... look, there's me with Sting... Moby... Dustin Hoffman – I was in a movie with him, you know ... Sean Penn... Stevie Wonder."

I'm getting the, em, picture at this stage, but he turns the page again anyway: "Look, here's me with Ed Norton... Bobby Brown... Linda Blair... Mickey Rourke... Heather Locklear... Jerry Springer – I've been on his show *four* times... Matt LeBlanc... Kid Rock."

This is getting a bit much. "Ron!" I say. "I've already read your book. I've seen all these. Can we just take this photograph and get on with the interview?"

"Sure, sure," he says. "But, you're Irish right? Look at this one!" He skips a few more pages. "That's me and Colin Farrell. He's from Dublin, right? That was just after he finished shooting *Miami Vice*."

"Cool," I say. "Now can we just take the picture?"

"Oh, one more thing!" Ron reaches back into his plastic bag and removes a small frame. "Look at this! I gave a lecture at Trinity College Dublin, and they gave me this. You know Trinity College, right? Really famous place, right? I was a big hit there. Full house. They gave me this after."

Closer inspection reveals that it's an honorary scroll from Trinity's Philosophical Society bearing his full name, Ron Jeremy Hyatt. "I've got a few of those at home from different colleges and universities," he proudly informs me. "I've even spoken at Oxford University. You know, in England? Oxford University?"

"Ron, please!" I plead. "Can we just take the fucking picture?"

"Oh sure, no problem!" He puts the bag down and we assume positions. As the photographer snaps away, Ron asks me, "Hey, do you know those Rodge and Podge guys? I was on their TV show in Ireland. It's a really big show, right?"

A few minutes later, Ron walks into my hotel suite. I'd been planning to do the interview downstairs, but he's already been asked for an autograph by a passing guest ("Happens all the time, everywhere I go!"), and time is too tight to risk any further interruptions. Besides, the breakfast room is closed.

"Hey, this is a nice room!" he whistles, approvingly. "How much you paying to stay here?"

"I'm not really sure," I admit. "Someone else is picking up the tab, but I think it's about $800 a night."

Ron does a wildly exaggerated double-take, slapping one of his heavily bejewelled paws to his forehead: *"EIGHT HUNDRED BUCKS A NIGHT!!! ARE YOU FUCKIN' KIDDING ME?!"* He sighs dramatically and claps me on the back. "Hey, next time you're coming to LA, gimme a call. I'll get you a hotel just as nice as this for three hundred dollars. I know some really cool places."

Do you not have a place of your own in LA?

"I've got a place in Queens with my dad, and I've got a condo here," he explains. "But I stay in hotels all the time, anyway."

It turns out he's carrying some small gifts for me in his plastic bag. There's a bunch of novelty St. Patrick's Day greeting cards, all of which feature over-the-top images of Ron wearing lurid leprechaun costumes on their front. He also gives me a packet of Ron Jeremy cigarette rolling papers (inside of which is a tasteful photograph of him shoving his massive penis into a woman's mouth: *'HEY, BABY... SMOKE THIS!!'*). Always hustling, Ron puts his name to a wide variety of products – from skateboards and clothing to beef jerkies and hot sauces. Unfortunately, the line of Ron Jeremy 10" cigars has recently been discontinued because of the smoking ban. Also in the plastic bag is a DVD copy of *The Boondock Saints*, the 1999 gangster flick in which he has a small role (but not, presumably, a small dick). Although Ron holds the world record for the most appearances in adult movies – so far he's made more than 2,000 – he's also shown up in a number of mainstream flicks.

"This movie never got a proper theatrical release but, according to *Variety* magazine, it's one of the biggest selling straight-to-DVD titles of all time," he informs me. "It's got a whole bunch of Irish actors in it. Guys like Willem Dafoe, Sean Patrick Flanery, and Billy Connolly. I play a gangster in it."

"Well, I'll look forward to watching it," I say, putting my hand out.

"No, I wasn't giving this one to you," he says, putting it back into the bag. "It's my only copy. But you really should check it out sometime."

Last night he was at an industry party in the House of Blues on Sunset Blvd for the launch of his most recent film (he'd invited me, but I hadn't been able to attend). Despite its title, *Homo Erectus* isn't actually a porn film.

"It's a National Lampoon comedy," he explains. "You should've been there last night – it was a great party. It's got an amazing cast. Talia Shire is in it, you know from *Rocky*? And Gary Busey. And Ali Larter, of course, who's had two hit films – *Varsity Blues* and *Resident Evil*. She was also a cover of *Cosmo*. But when she did *Homo Erectus*, she'd only done *Varsity Blues*, she wasn't that famous. It's a caveman comedy. It's really funny. I play Oog, the best friend of the lead actor. Now, the guy who produced it had an Academy Award for Charlize Theron. He did a film called *Monster*. The director was Adam Rifkin, who's written for Spielberg and for..."

And on he talks, unstoppably. It's quickly becoming obvious that Ron doesn't just shamelessly namedrop every second or third sentence. Like an overexcited child, or coked-up comedian, he's also an uninterruptible, natural born motor-mouth. Fortunately, he's a very likable one.

"Here's a funny story," he says. "You'll love this. Ali Larter wouldn't do press for the movie. Who knows why? Now she got big – *Heroes* is a huge hit on TV. You get it in Ireland? Have you heard of it? It's, like, huge – *HUGE!!* Anyway, they pushed back the release of the movie for a year, and then Gary – Gary Busey – says to me..."

Several minutes and many namedrops later...

"So to get even, someone at National Lampoon took a picture of me and Ali side by side, sitting in our chairs during the making of the movie, in our caveman attire. But they superimposed my schlong coming outta my pants. And it's so hysterical! And it's not mine! First of all, mine is bigger, number one. It's not pointy, number two. And, number three, I wouldn't have my penis out during *THE MAKING OF A PG-RATED MOVIE!!*"

I thought it was an R-rated movie?

"It only went R after National Lampoon took it," he explains. "They asked for a lot more boobies to be in the film. Because they do R-rated films. But it was made as a PG. And I'm not gonna have my *thing* out! I wore a jock support! I was careful not to have my thing fall out of my caveman shorts. So I'm looking at it, going 'WHAT?' They did it because they were pissed at her. And she'd a lot of reactions to it. Her press people were really pissed off that she'd actually posed next to an adult film actor with his thing outta his pants. It was so funny. And then somehow Perez Hilton got hold of the pictures. You've heard of Perez Hilton? He's got this celebrity website, right? Millions of hits! *MILLIONS!!*"

We're interrupted by a knock at the door. Room service has arrived with Ron's breakfast – a large pot of coffee and a blueberry Danish. I've signed for it and the porter is gone before he realises that the coffee pot is only half-full.

"Look at this!" he sighs, disgustedly. "Look at this! It's not even half-full. I love that. They're charging 800 bucks a night and they're skimping on the coffee. I'd love to know what this cost... what did you just pay for this?"

"I think it was $25 plus tip," I tell him.

"Ha, ha! Oh my God! I'm not all that cheap, but I laugh my ass off at what these places charge!"

Surely you've made enough money over the years not to have to worry about such things?

"Yeah, sure. I could afford to stay here – a lot. But I wouldn't be caught dead. You see, I happen to be... hang on... *A-JEW!!!!!!* Excuse me! Sorry, I sneezed! But I look around for bargains a little bit. I think it's part of my training. But 800 bucks a night, 25 bucks for coffee... *sheesh!*"

He grabs my digital recorder off the table and speaks directly into it: "Make a note of that, folks! Okay, that was $25 for a coffee *AND A DANISH!!!* You charge 25 bucks for this, you wanna bring Jesus Christ along to heal people at the same time. Holy shit! What we were talking about anyway?"

Sensing an opportunity to try and actually get some control over the conversation, I ask when he lost his virginity.

"I was 16 or 17. I don't remember exactly, but it was with a girl named... well, I'll call her 'Marge'. In the book I called her Maggie, as a courtesy. Marge was the first. And it's a true story, I put the rubber on backwards. Because I didn't know that you unravelled it onto the penis. I unravelled the whole thing first and it wouldn't go on, so the lubricated side was against me, not her. So then when I put the penis in the edge of her vagina, I'm going back and forth – and I basically screwed the rubber. That was the part that was lubricated."

Were you always aware that you were so spectacularly well-endowed?

"Not so much," he shrugs. "I mean, I saw in gym classes, some of these black basketball players who were kind of built like me. I was like, 'Hey, maybe I should play basketball, I'm built more like those guys'. But they were dangling, they weren't hard. And I read that Xaviera Hollander, you know that famous hooker who writes for that magazine in Amsterdam, she said that often white men might be smaller in the flaccid state but when they get hard they catch up. So I couldn't tell for sure."

He did have his suspicions, though. After all, he could auto-fellate (something he's since demonstrated in numerous movies). "I knew I could kiss it," he admits. "And that was a bit weird. But I didn't have to be hard to do that. I could just bend over and give it a kiss. I had a weird conversation with my dad about that. I was in boy scouts, bending over to tie those high shoes, I was always able to kiss my schlong. I was going, 'I wonder if that's normal?' And I was talking to my dad on the telephone and I asked him. First thing he says to me, 'Is anybody else in the room with you?' I says no. He says, 'Good! Listen, let me explain to you, it's not really good or bad. It's not abnormal. It's just not really necessary. Because when you get to be 18 years of age, you'll find girls will kiss it for you'. That was the conversation."

Despite his obvious advantage, he says he wasn't a particularly big hit with the girls as a teen. "I was a little bit chunky. They used to tease me going, *'Ronnie Hyatt's on a diet/ Isn't that a riot?'* But I wasn't that heavy. And my parents gave me a very good physique. Because they were very healthy. But all through my teens, I worked summers as a waiter in the Catskills in these old Jewish hotels, places like the Paramount and the Concorde. I did all right with the women there."

When was the first time you watched a porn movie?

"I guess I was maybe 19 or 20 years old," he recalls, tearing off a mouthful of Danish. "My dad and I, believe it or not, saw *Devil and Miss Jones* and *Deep Throat*, the two old, old ones from the early days in the '70s. And I went to see them never realising that six or seven years later, I'd be doing porn myself."

You went with your dad?

"Yeah, people say it's kinda weird, but, you know, we had heard of these and we weren't going there to get turned on."

This was in a movie theatre?

"Yeah, they didn't have DVDs or VHS back than. In fact, I think dinosaurs might've been on the earth, too. It was way, way back."

And did you... ahem... jerk off?

He waves a hand: "Nah, that would've been too weird. We weren't going for that reason. We were going to see how these films are made. It was more out of curiosity. I was going to major in theatre at Queens College and it was just a curiosity thing. Because we knew they weren't using professional actors. We were laughing the whole time. Because there was all this big hubbub, all this press about these films that got prosecuted.

"It was current events, you know – in the news. And Jack Nicholson and Warren Beatty and Shirley McLaine had all put their names behind friends of the court, called an amicus brief, to help [actor] Harry Reems in his battles. This is all in that new movie that came out called *The Making of Deep Throat*. So it was like, wow, they busted a movie! It was showing at the World Theatre and a judge got rid of *Deep Throat*, took it out, it was banned. So the headline in the *New York Post* was, *Judge Cuts Throat – World Mourns'*. That was brilliant."

At the time, Ron was studying theatre in Queens College. After graduation, he went on to do a Masters in Special Education. Although he'd always dreamed of being a actor, he started off his professional life teaching children with disabilities.

"I still have a teaching license – it's permanent, but I probably could not teach elementary school at this point. They'd be afraid I'd go up in front of a class, drop my pants, and go, 'Hi boys and girls, say hello to Mr. Happy!' Ha, ha! What the world needs is more ha-penis!"

Despite all the jokes, it's obvious that Ron really enjoyed his teaching years. "It was nice. It was rewarding. I took the kids on field trips – learned about firehouses, banks, stuff like that. I'd just put 'em in my car. You could do riskier things back then. Nowadays, if you want to take any kids in your car, you've probably got to get a million permits, fire marshals, police escorts. Back then, I'd just say, 'Get in the damn car!' and take them anywhere. It worked out really, really good. I still feel I should do something for that world, now that I've made money. I liked it. I feel like I kinda deserted that world. I just quit teaching when I got the opportunity."

Ron's acting career began to take off in 1978, when his then-girlfriend sent a naked picture of him in to *Playgirl* magazine. His 9.75-inch penis ("I don't mind if you wanna round it up to 10!") proved a big hit with readers. So much so that his grandmother, Rose, had to temporarily move out of her apartment. Playgirl had listed his name as 'R. Hyatt of Queens', and the poor woman was plagued with phone calls and unwanted late night visits from cock-hungry young females.

"She had to move out of her house after a day – for a month! My father told me, 'If you wanna get into this naked, crazy business, so be it, but if you use the family name again, I'll kill you!'"

Pretty soon some unusual offers began to come in. Ron swiftly abandoned his teaching career to become a porn star.

"It wasn't so much the money. Porn wasn't my first choice. I got my Bachelors in acting and I did theatre off-Broadway. One of my teachers, by the way, was Joel Zwick – who directed *My Big Fat Greek Wedding*. He had a thing called Café Le Moma in New York, and he taught me movement at Queens College. So I got my degree. I was doing off-off Broadway. And the job market is horrible, you really starve. So when my ex-girlfriend sent that picture of me into *Playgirl* and they published it, I thought being nude wasn't so bad. That was back in 1978. It's in my documentary (*Being Ron Jeremy*), if you saw that."

His first decent offer came from a reasonably well-known, low-budget, B-movie director named Jim Sandberg. Ron thought this could be his big break, but then Sandberg informed him that he'd recently decided to finish with B-movies and become an X-movie director instead.

"I asked my dad his opinion. It was a way to get some acting. Back then there was no videos, it was all theatre. And there were storylines. They had scripts sometimes, you know, so you felt like an actor. You'd work 10 days on a movie like *Bad Girls, Fascination, Amanda By Night, Co-Ed Fever, Sizzle*, I could go on and on and on – you'd work nine days as an actor and then one day you'd have sex. So you felt kinda like an actor. Maybe I was justifying or rationalising to myself, but I felt like an actor. Nowadays, most of the scripts are like, 'Here's a dollar, here's a cup of coffee – blow me!' There's no dialogue. It's changed a lot."

Resolutely straight – he doesn't touch drugs or men – Ron has since gone on to appear in well over 2,000 adult movies. Most male porn careers end at the age of 36, but thanks to his amazing cock control and stallionish stamina (he can go hard or soft in an instant, always ejaculates on cue, and once fucked 14 women in a row for a film called *Put It In Reverse III*), he's still going strong.

There used to be an industry joke that went, "there are three things some female porn stars won't do – bestiality, sadomasochism and Ron Jeremy." He's learned to laugh about his lack of obvious sex appeal: "Hey, I'm living proof that anybody can get laid! I used to be thinner, but I made the move from the gym to the buffet."

He tells me that one of his weirdest porn experiences came when he was filming a movie on a yacht off the Majorcan coast. His co-star was seriously seasick, but the show had to go on. "Rather than blowing me, she was blowing chunks," he laughs. "I was having sex with her from behind while she was throwing up over the side of the boat. The director had to film all her reaction shots later."

Of course, although it's what he's most famous for, nowadays there's far more to Ron Jeremy's career than just porn. In addition to his occasional mainstream movie roles, music video appearances (he's been in videos for Moby, Mercury Rev, Guns N' Roses and many others) and merchandising, he's recently added 'reality TV star' to his chequered CV, following well-received stints on hit shows *The Surreal Life* and *The Farm*. Despite all of his success, he's furious that his old alma mater has more or less disowned him.

"Queens College doesn't acknowledge me in any of their literature, and it kinda makes me angry. They'll list bestselling authors – I'm one, but never once got in there. They'll list people who have good careers – Jerry Seinfeld and Rodney Dangerfield went to Queens, a lot of the writers at Paramount went there. And I've done a lot of mainstream stuff as well, but they never acknowledge me. They only ever contact me to give money to the alumni association. I just reach into my pants and go, 'Here's your money right here!'

"It's like I don't even exist," he continues. "How many people are bestselling authors on the *New York Times* list? And my book came out the same time as Hilary Clinton's and Barack Obama's – all these non-fiction books. That wasn't easy getting that (*points to* 'New York Times Bestseller' *strapline on book cover*). I had to turn down all the lesser stores and just do autographs and signings at the stores they track. I didn't do any discount stores or any Hustlers (stores). I wasn't interested in the money, I wanted to get this – bestseller."

He goes to pour another cup of coffee, but there's only a dribble left in the jug. Once again, he screams directly into the recorder: *JESUS CHRIST!! EIGHT HUNDRED DOLLARS A NIGHT FOR THIS!!! IT'S NOT MY MONEY – AND I'M STILL PISSED OFF!!!"*

Queens College may want nothing to do with him, but Ron spends a lot of his time debating in other universities.

"Debating has been a big part of my life. Go to a computer, put in my name and the word 'college' and you'll see. It's *huge!* Five thousand kids sometimes, big turnouts. The computer will even tell you about this one time I started a riot because some kids couldn't get in. They had to take me home in a police car. Susan Cole, the feminist, said, 'Ron, you're a damn rock star!' It was so funny."

Needless to say, it was a pornography debate that brought him to Trinity in 2004. "I had some fun in Ireland!" he laughs. "They kept asking me when I spoke at Trinity College, 'Are you gonna make a porn film here?' So just to have some fun and scare the bejaysus outta the church, I was saying yeah. Because Ireland's got a very powerful church. You guys didn't even have legal rubbers until recently! So you guys are one of the most prudish countries in the world. And I respect that. So I said maybe I'll find some beautiful green fields in Ireland with the ocean in the background and just shoot a softcore. Nudity only. No hardcore, no sex. So I was very specific about that. I didn't wanna say 'Hell no!' But they kept asking me questions like, 'Are the Irish girls pretty enough?' I was saying of course the Irish girls are gorgeous, of course I could do a porn from here, but you guys are a little bit prudish compared to the rest of the world, so I don't wanna offend community standards. Why do I have to go where I'm not wanted? There's gorgeous scenery in other parts of the world, too – and I could always fly Irish girls to America anyway.

"But I'd do a nude movie – you know, a real strong R-rated. Boobies bouncing and girls running through fields with sexy bodies. But no penetration. None of this! No... *(makes popping sound with his cheek)*. None of that. I wouldn't be caught dead shooting a porn movie in Ireland. Why risk the law on your case? Even in America, I just shoot in LA and New York. Cause some states have a problem. Like the Bible Belt."

When Ron speaks at American universities, he's usually debating feminists or members of the XXX Church (an anti-pornography Christian group).

"I'm probably the number one defender of porn in America right now," he says, proudly. "Martin Bashir, who interviewed the Queen of England and Princess Diana and Michael Jackson – which he got sued for – flew to Yale to mediate my debate with the XXX Church. It was on *Nightline* and CNN!"

Funnily enough, he maintains that he gets on extremely well with his debating opponents.

"In a way, I respect what they're doing. They're doing what Jesus would've done. If you think there's a problem, go to where the problem is. All these other Christians who hate porn, they tell their church how bad it is. They don't have to tell them, they already agree. Craig Gross, the founder of the XXX Church, goes right to where supposedly the problem is. He tries to get people out of the biz, to counsels girls, and all that. He's really a great guy. We're actually really good friends, though you wouldn't think so when we're on stage.

"But the way I see it, it's a freedom of speech issue. It's secular, it's not religious. People who hate porn, 99% of the time come from a religious background. That's not what makes these countries great. These countries are based on separation of church and state. You can love religion or not, it's your choice."

Not that Ron has anything against religion. "I have a lot of religious friends. Tammy Faye (*the late evangelist who appeared on* The Surreal Life *with him*) was a great friend of mine. And I believe in the man upstairs. I do have a relationship with him. A lot of people in porn do. They have families. And they don't think that the Lord has a problem with consenting adults having consenting sex for consenting adults to watch. Let me know where's the problem? But if you're gonna follow the Bible to the letter... at these debates, one of my favourite bits, is when I say to these religious types, 'Now you don't like premarital sex of any kind, do you? You don't believe in any kind of sex before marriage?' and the people I'm debating say yes. So then I say, 'I'm glad you said that. With a show of hands, who here in the audience has ever had sex outside of marriage?' There's usually about 5,000 college kids in the audience and every single hand goes up. I look at the person and go, 'I'm not your problem! *Thank you! Limousine! Where's my cheque?*' They can't beat me! Ha, ha!

"Seriously, though, I really don't think the Lord above has a problem. Nobody's doing anything to hurt anybody, it's all just entertainment. And my other logic is, anything I do – you do. And that means you, too. You're a journalist. I'm not sure how crazy you are in your personal sex life, but I probably do the same things you do. I probably do the same things everyone else does. Just because I have a camera rolling, I'm a bad guy? I even say this to Craig Gross. He's been with one woman his whole life. He was a virgin before he met her. But we're probably about the same. I've had sex with about 4,000 women, he's done his wife about 4,000 times. Same thing. Same amount of pop shots! So there's nothing unusual in what I do."

The conversation ping-pongs for a while. He's against the Iraq war ("Bush is probably the worst president we've ever had – though, in fairness, he's been good to Israel!"); he doesn't have a current girlfriend ("Relationships are hell – especially when you're in my business. I do have a turtle, though!"); he was a great friend of the late Mo Mowlam ("We sang a song together on *The Frank Skinner Show*"); the lowest point of his life came watching his mother slowly die ("I was 26 and it was just awful to see this grand woman get struck down with Parkinson's Disease. Actually, Janet Reno has it – and I spoke to Janet about it, I met her. And Michael J. Fox. To see a woman who was so phenomenal was just so sad").

The telephone rings. My sister and her family have arrived, and are waiting for me downstairs. I ask them to give me a few minutes. What are your ambitions now, Ron?

"Just to continue acting," he says. "I'm doing it. I've got a lot of big films coming out, I've got more TV shows. *The Surreal Life* really opened a lot of doors for me. Because it was always a thing of, 'We can't put a porn star in a steady role in a TV series on network TV'. But *Surreal Life* took a chance – and that was a WB network. It got the highest ratings ever for that time slot, and they gave a lot of the credit to me and Tammy Faye, the evangelist who I got along with. You know, here's a porn star and an evangelist becoming friends. She used to go on *Larry King* and even say, 'I love Ron Jeremy and his pet tortoise' – cause my turtle was on the show, too. And Tammy helped me feed the tortoise, she said prayers over the tortoise, too. She used to say to me, 'Ronnie, tortoises have souls, too'. She was so cute. You know who Tammy Faye is? What a sweet lady. She died. A real hunny-bunny. So it opened up a lot of doors.

"But to finish your question. I love performing and I love being an actor. That's my desire. So if I could just get acting work. If you were sent down by the Lord or a clairvoyant or someone who could see the future, and said, 'Ronnie, you're gonna do like two or three films every year – one for Spielberg, James Cameron and all those other major directors, you're gonna work for'. I'd probably give up touring, give up doing the debates, and I'm done, that's it! I'll go to the beach and hang out with friends, play with my turtle, play with my buddies and just do that. Because that's all I want to do – just act, act, act. Films are the best, then TV, and porn if nothing else comes along."

Are all of your friends celebrities or do you have any normal mates?

"I've a mixture of both," he shrugs. "But you know, like, a lot of them are Hollywood friendships; they're not really that great a friend, but they can help your career. I hate to say it, but in Hollywood it's so important. Acting, music, sports

– they're not like any other career on this planet, because everyone wants to do it but there's very few jobs available.

"You wanna be a doctor, lawyer, teacher or whatever, you go to school, work damn hard, study your shit, don't go to discos, study, study, study, get good marks in a good school, you're gonna succeed. You go to Harvard to study law, I don't give a fuck if you're the bottom of your class, you're still gonna get a job. Some things have a set programme that works. Here's a formula – it's going to work. Acting? No! Music? No! You can spend 20 years at Lee Strasberg and get a doctorate in theatre or classics, but that doesn't mean you're gonna get a job.

"Look at Cathy Moriarty. She's working as a waitress and then Martin Scorsese sees her, thinks she has a great look, and gives her a job as Robert De Niro's wife in *Raging Bull*. Next thing you know, she gets famous. And she tells the whole world that. And all the people who spent years studying Strasberg – learning how to do jazz, tap, modern dance, ballet, choir lessons, singing lessons – are going, 'She's a WHAT? She's a WAITRESS?'

"So acting is based on a lot of luck and also on your connections. I call them 'Hollywood friendships'. Because you know they wouldn't be your friend if they weren't in a position to help you. I'm friends with a lot of directors. A couple of them would be my friend no matter what they did for a living. But some of the directors I'm really good friends with, I'm only friends with because they're directors. They could probably spit in my eye and I'd say, 'Thank you, can I have another?'

"The old joke in Hollywood is it's not who you know, it's who you blow," he continues. "That's if you're a girl. As (comedian) Carrie Snow used to say, 'If I could blow my way to the top, I'd already be there'. As a guy... actually, it's the same thing if the guy is gay. Nah, I'm kidding. It's just a lot of hustle, a lot of real hard work. But I don't knock myself for this because it's necessary for my career. If someone's an asshole, but can really help my career, I'm gonna continue being their friend. So it's hypocritical in a way, but what you gonna do?"

On that note, we have to leave it. There's so much more I'd like to ask Ron Jeremy, but I haven't seen my sister in months. He fully understands – and apologises once again for being so late.

"Hey, what's your sister's name?" he asks, as we walk towards the elevator.

"It's Emma," I answer.

"Hmmm... Emma... Emma," Ron stares off into space as if he's trying to remember something. Then he clicks his fingers and goes, "Yeah – *did her!*"

I shoot him a mock glare, and he playfully punches my shoulder. "Hey, you didn't mind that, did you? I use that line with everyone! It's just a thing that I do. There was this one time I met Coolio and ..."

{SEPTEMBER, 2008}

CHAPTER TEN:
Steve Jones

Hot Press's encounter with the legendary Steve Jones begins slightly earlier than scheduled, and live on air. I arrive at the Wilshire Blvd headquarters of hip Los Angeles radio station Indie 103.1 at 1.40pm, a good twenty minutes before *Jonesy's Jukebox* – the decidedly offbeat show the Sex Pistols guitarist has been hosting five days a week since 2004 – is due to end.

When the station's PR person leaves me sitting outside the door of the studio, Jones unexpectedly pops out to say hello. Wearing a thick pair of horn-rimmed glasses and about three days worth of stubble, the 52-year-old is tall, stocky and healthily tanned.
"Alright, mate," he says in a London accent unchanged by almost three decades of California living. "Get yerself in here and put some cans on. We're having a bit of a wind-up at the moment, but don't say nuffink."

There are few radio DJs who'd casually invite a journalist they've never met before into studio right in the middle of a live broadcast, but Jones isn't your typical jock. Through a combination of disarmingly down-to-earth charm and a freewheeling disregard for the normal conventions, the punk guitarist and ex-junkie who once seemed to have No Future now finds himself acclaimed as one of the most original and influential personalities in US rock radio.

The station management have given him a free hand to do, say or play anything he wants, once he stays within FCC rules. It's not uncommon for Jones to spend several minutes noisily eating a sandwich live on air, whilst reminiscing about the pork pies he used to consume as a youth. Or to start strumming a guitar, making up a song as he goes. Earlier today he had The Breeders live on air, and they spent the entire interview talking about giving up cigarettes.

I enter the studio – a small, dimly lit room wallpapered with music and Chelsea FC posters – ever so slightly worried that the wind-up is going to be perpetrated on me. Jones quickly introduces me to producer Kevin Begley and his current guest, Paul Potts – the Vodafone salesman turned professional tenor through winning ITV's *Britain's Got Talent* (he's in LA playing a showcase).

The Dead Kennedys' 'Holiday In Cambodia' is playing and I suddenly realise what the joke is. As the song draws to a close, Jones gives the nod to Begley, who whacks up the volume full blast just as vocalist Jello Biafra starts shouting, *"Pol Pot! Pol Pot! Pol Pot! Pol Pot!"* Jones cackles away, but Potts is only slightly amused – actually, he seems more baffled than anything else – and the brief interview that follows is more like a casual chat in the pub. But that's how *Jonesy's Jukebox* goes.

Twenty minutes later we're sitting in a small office down the hallway. "So, did ya fly over especially to meet me?" he asks. "Em... no," I reply. "Cunt!" he laughs. "All right, let's get on wiv it..."

OLAF TYARANSEN: So The Sex Pistols are headlining at Ireland's Electric Picnic in August.

STEVE JONES: You know what? I have no idea where we're playing. Someone sent me all the stuff, but it keeps getting added to. A week ago it was 19 festivals and now I think we're up to 25 or something.

Have you played Ireland before?

In 1996, I think the Pistols were banned from playing Ireland. Maybe not banned, but there was some weird reason we weren't playing there. But I went to Ireland with the Greedy Bastards *(an unholy 1978 'supergroup' comprised of Jones, Paul Cook, Phil Lynott, Brian Downey and others – OT)* years before. We played at the Stardust – the place that burnt down – and U2 opened up for us. It was when they first started. I had a good time there. Course, that was when I was drinking.

You've been sober for 17 years now.

I actually haven't had a drink in 23 years, but I've been off everything for 17. Seventeen-and-a-bit.

You've even quit smoking cigarettes, as I heard you tell Kim Deal on the show earlier.

Yeah. You smoke – I can smell it on ya!!

Pistols fans must be amazed that Steve Jones has got a proper job and has to show up punctually for work every day.

I can't believe it myself. It wouldn't have happened when I was 25. I'm 52 now, so I was 48 when I started this. You've gotta grow up sometime.

Were you surprised to get the opportunity?

Yeah. It's like what Paul Potts was saying earlier. You never know what's coming around the corner. 'Cos it wasn't something that ever occurred to me: "Oh, I wonder if I should try getting on radio?" And then I got a phone call from someone who I knew from the music business, who knew the programme director at the time. I just said, "I wanna be a DJ" – the words just came outta my mouth – and that was it. Three weeks after I said it, I was on air. And here I am, four years later.

How bad were your addictions?

I was a mess – heroin and all that – for many years. But I'm grateful that I've come through the other side.

What prompted your rehabilitation?

I've no idea. Luck of the draw. I've never wanted to die. I've never been that gloomy. Even in my worst days of kicking heroin. I might have thought about dying, but I always had a bit of hope. I always knew things would be alright in the back of me head so... I guess some guys don't get that feeling, and that's when they top themselves or whatever.

Were you shooting smack or just smoking it?

I was shooting it. For about eight years.

Were you wealthy from the Pistols?

Nah, not at all. I was just pretty much a junkie, selling everything I had to feed the beast.

Are you religious?

Nah. I really don't believe in it. I hate to say it, but I'm just not a religious guy.

Are you a spiritual guy?

Em… I guess so. I mean, I sometimes have a conscious contact with a higher power. 'Cos I'm not God. So I do that –but I don't believe in all that stuff. I don't believe in any religion. Catholic, Christian, whatever. It's all bullshit. It's a form of control from many, many, many years ago. And it's all warped and distorted and perverted. And it causes wars.

You've said before that music saved you from a life of crime.

That's a bit of a cliché, but I guess it did in a way. I think coming to America saved me from a life of crime. When I saw a documentary on the prisons here. Christ! That scared the shit outta me!

Have you ever been in prison?

Em… young man's prison – in Ashford. I was in there for a month or two. It was like a real nick – it had the nick doors and everything. I didn't like that. That was the last place I was ever in. I was in an 'approved school' for a year-and-a-half. And in a remand home a few times.

Is it true that you stole your first guitar from Mick Ronson?

No. My first guitar was the white Les Paul, the one that I had, which came from Sylvain Sylvain from the New York Dolls. Which Malcolm McLaren brought back with him. He was managing the New York Dolls for about 10 minutes, and then he brought that guitar back and he gave it to me. So I actually didn't nick that guitar. Though I have nicked a few guitars. I never nicked a guitar from Mick Ronson. Where'd you hear that?

I read it on… erm… Wikipedia.

Well, it's wrong! Do you know anyone can type anything they want on Wikipedia? Anyone can go on there at any time and add or take off anything that's on Wikipedia, which is really weird.

I would've thought the anarchy of that would appeal to you.

Not really, 'cos you can get in trouble by someone writing something about you. Like saying you're a fuckin' child molester. If you don't read it, how ya gonna know?

Do you keep an eye on what's written about you online?

Not really, no.

On the show yesterday you sounded pissed off about social networking sites and were talking about deleting people from your MySpace friends list.

Off the MySpace, yeah. If they don't put me in their top eight then I get rid of them. 'Cos I'm not asking to be their friend, they're asking to be my friend, and if they wanna be my friend they should at least put me in their top eight or 16 or whatever it is. Yeah, I'm not into the numbers like a lot of people seem to be. And I don't know what you gain from it, really.

Rumour has it that you're a fan of health food restaurants.
Yeah, not all the time. I eat a bit of everything. I'm not a vegetarian. I love the weather here. I like the openness of it. I like being by the ocean.
Are you an American citizen?
I've got a green card.
I'm surprised you were able to get one!
Why?
Well, coming from such a notorious background.
I'm respectable now. I don't think they care. When I first got here, I was a bit dodgy. It took me a while to get the green card.
Do you hang out with Johnny [Lydon] much?
Not a lot. We speak a lot on the phone, but I don't see him a lot. But I'll be seeing him a lot this summer.
Is it true that you're recording new Pistols' material as well as rehearsing the old stuff?
Well, we haven't done that yet. I think we might be closer than we ever have been before to maybe knocking out some new ideas. We haven't as yet, but hopefully we will. I'd like to do some new songs just out of curiosity, you know?
What are your thoughts on Malcolm McLaren these days?
I couldn't give a toss about him, to be honest with you. He's just wrong. That bloke is just *wrong*.
He certainly came out of *The Filth And The Fury* very badly.
He comes out of everything badly. He claims he's the big messiah and all that, as he's doing some two bob documentary – getting a couple of grand under the table. It's pretty pathetic. I used to defend him, but I couldn't give a toss about him anymore. He just has a go, he don't know what he's saying, he don't care who he's hurting. It's all about his ego – and it's lame.
When's the last time you saw him?
He actually came on my show a couple of years ago. I went off him after that.
Did something happen on the show?
No. A little while after that. He said a few things in some interview after being on here about… something. And it was just lame, you know. And I'd always defended him where people didn't. He's just lame. I don't even wanna talk about him *(shakes head disgustedly)*.
Are you in a relationship these days?
Nah. I was always pretty horny back in the day. I'm still pretty horny today, but I can take it or leave it. I ain't got the energy to run after 'em these days. Which is fine. A lot less hassle. I'm kind of happy about that. Because you can waste a lot of time just trying to get laid, you know. There's no reward in it. But I'm kind of happy these days. Happiest I've ever been, I think.
Is that down to this radio gig?
Yeah, it gets you out of your shell. I'm an isolator. I like to isolate and not just be around anyone. And this forces me to be around people. It's better for me. And they say, as you get older… you know, the people who live a long time are active. So as you get old you should stay active. It's when you kind of give up that you shrivel

away. So I'm gonna try and take that to heart.

Who's been the worst guest on *Jonesy's Jukebox*?
Um...there's literally only been about four or five. I've had hundreds of guests. It's a toss up between Jerry Lee Lewis, the guy from The Replacements *(Paul Westerberg)*, Eric Burdon *(Animals vocalist)*. It's a toss-up between them three.

Were you rowing with them on air?
It got a little bit heavy with Jerry Lee. I put my foot in it by asking him about what was it like going to England when you were married to your 13-year-old cousin. He was just like a bull with the red flag. And it was a bit hard to get him back on track. I mean, he's not the most talkative guy. You ask him a question, and you get these 'yes' and 'no' kind of answers. So that was tough. But everyone said afterwards that it was intense and it was great radio, but I just didn't like being the one that asked the question.

You're sitting at very close quarters in the studio, as well.
It's very small, yeah. But that's what's good about it. It's intimate, you know. And I can't knock Jerry Lee Lewis – I love them real old rock and rollers. And I've enormous respect for them. But it was difficult.

Who was your best interviewee?
Oh gawd! There's been loads. I think one of my best was Cliff Richard, actually. I didn't know him, but I ran into him in a restaurant here. He walked in and I was looking at him going, "That can't be Cliff Richard." And I went up to him and said, "I've got a radio show here and I'm a big fan; why don't you come on?" And I think he thought I was taking the mickey out of him.

Did he know who you were?
Not really. He's kind of in a bubble. But he took me number, and I guess he did some homework, and about six months later I got a call from his publicist or agent or whatever saying he wants to come on. He was out here doing a showcase.

Were you serious when you told him you were a fan?
I genuinely like him. I love his voice. And I actually would like to do an album with him. Like an unplugged kind of deal, with me and a couple of other guys playing guitar and maybe some other things, and do some of them old songs. 'Cos his voice is still amazing. We did about six songs on the show. I was rehearsing the day before with my mate Naveen Andrews, who's in that TV show, *Lost*. And he's a really good guitar player. So I was like, "Cliff Richard is coming on! We've gotta rehearse some songs!" And he's good with all the little fiddly bits. And sure enough, he came on with a guitar. You couldn't shut him up, Cliff. He was brilliant. That was one of the best moments for me. I know a lot of people in America don't know who he is, but for me that was a highlight.

Do you ever swear on the show?
Nah. You get fined, you know. I haven't yet, somehow. It's actually more fun when you can't swear than if you could. I'd say it gets kind of boring if you was on Sirius Satellite *(home of shock-jock Howard Stern)*, where you're allowed to swear. I mean, there's been a few times when I'd have liked to say 'cunt'. But I don't mind it.

You've never slipped up?
Maybe once or twice. You get so relaxed in there, talking to people, that you

forget where you are. But the swearing thing happens more with guests. Guests that you wouldn't think are gonna swear, real straight goers, they get so relaxed – and they're the ones who swear. It's not like the rock and rollers. It's bizarre.

Are you still playing with Hollywood United Football Club?

Yeah. Played last Monday night. Scored a goal. We won 5-0 in the over 40's. There's three different teams. There's the young guys, there's us, and then there's a girls team. The older guys are called 'Dad's Army'.

Are they all celebrities?

Not really. Just a couple of guys. Anthony La Paglia, from that show *Without A Trace*. It comes and goes. It's mainly English blokes who've been out here for years and we love it – it's fun just having a bunch of blokes to play football with. Normal stuff. I need that in my life.

Do you miss the UK much?

Not really. I go back now and again. I miss pie and mash-ups, and going to football matches, and that's about it. Oh, and walking – I like to walk.

Are you still estranged from your mum?

No. We're talking. Gawd bless her. We talk about once every week or two weeks on the phone. And I see her when I go back there.

That's a bit of a turnaround, isn't it?

It is, yeah. On my part. I always felt like I was the victim, but I had to grow up a bit and realise that she did the best she could. She's alright.

You played on Ian Brown's *The World Is Yours* album last year.

Yeah, I did. A couple of tracks. I didn't see him, though. It was just flown over here and I took it in a studio and put the guitar on. Cookie *(Paul Cook)* played drums on a couple of tracks. I think Ian Brown wants to do a record with me and Cookie. Which I think could be good.

You seem to be entering a more creative phase.

I think in this day and age, if you're doing something like that, it's just a labour of love because nobody buys records anymore. I like Ian Brown. I like his voice. Like I say, I'm just trying to keep busy. It might never happen, but we've been talking about it.

What can fans expect from the Pistols' now?

Well, last November we did a bunch of shows. We played five nights in the Brixton Academy and one in Manchester and one in Glasgow. And it was great. We're playing better than ever. We're getting along better than ever. I think it's safe to say we're all growing up a little bit, and kind of being more accepting of each other. If it wasn't like that I wouldn't be doing it. 'Cos I don't need the aggravation anymore. You know, we're a dysfunctional family – and I love 'em all!

{AUGUST, 2008}

CHAPTER ELEVEN:
Courtney Love

"**O**h and I don't CAAARE what I ... HAAAVE to defend ... I will NEVVV-ER go hungry ... go hungry ...' Fuck! I just broke another damn string. Gimme a minute. Sorry – I'll get it right."

Courtney Michelle Harrison – better known as Courtney Love – is on the phone, and I have a serious pain in the head. The most notorious widow in rock 'n' roll is sitting on an unmade bed in her LA home, playing me a rough acoustic version of a new song she's written called 'Never Go Hungry Again'. Or trying to play it. Several aborted takes in, she keeps either forgetting the lyrics or breaking guitar strings.

She sounds stoned out of her gourd. She's possibly naked, or that's the impression I get from shards of the rambling conversation we've been engaged in for what – a couple of brief "pee breaks" included – must be almost two hours now. I'm sitting in my office, thousands of miles away in Galway, head-numbed from my mobile, so there's no way of really knowing what state of dress or undress she's in.

Conversationally, she's a rambling ADHD surrealist – a little like a more entertaining version of Grandpa Simpson. When not telling you what she's doing at that exact moment ("I'm just going into the bedroom – *ugh!*"), she hops, skips and segues from topic to topic, story to story, scandalously, libellously, liberally namedropping a veritable A-Z of celebrities. Most of those she references are on first name basis (Ed, Bono, Kate, Billy and, of course, Kurt), but some are surnamed (Gibson, Downey, McGuinness, Spielberg, Geffen).

"Gibson gave me a really fuckin' hard time over that – so did Larry, actually – but I remember this one time with Kurt, we were talking to Navarro and fuckin' Flea, and they were saying that Madonna had told them that ..."

Like a spoken word *Vanity Fair-National Enquirer* combo, Love could namedrop as an Olympic sport. BP Fallon put it best when he told me, "Courtney does more rabbit than the Easter Bunny." He meant it as a compliment.

Of course, I brought this earache on myself. We've spoken at length over the phone on a couple of occasions recently, but I'm still not entirely sure she even knows who I am ("Olaf? What kinda fuckin' name is that?"). Last month I interviewed *Hustler* publisher Larry Flynt at his office in LA. We hit it off, and Flynt asked if there was anything he could do for me. Hoping to secure an interview, I asked him to give me Courtney's private number (she was nominated for a Golden Globe for her portrayal of his late wife, Althea, in Milos Forman's 1996 biopic *The People vs. Larry Flynt*). When I rang her, she wasn't very happy. "What the *fuck* is Larry doing giving journalists my number?" she asked. But then she talked until my phone battery died.

This time she rang me, at 10am Irish time on a Sunday morning. I haven't been in bed long...

As she attempts to restring her guitar ("hang on a second, I'm almost there ... *FUCK!* ... I'll get it ... I'll get it"), I realise that my ear is burning, my brain is melting, and my head is spinning. It's the longest phone call I've ever had and it's hurting me: I have to go. I hang up, switch the phone off and go back to bed where I belong. A lengthy text comes the following day. Her black Am-Ex card has been refused in some hotel somewhere and Frances Bean, her daughter with Kurt Cobain, is pissed off. As sorry as I feel for her, there's not all that much I can do about it.

A couple of weeks later, having spotted some worrying paparazzi shots of her looking tired and emotional outside a Malibu restaurant, I try to call her again.

The phone is disconnected. Somehow, I'm not all that surprised.

Eighteen months later. Hole are about to kick off a short UK tour to support *Nobody's Daughter*, their first album in more than a decade ('Never Go Hungry Again' has made it as the bonus track) in the Glasgow O2. I'm standing backstage with two other journalists in the hallway outside Love's dressing room, waiting for her to return from the soundcheck. We've been allocated just twenty minutes each and, although things are running worryingly late, I've opted to go last. If I go first or second, there'll be a media rival at the door the moment my time is up. If I go third, our previous telephonic history might mean she'll give me some extra time.

Her management have issued some guidelines – questions about Cobain, drug use, her estranged 17-year-old daughter Frances Bean (who reportedly recently tried to "divorce" her), her arrests and their legal ramifications are all strictly verboten. Still, the surprisingly good new album aside, there's plenty more to ask Love about. She hit the tabloid headlines last week when she told American shock-jock Howard Stern live on air that she was sleeping with Bush frontman Gavin Rossdale, while he was engaged to his now-wife Gwen Stefani. Since then, her ex-boyfriend Billy Corgan (who co-wrote some of the tracks on the new album) has attacked her on Twitter – variously accusing her of being a drug addict, a has-been, a plagiarist, and of having "no honour." In addition, he accused her of abandoning her daughter – though the content of the 'tweet' probably says more about him than it does about Courtney: *"Only u could abandon such a beautiful, incredible child who is smarter than u, cooler than u, and better than u. Oops, did I say too much?"*

Eventually the time arrives. When I enter the dressing room, Courtney's sitting cross-legged on a white couch. Wearing an expensive-looking beige Chloe jacket, sombre black top and trousers, and clear designer glasses, the peroxide blonde looks more like a slightly frayed PR girl than a grungy rock 'n' roller. She immediately stands up, as if to leave, and informs me that she doesn't want to talk. "You know, I'm really tired and I've just done a whole bunch of interviews," she says. "And I've got a fuckin' show to play tonight."

"Courtney, it's me – Olaf from *Hot Press*," I say. "We've spoken a few times on the phone. Larry Flynt gave me your number – remember?"

The blank look on her face indicates that she may or may not have the foggiest what I'm talking about. Even so, she walks back to the couch and lays down on it, curling up like a cat. Are we doing an interview or not? Best to proceed as though we are. So how's it going, Courtney? "I'm alright," she sighs, laying her head in her hands and closing her eyes. "I've got Joni Mitchell playing in my pocket."

This much is true. Her iPhone is emitting an irritatingly tinny version of 'Clouds' as we speak (as it will throughout most of the next hour). It's interrupted by an electronic bleep as a text message comes in. She reads it and shakes her head sadly: "I have a moody man in my life."

Billy? Gavin?

"God no!" she laughs. "A moody man. A proper man. He's a man's man. Little bit of a jet-setter. Like some of the people he hangs with are absolutely *wack*."

She reaches over and touches my arm with a heavily bejewelled hand. "We were at this party in Paris the other night. It's sorta the same crew that Bono and Sting and Trudy and other people hang with – and I hang with – but then there's extra sort of Eurotrash crew that hangs with us. They're desolate and they ... huddle together. They're like these insanely rich Rothschild-type people who do lots and lots and lots of drugs to huddle away from the rest of the world. And it's almost like it fascinates him – and we're arguing about it. You know, I just think it's ridiculous. It's ... *ridiculous*."

Indeed. It must be a bit off-putting for you receiving nasty text messages just before a big show.

"No, it's fucking off-putting for him to text me going, *'I need a break'*. You're in fucking Istanbul – you're getting a break. *Fool!*"

She won't reveal who this foolish new boyfriend is. "You wouldn't know him. He's a businessman, not a celebrity – well, I guess he's a celebrity in what he does. He's a lot older than me – he's, like, *50*."

Well, you're 45, aren't you?

"Five years older than me. But I mean the *Village Voice* has called me 'The Queen of Generation X'. And I'm a boomer by one year – '64. So I think we've a generational issue."

Will you go over to see him in Istanbul after this tour?

"I'm not travelling over to see him," she snaps. "I'm playing, like, Brixton. I've a *job*."

Speaking of which, let's talk about the new album. Was there a time where you doubted *Nobody's Daughter* would ever get released?

"Yeah, lots of times."

Are you happy right now?

Another text comes in. "We'll see if I'm fuckin' happy now!"

Oh, cheer up, Courtney!

"I'll be alright," she sighs, smiling wearily.

She reads the text: "He's written, *'xoxoxoxo always!'* What the fuck! How do you respond to that? Quick – tell me a smartass way to reply to *'x-fucking-o'*."

Although I'm not supposed to mention drugs, for some reason, hillbilly heroin comes to mind. "Well, Oxycontin has o and x in it ..."

"Oxycontin. Oh yeah, that's good. Ha! Let's send that... *fucker!*"

A full minute passes in silence as she taps out a message, pausing only to gratefully accept a Benson & Hedges (which I light for her). "Sorry about this," she says. "Ask me something."

Sure. Back in the early '80s, when she was based in Dublin, Courtney remembers briefly working for *Hot Press* as a photographer. Can she recall the shoots she did?

"I did three shoots," she says, "of Toyah Wilcox, The Pretenders and U2. Oh, and also The Teardrop Explodes at McGonagles. And then Julian Cope gave me the keys to his apartment and I ran away to meet some Vietnamese people for Christmas. Because they brought Grateful Dead records for my father. It was a squat on Stephen's Green – it's worth about €20million now."

Not anymore!

"Really?"

I quickly abandon my explanation of the Irish property bubble when she yawns.

Will Hole be playing Ireland?

"Yeah, I'd love to."

What's going on with Billy?

She looks up and pulls a face: "I don't know. What *is* going on with Billy? He's a fool. That [Tweet] was a bit below the belt."

Maybe he's pissed off about what you recently told the *NME* about his sexual prowess?

"I said he was good in bed, didn't I?" she protests. "I don't think that's below the belt. Below the belt is bringing my child into it."

Have you spoken to Gavin recently?

"Rossdale? No. It was very interesting what your tabloids made it into. Me and Gavin dated for eight months. And there was some overlap between when I dated Edward (Norton) and he dated Gwen – but never when they were engaged. So we were like sorta fuck buddies. He was playing the field. He was seeing Gwen, he was seeing me. It was common knowledge. So it was a bit of an overlap back in the '90s. No big deal. I would never sleep with a ... Actually I did once sleep with a married man, that was a terrible thing. As advertised – *disastrous!* And Gavin was lovely.

"And so Stern was asking me who was the best kisser in rock 'n' roll? I told them if you put me on Stern... Like, he is my friend. You know, I don't have a big inner-censor on Stern. It's almost impossible to go on there and not, you know, say something. So I wasn't trying to court controversy. Stern asked me 'who is the best kisser in rock 'n' roll?' And I was hard pressed to think of one, and then I remembered this one night that Gavin made roast chicken and it was really, really good, and then we snogged and he was really good at it. And he'd improved vastly from the last time we snogged. And so I thought, 'well... Gavin'. But certainly not when they were engaged or anything. In fact, Gwen forbade him to see me, and Edward Norton forbade me to see him. So that was that. But we dated straight-up for eight months."

Are many of the new songs inspired by these sexual shenanigans?

"By Gavin and Billy?" she says, incredulously. "Nothing!"

But you worked with Billy on the album?

"Yes. He wrote the tail of 'Pacific Coast Highway', which is quite good. And he wrote the skeleton of 'Samantha' – but I wrote the *'people like you fuck people like me'* part. Linda (Perry, the songwriter and producer) wrote the bridge, but he contributed for 66-and-three-quarters clicks – I know that because he counted. Of course he did! But I dunno. I dunno if talking about someone's sexual prowess allows somebody to go off their spiritual programming, you know, and go below the belt and talk about my child in a creepy manner.

"He's always wanted to be a part of some Kurt and me soap opera that he's not a part of," she continues. "You know, (Smashing Pumpkins 1994 album) *Pisces Iscariot*. But I mean I really don't wanna do rock stars fighting. I did do something (on Twitter) and then I deleted it immediately. I know Frances doesn't like him talking about her and she certainly doesn't like him. He made her cry one time – like *deliberately*. And I think he's creepily obsessed with her. He just needs to leave the kid alone. That's all she wants right now. Leave her the fuck alone!"

Suddenly seeming upset, she rises off the couch and strides across the room. For a moment I think she's walking out, but she swiftly returns and plonks herself down again. Maybe time to change the subject. Is it weird to be back in the limelight again as a musician rather than a tabloid celebrity?

"No, it feels good. Other than film, this is what I like to do. Like, I don't know why I'm so famous and have people talking about what I do every fucking day, or every week, for like twelve fucking years when I've not done anything of merit. Actually, I got a letter from McGuinness and Bono – to my manager at the time – and it said, *'Elvis, Sinatra and Courtney'*. And then McGuinness always seems to be so disappointed in me. But I did just get a big huge agent so maybe he'll stop giving me that beleaguered look."

Between various arrests, scandals, legal problems and stints in rehab, it took you a long time to get yourself together. There are people who say that you're your own worst enemy...

"Sure," she nods. "What I'm hoping what I'll be able to do is what Downey was able to do – despite the difference in sexes. My agent seems to think so. And I'm very, very athletic. Nobody's as athletic as Downey is now though. If you watch the fight scene in *Sherlock Holmes* – Jesus fucking Christ!!! He's doing this thing called 'wang chung'. It's like *'everyone wang chung tonight'*. Endorphins are free, you know. So I chant every day. Today I took a little run but..."

Another message comes in on her phone. She reads it and laughs, shaking her head. "I really do think I'm gonna take a vacation from this man. Hold on a second." She starts to text a reply. "It's weird going out – not going out but having a relationship or whatever you wanna call it – with a businessman. Because they're not... they're not *creative*."

It was recently reported that you had some kind of thing going on with (Venezuelan president) Hugo Chavez. What's the story there?

"Chavez? Yeah, he wanted me to go to Caracas about a month ago for the *Playboy* interview, and get on a plane at 8am. I think he thought I was a hooker.

And Oliver (Stone) put me right in the line of fire. Where he knew Chavez would see me and I think Chavez would think I was a hooker or something. But then he went on *Larry King* and said, 'Oh, I kissed a girl in a rock band last night. I love America'. And then he started sending me flowers. I don't really know anything about him. I know he's been the President thirteen times in a row which doesn't bode well for democracy, but hey."

Actually, he was only elected in 1998.

"No, thirteen times, I was told," she insists. "Thirteen presidencies." She laughs: "Oh, what the fuck do I know? I read the *Post* not the *Times*."

A text comes in on my own phone. She's still typing away on hers so I take the time to read it. It's a news alert: the Iceland volcano has just erupted again and UK airspace may be closed down by the ash cloud.

"You're fuckin' kidding me?" she says, when I pass on the news. "The fuckin' volcano! How many days will we be stuck? Oh, you're kidding? How long will it take? Oh fuck, I've gotta tell somebody about this."

She starts poking at her phone again. "We can keep talking. I'm pretty good at multi-tasking."

You're producing a Kurt biopic at the moment. Are you heavily involved?

"Sure – I'm a producer."

Who's going to play Kurt, and who's going to play you?

"I think (James) McAvoy for Kurt, and we'll see what Scarlett says about the script."

Are you still living in LA?

"No, I moved back to New York a year ago. I live in basically a pied-a-terre that's good for clothes and guitars and things."

Were you sad when Malcolm McLaren died?

"Yeah. I'm a little jet-setty myself. I'm not punk for life. But then McLaren was a little jet-setty by the time he died. We all give in."

She puts the iPhone down, gets up off the couch and kicks open a suitcase on the floor. "I'd better get some clothes sorted for the show."

Courtney removes her jacket and throws it onto the back of a chair. "This is Chloe," she explains to me. "I just raided Selfridge's last night. I got off the plane and went straight to Selfridge's."

You seem to have adopted a new look. More sober.

"Yeah, I was into a different kinda clothes – my kook. I was into taking Victorian and Edwardian clothes and kinda up-cycling them. And then I spent a lot of money and time on seamstresses and things like that. And then I just lost it because, you know what, I wasn't gonna get laid that way."

Surely it's not difficult for you to get laid?

"It's not difficult for me to get laid, but like it's a rarefied strata," she explains. "Some women aged 45 have like a pool. I have sort of like an espresso cup. Like, I know everyone in it. And because I'm very, very, very, very particular about who I'll go out with, and who I'll be with, it makes it hard because I'm just extremely… *particular*."

You hinted at a lesbian fling with an English supermodel in a recent interview…

"Oh, it was Kate Moss," she says, waving a hand. "She doesn't care."

Lucky you!

"I know, right!" she laughs, rifling through her case. "It's a great story for the grandchildren so… yeah. But there's another English supermodel that I had this… there was this indie director and he was doing a lot of drugs at the time. Kate wasn't doing a lot of drugs. It was just a thing that happened in Milan in the '90s. It happened and it was fun and whatever. And she talks about it and so I hope she doesn't get mad that I outed her about it. But she was like 'Oh, remember Milan? Remember Milan?' And I think Gavin was there and Nellee Hooper was there and it was like … you know. I feel like such a kiss and tell. But anyway, this one I'm not gonna name names. So this indie director became quite big, and then another English supermodel, and it was a really sordid nightmare, a horrible scene – and that was the end of me and the indie director. But he invited this one English supermodel over and she was just a fucking… oh god, she was just a vituperative… ugh! Kate's great, though! Kate's a good friend of mine. I almost bought Kate's house."

Really?

"Yeah, I almost bought Kate's house in St. John's Wood. But then… I *don't like* St. John's Wood. And also, this is before the Frances thing, but unless Frances was really into living miniature style… (Moss's daughter) Lila had grown, but her room and the nanny's room were so tiny up on the third floor. And plus I don't like St. John's Wood. I'd love to live in Marylebone – that'd be nice. Costs a lot of money, though."

Speaking of money, you've been more or less broke a few times in recent years. What happened to all of those Nirvana royalties? She runs a hand through her hair and pulls a face: "Oh, it's a long story. I was saying to this person, 'You know what, I lost a billion dollars but I'm letting it go. How many times have you lost a billion dollars? Like… just shut up. *Shut up!* Lost a billion dollars… it's gone… *let it go!!*' And I found a quote somewhere from Donald Trump where he said something like you've gotta lose a billion to make a billion. So anyway, a billion dollars takes, like, 23 years to grow."

How do you figure a billion?

"The *London Times* valued Kurt's estate at £900million, and then my estate's worth another £26million. So it's not really a lot, but it's money. Actually we did this thing in Las Vegas the other night where you show up at a club for money. It was the first time I'd ever done that and… I must show you a picture, it's fucking ridiculous. There was like $10,000 worth of alcohol. It wasn't even sick money – it was recession money. It was like fifty grand. It wasn't like Paris Hilton crazy money – it was fifty fucking grand! So it paid for my clothes in Selfridge's last night, put it that way. But it's good because I'm living on my own money and… Let me just show you this. There was this kid who's drawing these crazy cartoons of me."

She retrieves the iPhone, sits back on the couch, and starts scrolling through some pictures. Unfortunately, I'm unable to see them. She seems utterly oblivious to the fact.

"That's me at the Chateau… oh god, this is us playing at the Fred Durst crowd the other day, we had to catch a plane so we played at like noon. It was 20,000 but it was 20,000 fuckers in baseball hats – in Pizza Hut Park, I might add – next thing will be fucking Chuck E Cheese Stadium! – and these are the shoes I bought in Vegas, they were like three grand – and they only make them in Milan. And then this is me smoking – post coital… this is the Boom Boom Room in New York… this is me on *Letterman*… this is me driving a boat in Malibu… here's me tits akimbo at the Chateau."

Eh? I immediately get out of my seat and squeeze in beside her on the couch.

"This is this great video director… like video fine art… I thought Bono would get him – and then *Kanye* got him… and then they fuckin' played Kanye just to *piss me off* that night. This is me wearing a man's bespoke shirt – I do like a man's shirt. I got this Birkin bag from a girl who was the mistress of a very famous painter, so she got it on her back. Frances has two Birkins… this is Florence (Welch) – she fucking kicked my ass. This is me and Al Gore's daughter… me and Navarro… Stipe… this is me drunk on Rose in my room… I just started drinking it recently. Here's another of those cartoons…."

This celebrity slideshow goes on for several minutes. She comes across a photo of Frances. Although the album title refers to herself, she reportedly lost custody of her only daughter last December. Would you like to have another child, Courtney?

"Sure, I'd like to have another child," she smiles. "Absolutely. I'd like a boy. Oh, this is me on the back of a Grateful Dead record."

Courtney's father Hank Harrison briefly managed the Dead back in the day. She shows me a photograph of her three-year-old self, presumably taken backstage at some San Francisco festival, on the back cover of their third album *Aoxomoxoa*. Have you spoken to your dad recently?

"God no!" she snorts, haughtily. "Oh, here's me getting tattooed. I just got my midlife crisis ones – I got one that says 'Let It Bleed' (*shows me her upper arm*) – I don't like the song, I just like the title. Oh, here's me with Gaga at the Brits."

What do you think of Lady Gaga?

"I think if she wants to do it, God bless. I had to introduce her at the Brits. It's like she wakes up every morning and says, 'Alright boys, do me – and make it cost the most!' God bless, I don't want 25,000 purple pearls encrusted on me. That's what my kook was for and then I got real simple – rockin' navy, rockin' cream, rockin' secretarial. One thing I found with the kook is you don't get laid so much."

She puts the phone down and stands up again. Unembarrassed, she pulls her top off, walks to the mirror, and starts putting on make-up. She's onstage in less than an hour and I'm already well over my allotted time. Would you like me to leave, Courtney?

"No, no. It's cool. Keep talking."

The ass has really fallen out of the music industry in the last few years…

"Yeah, I know," she says, plastering her face in foundation. "That's why we're doing things like going to fuckin' (Vegas nightclub) Tao for fucking fifty grand. It's not even stupid money. Ten years ago it would've been a hundred and fifty grand, you know – whoop, whoop! But I mean four people sitting there drinking Pellegrino – that's just fucking sad, bitch! But don't tell me I can't do grace under pressure because me and Micko (Larkin, Hole guitarist) got up and did 'Pacific Coast Highway' and we'd all these people going *'Zoo-ey-zoo-ey'*, and then I got really fucking perverse and did *Cohen*. No, we're not doing 'Hallelujah', thank fucking god! *Enough* with that song. I don't even think Leonard does 'Hallelujah' very well. And to be honest – and I'm very, very much a Leonard Cohen-ologist – I thought that Jeff Buckley's... I mean, Jeff Buckley and me went to see *Hamlet* one night..."

A hilariously colourful two-minute stream of consciousness rant follows, taking in Kurt Cobain's *In Utero* notebooks, her mother's Shakespeare collection, and something about Leonard Cohen's poetry...

"... anyway it makes a good story but it's just not true. So anyway, me and Jeff Buckley went to see *Hamlet* and the whole way back he was complaining... he was really grumpy because I got a better seat or something like that, I dunno... but anyway Melissa (Auf der Maur of Hole) wanted to date him after that – because I just spent, like, a night with him – and Melissa wanted to date him, I was like, 'go ahead, he's a *grump!*' So when I heard 'Hallelujah'... and the first time I really heard 'Hallelujah', (art photographer David) LaChapelle had me in the studio holding this Kurt imitator in my arms and I could do nothing and I couldn't even leave and David was going *'La Pietà! La Pietà!'* and I'm going, 'David, this is not *La Pietà* – this is a fucking Kurt imitator!' and if you go onto his last MySpace, which is like 2006 or something, he says..."

Eventually her phone beeps again and she stops to read a text. By the time she's replied, she's lost her thread. "Do you ever get nervous before shows?" I ask.

"No, because I usually run late and so don't have time to get nervous," she explains, pouting her lips to apply vibrantly red lipstick. "You know, this is Glasgow and, to me, Brixton more than New York or LA decides if you're gonna play Wembley – which decides if you're gonna play the Garden. And I'm very English that way. I don't look at, like, *Terminal Five* as deciding if you're gonna play the Garden. Now, Billy Joe (Armstrong) offered it, if I wanted to play Wembley, but I'd have to play under Joan Jett and he sort of did it as an afterthought because me and Billy Joe became great friends – again! Because we'd always been pals, but we became really good friends one night me and Bono and him hung out. They ended up doing a single together after that night.

"And then I went to see him in Madison Square Garden and he did like three-and-a-half hours and then he lit up a cigarette and it was like – *astonishing*. And I wanna get to that point. So I did my Courtney run today but I totally forgot to do my chants. And I'm staying in this really weird hotel – it's the one PJ Harvey stays in – and it's like *The Shining*. It's not like Claridge's or somewhere, it's like this really weird hotel. It's like cheese and pickle sandwiches, you know. So anyway me and..."

A couple of minutes of non-stop verbals later, Courtney Love kicks open another suitcase. "I have, like, nineteen bodybags of this shit," she laughs. "This is just one of them."

She removes some brand new underwear, still tagged. "I wonder should I wear this… or this?" I tell her I prefer the sheer black panties. "Good choice," she says.

Rifling through some dresses, she starts talking about her recently abandoned kook look again. "I realised that I just didn't want to be that anymore – and I also wanted to get fucked. It's not just that, I wanna act again and part of acting is looking reasonably, you know, together. So it makes me work harder to not have the kook."

Courtney made her film debut way back in 1986 with a small role in Alex Cox's *Sid & Nancy*. She's made a few movies since, but her acting career basically stalled after her Golden Globe nomination for *The People vs. Larry Flynt* in 1996. She tells me she bitterly regrets turning down roles in *Girl Interrupted* and *The Matrix*. She blames the latter decision on one of her exes. "It was nine months in this remote part of Australia and I remember Norton telling me, 'Oh don't do it, Val Kilmer's in it!' Like, Val Kilmer *wasn't even in it!* I mean, was that a reason not to do it? A lot of people were like, 'what happened with the film thing?' I was like, 'what happened with the fucking film thing is I had a boyfriend in Edward Norton who wanted to fucking tame me, as many men have tried to do, as many men still do try and do, and…' You know, 'let's chain the rock star!' Oh my god, Mrs. Norton – she *used* to be Courtney Love. That's really what was going on in that relationship. And a lot of people were saying, 'Oh, he saved you, he saved you!' No, he didn't save me – he wanted me to be his waspy wife."

She indicates the six tattooed flowers adorning her breasts and upper arms. "The thing is, as much as I love Edward, each of these represent somebody that I love very much. I have six people in my life that I love very much – except I keep flip-flopping on five. And then six is maddening."

Cobain isn't represented by a flower. She still has the famous 'K' tattoo just above her belly button.

"The thing about the K is that it's half-faded and that's because Edward didn't like to look at it when we had sex so I went to get it taken off. And then I was like 'fuck that!' So I keep it so it's like half-off/half-on so I remind myself that I almost took it off. You know what I mean?"

I do indeed. Has the whole Kurt thing become a bit of a millstone around your neck at this point?

"Well, it has and that's one of the reasons that I thought about selling all his publishing which no-one's ever done. And Howard Stern was like, 'no, no, no'. At the same time, it's extraordinarily expensive publishing and I doubt anyone could meet my price. You know, Bono tried to buy it from me first time round."

Did he really?

"Oh yeah – for about two cents. Don't take the pink Cadillac, Courts! Now, I do love Bono, and I love the boys – I love all of them. I love Edge's brother, Dick – he's so smart, do you know him? Such a guy. Oh my god! That night we did the Gavin Friday [50th birthday party at Carnegie Hall] thing? And Bono was always telling me for years and years and years that I should meet Gavin. And I was always afraid to, because Gavin, to be honest, really intimidated me more than any of them. And then when we played with them, of course … I suggested Magazine's

'The Light Pours Out Of Me' as opposed to an old Virgin Prunes song – and it was fuckin' brilliant.

"And the night before, me and Micko had played with Slash and friends in Vegas, and the next night straight to Carnegie Hall with Lydia Lunch and Lou Reed and, you know, a lot of brilliant songs. And each member of U2 was billed with their own names – so Larry's Larry, and Adam's Adam, and, you know, shit like that. And Micko plays with Slash and then plays with Edge – so he's playing through giant Marshalls and then he's playing through Edge's little stuff and he's playing for girls with big titties ..."

Speaking of Micko, he's just entered the dressing room. A pale, skinny, big-haired Irishman in a long grey trenchcoat (his family are originally from Wexford), he speaks in a slightly stuttery London accent. "Em, Courts, we're on fairly soon," he tells her. "Maybe we should start thinking about, you know, putting a set list together."

Courtney has other concerns. "Hey, Olaf says the volcano has erupted again and we might not be able to get home," she tells him. "I've gotta go pee."

She disappears into the adjoining bathroom. I chat with Micko for a few moments (he's obviously wondering what I'm still doing there). He's unbothered about the volcanic ash cloud. "I'm actually planning on staying in England for a while. That place in New York is killing me. It's just not right for either of us. It isn't even the fact that it's small, it's just not nice. The furniture is small – it's kind of weird."

Oh, do you live together?

"Yeah, we live together in this place off Union Square."

I'd imagine she's an interesting housemate ...

"Yeah. She's like my best friend. She's awesome."

Courtney comes back in. She tells me I can stay if I want ("fuck, I don't care"), but I feel it's bad manners to hang around a band's dressing room just before a show. Before I leave, though, she wants to make it clear that she absolutely loves Bono.

"I actually started this craze called 'The Bono Talk' and so if you go back quite a few years on the internet it'll say in quotes 'The Bono Talk' – and if you look it up, it's like 'The 10 Commandments of Bono'. And he's absolutely on point – *'thou shalt be afraid of TV'; 'thou shalt not be a dickhead'; 'thou shalt not go for the pink Cadillac'*. But the tragedy is, despite contributing this to the nomenclature, I've never actually had the Bono Talk – I've only *watched* the Bono Talk."

She mentions that Hole are – or maybe were - in consideration to support the next leg of the U2 tour. "I'd love to do that," she says. "It would be an absolute fuckin' dream to support U2. I would love that. But I'm sure you get this bollocking from someone you'll never see again the first day – [*adopts crazed voice*] 'You're not more important than the band, *godammit!!!*' And then you never see them again."

It's time to take my leave. "Give us a kiss, Courtney!" She obligingly smooches me goodbye, smudging red lipstick on my mouth.

Final question, Courtney ... do you have a motto in life?

She barely pauses before replying: "It's the standard one – if it doesn't kill you, it'll make you stronger. Sorry to be a bore!"

Courtney Love is a lot of things – smart, mouthy, controversial, talented, crazy – but she's most definitely not a bore. The Hole show, incidentally, is truly spectacular. Glasgow loves Love. And as she explains from the stage, she loves Glasgow.

"This is one of two cities in the world where I've stage-dived – and nobody's tried to feel my tits, rip my dress, or finger me!"

The Hole story has yet to be written ... but there's plenty to be getting on with for now.

{MAY, 2010}

CHAPTER TWELVE:
Martin McDonagh

Martin McDonagh wants you all to know about New York indie rockers The Walkmen. "It's the only reason I agreed to do this interview," the 38-year-old playwright and film director chuckles, pulling up a seat in the reception area of Galway's plush House Hotel. "I just wanted to give my favourite band a plug in *Hot Press*."

Hopefully, he's also planning to talk about the new Druid production of his play *The Cripple Of Inishmaan* – a typically dark, and occasionally savage, tragicomedy which imagines the reactions of petty and insular Aran Islanders to the filming of Robert Flaherty's 1934 movie *Man of Aran* – but I tell him to go ahead.

"Have you heard of The Walkmen?" he asks, in his strong London accent. "I used one of their songs in *In Bruges*. They're this really great American band, who've got four or five albums out now. I seriously think they're one of the best things out there. They're a lot more intelligent, but kind of have the same sound as a Strokes-like outfit. But somehow they're totally obscure. I don't know why. Maybe because they're more poetic than The Strokes."

Anybody else you'd like to big up while you're at it?

"Actually, yeah, there's another good guy called Micah Hinson. I saw him at the Electric Picnic, and I've seen him a bunch of other times. His first album, *Micah P. Hinson and the Gospel of Progress*, was really great."

Although famously prickly, McDonagh seems to be in very good form tonight. During the pre-interview photo shoot in the hotel bar, a couple sitting nearby asked the tall, silver-haired and handsome writer if he was someone famous. "Nah, I'm just a wannabe," he deadpanned. Needless to say, McDonagh hasn't been a wannabe for well over a decade. The last time we met was back in 1996, around the time his controversial first play, *The Beauty Queen of Leenane*, was wowing audiences both here and in London, and critics were dubbing him "the Tarantino of theatre."

People were predicting great things for the young London-born Irishman, pretty much all of which have come to pass. At 25, McDonagh (who'd dropped out of school aged 16) already had six other plays written and ready to go. Two more scripts made up what became known as 'The Leenane Trilogy', there was another trilogy set on the Aran Islands, and also a dark and twisted Orwellian piece entitled *The Pillowman*.

Over the course of the past 12 years, all seven of these plays have been repeatedly produced, acclaimed, damned, and enjoyed by audiences all over the globe. In

1997, McDonagh had four works professionally produced on the London stage in a single season. The hysteria surrounding his rapid success was such that he was frequently touted as being the first dramatist since William Shakespeare to do so. He's won more awards than he can probably even count. His first foray into movies – a short film called *Six Shooter* starring Brendan Gleeson – earned him an Oscar in 2006. Earlier this year, his debut full length feature film *In Bruges*, starring Gleeson and Colin Farrell, was released to hugely positive reviews and performed extremely well at the box office. Not that he's left the theatre behind. Druid's new production of *The Cripple of Inishmaan*, directed by Garry Hynes, is currently touring the UK and Ireland. The tour will culminate with a three-month run in New York's prestigious Atlantic Theatre.

OLAF TYARANSEN: I know you're still living in London, but do you come back to Ireland often?
MARTIN MCDONAGH: Yeah, a fair bit. My parents live in Spiddal so I'm back to see them quite regularly.
Do you generally go to see productions of your plays?
I'll go to see one in a foreign language someplace if I haven't been and the place appeals. I've been to see a couple in Tokyo. But all the productions, I've gotten involved in the original rehearsal periods. So I did that for the 'Leenane Trilogy' and, for this one. I've been in for pretty much all of the rehearsals.
Most writers are barred from rehearsals, aren't they?
Only by bad directors. And there's a lot of them, so probably most writers are. It's different in movies but, in fact, the playwright has an awful lot of power. They can only be barred if they allow themselves to be.
You sound like you learnt that lesson the hard way.
There was a production of *Cripple* in New York, the director didn't let me in from day one, and the staging turned out to be a debacle. So that's one of the reasons to get heavily involved in this production – knowing it was going to New York, as well as going around some cool places in Ireland. Because, certainly in New York, we hadn't gotten it right before. There were still things I wanted to bring out of the play that maybe we hadn't touched on quite so much in the original production. Just the darker, sadder aspects. And I think we might have some more work to do, but we're much closer to it now.
Do you workshop the scripts or change lines of dialogue?
I've never really workshopped anything. I've always been very anti-that. You should hold onto a play or a film script until you think it's completely ready, and be very rigorous with yourself about how good or bad it is. But once you come to the decision that it is good, workshop shouldn't enter into it.
Were you always confident in your work?
I was confident about how badly I was writing for a long time, but then about how well I was writing when it changed. And angry about how things that were way worse than what I was writing were getting put on. So that breeds a degree of confidence, I think. So yeah. I saw all the crap that was out there, and thought

I was better than that.

You had 22 radio plays rejected before you began writing for the stage.

Yeah, it was pretty tough. Because I was either on the dole or in the last year of civil service work – doing basic office admin crap to pay the bills. So it was either mind-numbing office work or poverty. I kind of enjoyed the poverty more than the mind-numbing office work *[laughs]*. But because of that process of writing almost one play a week or a fortnight, it kind of hones your ear for dialogue and plot structure and character and all that kinda stuff. So right at the end of that, I tried stage plays. And probably the second and third of those attempts was *Lonesome West* and *Beauty Queen*. Once I attempted this new art form or story form, things just kind of exploded, and that kind of pent-up anger and honing of the skills all kind of came together in some way.

You wrote seven complete plays in less than 12 months in the early '90s.

The 22 radio plays was probably a more concerted effort. It all happened in that year-and-a-half of being on the dole. So that was a freedom. Also my brother, John, had just gone to LA on a screenwriting fellowship so I had space. So it was a combination of being freed from work and being free in the house.

Are you and your brother competitive?

Luckily, for the past 10 years or so, I've stayed with the plays while he was involved in movies. He never really cared about theatre at all. Now we're kind of crossing over into each other's territories a bit more, but I've never felt like there was any kind of antagonism on that score. There may be on pretty much every other score in the world *(laughs)*.

***The Lonesome West* is about the petty antagonism between two warring brothers. Was that based on yourself and John in any way?**

I remember writing *Lonesome West* not consciously basing any of it on us or me and him, but then in the year after it came out, almost every single friend of ours said, 'That's you and that's him'. It's interesting. Maybe it came through the pores or something, the vitriol in that situation. But we were never like that. Our relationship has always been very much based on love, but we'd be very competitive, not so much in the writing actually, but in sports – football, tennis or something.

How many productions of your plays are running worldwide as we speak?

I'm not sure. I try to get my agent to keep me posted when there's ones going on in places I'd be interested in going to. Not blowing my own trumpet, but there's just too many to keep up with. You get strange dribbles of £60 or £150 from Bratislava or something. So it's not big wads of cash, but it does add up because there'll be probably 20 new productions a month. Remember the 'Leenane Trilogy' are all one set, four characters. Two of those plays have strong women characters, which really appeals to amateur groups. *Cripple* has four women characters – so those things help. So the fact that they haven't stopped going on has allowed me to say no to film stuff, or to have any of them turned into films.

Does it bother you that the Abbey rejected your work in the '90s?

I don't think it bothered me even then. I found it laughable. I lost the rejection letter that they sent to me when they rejected the 'Leenane Trilogy', but I remember it said, 'These plays will never have an appeal to a metropolitan theatre-going audience'. Elsewhere, it said they were 'stage Irish' and 'childish' and things like that. I just thought they were so dumb to have missed it. I was still unemployed when I got that letter, but I knew then that there was more to my work than they were saying.

You were probably used to rejection by that stage.

Yeah. I remember six of the radio plays being rejected in one day. I got one letter that rejected all six of them! That's pretty hard, because you're waiting probably three months for someone to send you back your stuff. So to get six rejected – each of which you had hopes for – is tough. But I found it laughable the stuff the Abbey was staging while they were rejecting my plays. Not just mine, but Conor McPherson's stuff, too. And I think Mark O'Rowe's early stuff. It seems like every single generation they miss it. Each time they get a new guy running the place – it's invariably a guy apart from Garry's [Hynes] tenure – they mess it up in a different way. Now they're supposedly cleaning out their house again and doing a much better job.

They still haven't staged a Martin McDonagh play.

They've been approaching me for the last year or two. But, for me, they don't prove themselves to have changed by saying, 'We want you now'. They'll prove they've changed by having brand new writers on the main stage and on the small stage. And to have three years of undiscovered new writing up there – and maybe then I'll consider them.

You mentioned Conor McPherson. Are you friendly?

I haven't seen him for ages, but the last couple of times we were on friendly terms. At the start, there was a little bit of rivalry. Down to drunken incidents in bars and things. But I like a lot of his stuff. He'd had health issues, so when something like that happens you realise that the rivalries you feel towards another writer are totally ridiculous. If you're gonna express antagonism in interviews or whatever, it should be towards governments or politicians who're actually doing some real damage, rather than towards some guy who writes things you don't really like that much.

Speaking of drunken incidents, didn't you once tell Sean Connery to 'fuck off' at an award ceremony?

That was at the *Evening Standard* Theatre Awards. I thought it was funny at the time. The whole awards thing seemed quite silly anyway. But I was also very nervous. I was up for the one award that night where you know you're gonna get it early – 'Best Newcomer' or something. So my brother and I got tanked up on vodka. It was an afternoon show. I remember having two big triple vodkas at about 11.30 in the morning. Then we went to the thing and started on the free wine. And free wine to us then was like, 'Wow! Free stuff! And it's alcohol!' *(laughs).* We didn't stand when they were toasting the Queen. We were kind of mumbling – nothing rude, but anti-Queen stuff. We had reasons for not wanting to toast the Queen. So Connery put his hand on my shoulder and tells me to shut up or leave. I apologised at first, and then my brother said, 'Don't take that from him!' So I kinda caught myself, realised he was right, and told Connery, *'Fuck off!'* But of course it was a roomful of journalists and actors. And at that moment there was one of those silences, and every single head kind of turned. Connery obviously didn't really know how to come back. So he went off and sat down. And that was about it. I went off and picked up the award, and I pretty much can't really remember much else of what happened from then on.

But the next day I thought it might be a little piece in the paper – just a little two-inch story on page 3 or whatever. But it was a big story. And even at the same time, I thought it was kind of a punk fuck off thing to do at an awards ceremony. I didn't really stress about it. I didn't think it would be a big deal.

The last time we met, you told me that you saw theatre as a stepping stone to movies...

Did I say 'stepping stone'? I suppose I might have said something like ... *(pauses)*. I've never actually believed that. Because they're not. Maybe, shortly before *Beauty Queen* came out, I was feeling that way about the theatre. But in the next couple of years, my attitude changed.

Were you surprised to win an Oscar for your first attempt (Best Short Film for *Six Shooter*)?

It was totally bizarre. How could it not be? Like you're making a short film, and the only reason for making a short film is to see if you can do it. For it even to be seen on Channel 4 or Network 2 isn't even on the agenda. It certainly wasn't for me.

Was the Oscar a bit of a disappointment, then?

Ha, ha! No! *Why?*

It happened so effortlessly...

I didn't even have a moment to think. It was like winning the lottery, but it's a lottery that you didn't even know you'd entered – or even had much respect for. Because for me as a film buff, I think of all those Orson Welles films that were shut out or were hated. Malick was another, and all of Scorsese's films. So of course it's a joke. But it's an enjoyable joke. For someone like me who loves all the people who never won, the idea of even making one feature film would be the be all and end all. And certainly Oscars or any of that kind of schtick would have no importance. Even now, to make a film that would last is the thing. Every single one of my favourite films probably didn't even get a single nomination. And were made by people who didn't give a fuck about awards..

Before you started shooting *In Bruges*, you insisted on three weeks of rehearsals with Colin Farrell and Brendan Gleeson.

That was mostly down to my nerves. I remember on the first day getting a coffee with Colin and Brendan – just the three of us, literally, sitting across a table and me thinking, 'What do I say now?' I literally had no idea what to do. So we just read it and then talked. But I think Colin and Brendan had the same thing. They were like, 'We're not used to this. This could kill our process' – kill the spontaneity. Brendan's background is more theatrical, so he was possibly less wary of it. But I think you realise the things you've picked up over the years in rehearsal rooms. And the thing I've always had script-wise – like knowing a script, knowing why a character is behaving this way or saying this specific thing. And having lived with the script in my head for almost two years, you know each line and you know why each moment is happening so you can answer all the questions. So basically it was just a nice period of every single question being asked and answered.

You're happy with the film?

I really like what we got with *Bruges*. It's basically their relationship.

What are you doing next?

Well, originally I wanted to take a couple of years off after *Bruges*. But I've got two film scripts that are ready to go. There's one I wrote before *Bruges* called *Suicide On Sixth Street*, and there's a more recent one called *Seven Psychopaths*, which is the best of the three, really.

What's it about?

Em... I'll not give you any more *[smiles]*.

There are some other plays and scripts listed in your biography in the programme that I didn't recognise – like *The Banshees of Inisheer* and *The Retard is Out in the Cold*.

Some of those are scripts that I've finished, but that I have to go back to, or scripts that are ready but won't be seen for say two or three years. I always used to like at the end of James Bond films, they'd say 'Coming next – *Octopussy*'. And it'd be two years, but as a kid you'd be going, 'Wow! *Octopussy* is the next one!' I thought that was so cool to plan two years ahead. So that's why I always have the future plays or film scripts listed.

Do you have a motto in life?

I always liked that Beckett quote: *"Ever tried. Ever failed. No matter. Try again. Fail again. Fail better."*

{NOVEMBER, 2008}

CHAPTER THIRTEEN:
Sinéad O'Connor & Shane MacGowan

When you spot the big blue Virgin Mary statue by the front door, there's no doubt that you've arrived at the correct address. "Come on in!" says Sinéad O'Connor, greeting your *Hot Press* reporter with a friendly peck on the cheek. "Shane's running late, but he should be here in a little while."

Well, there's a surprise! It's exactly midday on the 9th of May, and Shane MacGowan is running late. Actually, given Mr. MacGowan's notoriously decadent lifestyle, it's far more likely that he's *staggering* late. "No, no," Sinéad laughs. "Victoria just rang from the cab. They're definitely on their way."

Sinéad's Dublin home is bright, spacious and luxurious – all wooden floorboards, Moroccan rugs and high ceilings. The 40-year-old singer, still beautiful after all these years, leads us into her living room, and then immediately disappears off to do a quick phone interview with an American paper. Her double album, *Theology*, is being released in six weeks time, but promotional duties have already begun in earnest. Which is essentially why we're here. Today's cunning plan is that Shane will conduct the *Hot Press* interview with Sinéad, and I'm to be the referee between Irish rock's most notorious son and controversial daughter. I have my doubts about how this is going to work out, but, hey, it's so crazy it just might crackle. While Sinéad does her interview, I assist photographer Mick Quinn in rearranging her furniture for the photo shoot. There are framed images and statuettes of the Blessed Virgin everywhere, and her bookshelf is stuffed full of well-thumbed religious tomes.

Sinead's Mary fixation is nothing new. Some years back she played a chain-smoking Mother of Christ in Neil Jordan's movie of Pat McCabe's *The Butcher Boy*. When she was ordained by the breakaway Latin Tridentine Church in 1999, she took the name Mother Bernadette Mary. The Mary thing even seems to extend to her viewing material. There's a DVD copy of *There's Something About Mary* lying in front of a massive flatscreen TV. Sadly, her fixation only goes so far. I'd murder a Bloody Mary but, as a non-drinker, Sinead doesn't have any alcohol in the house. Her charming publicist, Tara, offers tea or coffee instead. Fifteen minutes later, Shane still hasn't arrived, but Sinead's phone interview is done. Apparently it went a lot better than the last one she did. "I had this Italian bitch giving out to me and telling me where I was going wrong in my life," she laughs. "I'd never even met this person. The fuckin' *cheek* of her!"

She seems to be in relaxed form. We talk about her brother Joe's latest novel,

Redemption Falls. "I'm only a few chapters in, but I can't believe how brilliant it is," she laughs. "I'm really proud of him. I've been plugging it in all my interviews. It's funny – reading it, I kinda forget that it's my own brother who's written it." Soon afterwards, Shane arrives with bubbly fiancée Victoria Clark in tow. Attired in a new – or at least unslept-in – blue suit, he looks healthier than he has in years. Having said that, he's brought two carrier bags full of liquid supplies (a couple of bottle of spirits and a case of white wine). "I told him that he wouldn't need all that booze," Victoria announces, "but then he said Olaf was going to be here!"

Tara fetches some ice and glasses, and Shane pours me an extremely generous quadruple vodka. "D'ya wanna mixer wiv that?" he asks. "What do you have?" He holds up a bottle of gin and sniggers. "Thanks, Shane, but I prefer not to mix my vodka with gin. At least, not before lunchtime."

He lets out one of his trademark gas-escaping laughs: *"KERSSHHHSSSHHHH!!!!"*

Victoria insists on Shane showing us all his new engagement ring. A fitting rock for a rock star, it's a purple bauble larger than a witch's boil. "It's even bigger than mine!" she laughs. When I suggest that maybe Sinéad could be the priestess who marries them, Victoria says, "That's a great idea! You can if you want!"

The photo-shoot takes about twenty minutes and is enjoyably chaotic. Midway through, Jake – Sinéad's 20-year-old son – pops in to say hello. His arm is in a cast.

"How'd that happen to you?" Shane enquires. "I was masturbating," Jake replies, deadpan. This prompts another loud, *"KERSSHHHSSSHHH!"* (it was actually a rollerblading incident).

Once the shoot is finished, we all tiptoe quietly down the stairs to a small basement back room to do the interview. Apparently, the new baby is asleep. Sadly, despite the fact that everybody present has posed naked at some stage in their careers, Sinéad rejects outright Shane's suggestion that we should all disrobe for the interview, a la Dave Fanning and U2. "No – fuck off!" she laughs. "Like... *fuck off!*"

There's a surprisingly heavy stone elephant on the table (Sinéad challenges us to lift it), but hopefully none in the room. In fact, there's a harp in the corner. There's also a painting of His Holiness Bob Marley on the wall, to which due homage is paid throughout proceedings.

SINÉAD: Alright, so how's this gonna work?

OLAF: Well, I guess Shane is going to ask the questions, I'll record the whole thing, and perhaps throw in a comment or question every now and then.

SHANE: Right... *(Getting down to work)* Anyone wanna drink? *(Unscrews bottle).*

OLAF: I think we should kick off by raising our glasses to Sinéad. Congratulations! The new album's terrific.

(Glasses and teacups are held aloft).

SINÉAD: Thank you very much.

SHANE: Yeah, I think it's a brilliant album. It reminded me a lot of *Astral Weeks*.

VICTORIA: Tell her what you said about the fear this morning.

SHANE: Oh yeah. Well, I was up pretty late and suddenly, for the first fucking time in many, many years, I started thinking that I might die, ya know worra mean. I'm likely to die one day – *KERRSSSHHHSSSHHH!* I was on the jacks, actually – *KERSSHHHSSHHHHH!* And then, anyway... I had a listen to your album, and it genuinely made me feel better. Em... I presume you did the Dublin sessions first, yeah?

SINÉAD: Well, I started recording the Dublin ones first, but they overlapped – and I wound up recording them both at the same time. We had three songs of the acoustic one done, and then we started the London one. So I was running between the two places. But the musicians in Dublin didn't know about the London sessions, and I never let the London ones listen to the other one either, because I didn't want them to be influenced by each other. So that was a funny one. I had to lie my way through the Irish sessions.

OLAF: So was it the plan all along to do a double album?

SINÉAD: No, it was an accident. At first, it was just gonna be the acoustic album. And then what happened with the guy, RonTom, who produced the London album, was he asked me to come over to make some demos with him. So I said, 'Well, I'll go just to see how we get on working together'. But the only songs I had were the ones for *Theology*. So we demoed those, but my plan was really just to see if I could work on a future album with this guy. But when he found out that that was the plan, he burst into tears and literally begged me to let him make the album. So in the end, I just said, 'Fuck it, let's do it.'

SHANE: RonTom? Is that just one guy or is it two?

SINÉAD: Yeah, he's just one guy.

SHANE: Who else has he produced?

SINÉAD: He used to produce people like the Sugababes and Gabrielle. And he was a DJ for a while. He's a lovely, lovely guy. He's very like John Reynolds actually – Jake's dad.

SHANE: Does John play drums on this album?

SINÉAD: On this album? He played at the show (in Dublin Castle) the other day. Oh, and he did play on one track. He's on the first song, 'Something Beautiful'.

SHANE: Yeah, that's definitely got his style.

SINÉAD: He also played on 'I Don't Know How To Love Him' actually.

SHANE: That is wild – it's a fucking wild song. I always thought that was a great song, but they always did such wimpy fucking versions of it.

SINÉAD: Yeah, yeah, yeah *(nods vigorously)*. That came out when I was about eight, and I remember thinking, 'That's my fucking song!' Ha, ha!

VICTORIA: Shane, you never finished telling us what happened on the jacks!

SHANE: Oh yeah! Well, it was just a horrible, crawling sort of... Em, I was reading about (Colombian cocaine baron) Pablo Escobar, right. About everyone coming up telling him he was gonna get blown away, yeah. And his own people were dropping like flies all over the place. And I just suddenly got this horrible crawling fear of death, ya know worra mean? And I went upstairs and just bundled myself up in an embryonic heap, and went to sleep. And then Vickie got up and came into the room and I said, 'Can you stick the album on again?' And it had that kind of natural calmness to it. More or less made you glad to be alive. It went straight to my heart. No bullshit. Was that a... *(pauses and takes a long drink).* And I liked the title – *Theology*. It's straightforward, ya know worra mean? I liked 'The Glory Of Jah' and all that stuff, too. *(Pauses again and then looks accusingly at Sinead).* You're supposed to kinda say something – KERSSHHSSHHH!

SINÉAD: I'm waiting for a question.

VICTORIA: What you're saying is that it took away your fear of death!

SHANE: Yes, yes. Right. Exactly. That was what I was saying. It took away my fear of death. *KERSHHSSHHHSSHHH!*

(Everybody laughs)

SINÉAD: I reckon the thing about death is to relax and enjoy it, actually.

SHANE: YES! I know. Well, that's what I'm saying. To sorta chill... *(Long pause)*

SINÉAD: I don't know what to say, Shane. I don't know what to say. You've got to ask me something, I think.

OLAF: What are your feelings on life after death?

VICTORIA: What are your favourite recipes?

SHANE: *KERSSSHHHSSSHHH!!*

SINÉAD: What are my feelings on life after death? I don't know. Nobody knows for sure, but I think that when you die, you become pure compassion. And also you become light. That's what I think. And I also think that there's some source to which we all go back, but I don't know what that is. But I do really think that death is just like taking your clothes off. But we've been conditioned to be frightened of it. You know, we've been brought up to believe that it's a terrible thing. And it's hard for those left behind, alright, because you miss the person you love, but I think the person who's gone is actually peaceful and happy. I think it's sad that we're so conditioned to be frightened of it.

SHANE: Well, I'm not normally frightened of it...

SINÉAD: Me neither, but sometimes we are.

SHANE: But there's various things to help you. Like, I think that music is a healing force. And, like, since fear is the only real thing to be afraid of... *KERSSHHHSSHHH!* Fear is all you have to confront. All the rest of it, you don't have any choices, really. Ya know worra mean? You go with the flow, yeah?

SINÉAD: Em... exactly.

SHANE: Yeah, but anyway, your album knocked me out. It really knocked me out. Obviously there's a couple of tracks that grab you instantly, but it's also one of those albums that you can sorta relax and listen to whenever you need a bit of cheering-up.

SINÉAD: Well, that's what I think the Rasta records are like. That's what I listen to if I'm freaked out. It always works.

OLAF: Did Sly and Robbie play on this album?

SINÉAD: On this album? I don't know, actually. It was RonTom that kinda got everybody in. I was leaving them to record for two weeks, kinda thing, and then going over and doing the vocals. So he was kinda the boss. So I couldn't tell you half the people who played on it at all.

OLAF: Lots of different musicians, then?

SINÉAD: Yeah. But I think music is a bit like that. If it's good then music is like arms around you, isn't it?

SHANE: Yeah, yeah. It is! You get your cellos and fiddles and all the rest of it, coming in and doing it when they need to come in. But basically it's just... *(shrugs and takes another long drink).* But basically, I think your voice has really matured. Like, it's either gonna mature or you're gonna lose it! *(laughs)* But no, it's really matured and it's just got that quality. It's just the... the voice of a woman. Ya know worra mean?

SINÉAD: Yeah. I think so.

SHANE: And I'll never pretend to understand a woman! *KERSHHSSHHHSHH!* There's two races of human beings on this planet – and that's woman and man! *(laughs).*

OLAF: Can I ask a nasty journo question here? You two seem to be getting on great today, but you've been at loggerheads in the not so distant past...

SINÉAD: We've never been at loggerheads!

OLAF: Come on! Yes, you have!

VICTORIA: Honestly. We've never been at loggerheads. We never all stopped seeing each other.

OLAF: So was that whole smack thing just something that was blown up out of all proportion by the tabloids?

SINÉAD: Yeah. We never really had an argument in our lives, did we, Shane?

SHANE: Not a serious one. I made a stupid joke and it all got blown up into something stupid.

SINÉAD: Did I get pissed off?

SHANE: Yeah *(laughs)*. But I mean, why not? It was sexist and it was... *KERSSHHSSHHH!*

(Everybody talks over each other for about 30 seconds).

OLAF: Hang on a second! Putting this bluntly, didn't you, Sinéad, shop Shane to the London cops for taking smack a few years back?

SINÉAD: Yeah, but...

VICTORIA: She did, but what everybody ignores is that I was the one who asked her to do it! I didn't have the courage to do it myself, so she did it for me. That's what happened! She did it! And it worked!

(Everybody talks over each other again, rendering the tape unintelligible).

SINÉAD: Seriously, though, we never really fell out or anything, did we?

SHANE: The one argument we did have, you were actually right.

SINÉAD: I can't even remember what it was about. What did we argue about?

SHANE: About the smack... *(laughs)*

SINÉAD: Ah yeah! Even then, we didn't actually argue...

SHANE: No, no. You just went to the cops... *KERSSSHHHSSSHHH!*

SINÉAD: Quite happily. But we didn't have an argument about it.

OLAF: It's not really like either of you to do anything particularly quietly, though. Not always by choice. For example, Sinéad, you just had the tabloids all over you because you bought a new house near where an old murder happened, and they made a big thing about you buying a 'murder house'. And as for you, Shane, every time you fall out the door, there's a story about you. Does that bother either of you?

SHANE: Nah, doesn't bother me at all. Does it bother you, Sinéad?

SINÉAD: It doesn't bother me all the time, but sometimes, yeah, it does bother me. It depends on what the *thing* is.

OLAF: Do you think that kind of shared tabloid intrusion into your personal lives is a bonding thing? You know, one of the reasons why you're friends?

SINÉAD: I don't think that has anything to do with why people are friends. People are just friends because they like each other or because they have some kind of connection.

OLAF: Incidentally, do you know Britney Spears?

SINÉAD: No.

OLAF: Do you have any feelings for her? Sorry – just when she shaved her head recently, she reminded me a little of you...

SINÉAD: I've always had feelings for her, in terms of feeling sorry for her for the way they treat her. I feel sorry for her for the way she's stuck. If I were her, I'd move out of America and go live somewhere else. Like, Longford.

VICKIE: *Longford!* Ha, ha!

SINÉAD: Yeah. Well, I just feel sorry that she can't get away from all that shit. I mean, her family live in the equivalent of Longford. What are her family doing? I feel sorry that she's trapped in that. It's disgusting, really, what people are doing to her.

OLAF: But pretty much the same thing has happened to you in the past. Did you ever freak?

SINÉAD: Yeah, constantly. I have a permanent freak. Ha, ha! I was completely freaked for years. Totally.

OLAF: But you can take the piss out of it now. For example, recently on *Podge & Rodge* you ripped up a picture of Louis Walsh – a reference to that time you ripped up a picture of the Pope.

SINÉAD: I'm sure they'll make him rip up a picture of me at some point.

SHANE: You ripped up a picture of Louis Walsh on *Podge & Rodge*?

SINÉAD: Well, only because they asked me to. It would've been rude to say no.

SHANE: They're a pair of right bastards, actually. *KERSSHHHSSSHHH!* They can't take it either. They give it but they can't take it.

OLAF: They kind of shortened your appearance on the show, didn't they, Shane?

SHANE: Yeah. They 'ad to. *(laughs)*

OLAF: Are you a fan of Irish television, Sinead?

SINÉAD: I mostly just watch the news actually.

OLAF: Are you following the 'Miss D' abortion case at the moment?

SINÉAD: Actually I mostly watch the English news, but I am aware of that case, obviously.

OLAF: What's your take on it?

SINÉAD: My take on it is the same as it's always been. A person should have the right to decide whether they're ready or not to have a baby. And whether they can deal with it. Especially in a situation like hers. It's different to any other regular situation, you know. But at the same time, I don't think that I have the right to be telling anybody what's right or what's wrong. It's nothing to do with me, in lots of ways. But I feel sorry that somebody doesn't have the freedom of movement, never mind anything else. The idea that somebody could be stopped from travelling for any reason is kind of archaic.

OLAF: Shane, you've been stopped from travelling a few times ...

SHANE: Not in a long time.

VICKIE: Isn't Shane meant to be doing the interview, Olaf?

OLAF: I'm just keeping things moving, Victoria.

SINÉAD: He's just keeping it moving.

SHANE: Yeah. Let's keep it moving. Anyway, the Irish thing like... There's a huge relationship between... Well, particularly, like, I love country and rock & roll and jazz. They've got a totally different noise in the West Indies than we have over here – musically, I mean. And that's why I was making the comparison with *Astral Weeks* or something. Where you're really just letting it all out...

SINÉAD: Yeah. What are you getting at?

SHANE: Just that it sounded like it was fun to make.

SINÉAD: I know what you mean. That somehow you're not thinking just in terms of the role of your Irish musical culture. Like you're not necessarily just making traditional records, I guess. Is that what you mean?

SHANE: Well, everything's traditional, isn't it?

SINÉAD: Yeah, in a way. I saw Kila the other night – they played support at Dublin Castle. Fuck! They were like traditional Irish music on acid! They're totally like an acid trip. They were completely mad. It was brilliant!

SHANE: Well, poitin has got its uses. *KERRRSSSHHHHH!*

SINÉAD: In fact, I had a sip of poitin once and I was completely pissed.

SHANE: Yeah, but you ought to have taken it further. You drink enough of it and... *(mumbles unintelligibly before lapsing into a brief silence).* But anyway, we're pretty psychedelic people, aren't we? Well, everybody is actually. But that's what you find out when you travel.

SINÉAD: Definitely. Though I guess we're not as psychedelic as we would be if we were all doing acid. But I reckon Kila have done a shitload of acid! Ha, ha! I had flashbacks when I was watching them the other night. Oh man! Or else they'd done a lot of mushrooms.

SHANE: Do you remember the ancient Irish idea we were talking about before?

SINÉAD: What was that?

SHANE: It was me, you and Vickie. And I was reading out a translation of an old Irish poem by this guy who was saying that poetry, music and all the rest of it is all the same thing. And it's the listener who makes the meaning out of it. Do you remember that?

SINÉAD: Em... yeah. Did I argue with you over that?

SHANE: Nah, it was just a very beautiful poem. But I think I was on my high-horse about Irish poetry and all that. I think it was O'Raftery or one of those old guys. And we were all having a great time, yeah? And I read it out, saying, 'Isn't that amazing?' And you and her said, 'Yeah, he probably went and had a wank afterwards!' *(laughs)*

VICKIE: We didn't say that!

SHANE: Yes, you did. And actually it was probably true.

KERSSSHHHSSSHHH!

(Everybody laughs and talks over each other again).

SINÉAD: I remember that time your dad came round.

VICKIE: My dad tried to get off with her!

SHANE: Oh yeah. He had Hitler's cufflinks!

OLAF: Hitler's cufflinks?

VICKIE: He brought her a pair of Hitler's cufflinks as a present!

OLAF: Do you mean cufflinks that belonged to Hitler, or a pair of cufflinks with Hitler's image on them?

SINÉAD: They had belonged to Hitler. This was Victoria's dad's way of trying to chat a girl up! Ha, ha!

SHANE: But they had no power of their own. Do you understand? You consult your power. The swastika is an ancient fucking symbol of love. It's a mandala, like a cross is a mandala.

SINÉAD: But the Nazis turned it the other way round, that was the thing.

SHANE: That's actually a bit of a myth. Because whatever way you turn it around... em, you can't turn it around because it's symmetrical. Like a cross or a circle or a mandala. But he was into all that stuff. He wanted to find things like the Spear of Destiny and use them for evil purposes. Em...*(sips drink)*. Who the hell are we talking about again?

SINÉAD: Hitler.

SHANE: Oh yeah *(laughs)*. He tried to get the Holy Grail and the Spear of Destiny – you know the spear they stuck in Jesus' side – and the Arc of the Covenant. And the Nazis were really looking for them. What was that Harrison Ford film again? *Raiders of the Lost Ark*. That was actually based on truth. The real nutters at the top felt that they were the natural follow-on from all these supposedly great empires – like the Roman Empire or whatever. And they tried to gather all the symbols together. How did this come up again? Oh yeah, Hilter's cufflinks. And Vickie's dad. That was really funny!

SINÉAD: It was horrible. Ha, ha!

(Conversation goes off the record for a time – though the gist of it is that Vickie's father got nowhere with Sinéad, and Shane somehow wound up owning Hitler's cufflinks).

SHANE: Anyway, as I was saying, those cufflinks are my pension!

SINÉAD: No, Shane. Your songs are your pension!

SHANE: Yeah. Well, we all know that the music business can be a bit slow in delivering the cash.

SINÉAD: Yeah, but do you remember that time they did that survey of the 100 most loved Irish songs of all time – voted for by Irish people. And something like three of your songs were in the top eight – including the first and the third. And the first one was 'Fairytale Of New York'. That's your fucking pension! Your songs are worth a lot more than bloody Hitler's cufflinks.

SHANE: Yeah... but not to a Nazi! *KERSSHHHSSSHHH!!!*

OLAF: You should flog them to George Bush.

SHANE: Yeah, George Bush and that lot are all on exactly the same trip.

SINÉAD: Maybe the best thing you could do with them is chuck them in the fucking ocean!

SHANE: Yeah, but I've already done that with a Satanic badge, yeah? It was driving me nuts. This was years ago. And I was totally out of it when I accepted it from a very good friend – who was a very sound guy. And then I started feeling like I was possessed by a demon. It was in London actually, when there was a lot of Satanism going around at the time. Me and Vickie were walking over a canal bridge and I was going, 'This is driving me nuts, I can't take any more of this!' And she said, 'Why don't you just take the devil badge off and throw it in the bloody water?' Because traditionally, the devil or his accomplices hate water.

SINÉAD: Apparently they also hate Latin. That's why they used to say the mass in Latin.

SHANE: No – they used Latin! The Germans screwed it up totally, because... *(goes off on a brief incoherent rant about demons, Nazis and swastikas).*

SINÉAD: But anyway, Shane, to get back to my point, the only thing you can do with Hitler's cufflinks is chuck them away. Let's face it, you can't sell those to anybody.

SHANE: *(Pulls blank face)* Why not? *KERSSSHHHSSHHH!*

SINÉAD: Because it's bad – and it's badness. And if you give them to somebody, whether for money or not, you're giving badness to somebody, like. You may as well chuck it in the ocean – then you don't have to give it to anybody.

SHANE: I'll have to think about that one, yeah.

SINÉAD: And I'll betcha if you did do that, you'd find the money in some other way. Probably more money than you'd get for the Hitler cufflinks.

SHANE: Hmmm... *(Considers this for a moment)* You're bloody right! *KERSSSHHSSHH!* You're dead right!

SINÉAD: Chuck 'em! Ha, ha!

VICKIE: I think you should talk about where you two first met...

OLAF: Great idea!!!

SHANE: That was at the Forum, I think.

SINÉAD: I don't remember.

VICKIE: No, it was in our flat on Liverpool Road. BP Fallon brought her around.

SHANE: No, we met in Dublin definitely. Lillie's Bordello or somewhere.

VICKIE: No, BP brought her around to our house after she'd put out that single. The one which made loads of money.

SHANE: What? 'Nothing Takes The Place Of You'? *(laughs)*. That Prince thing? Nah, you were already big news in Ireland with *The Lion and the Cobra*. The first time I really clocked into you was the video for 'Mandika'. You were playing the electric guitar. You actually looked like Noddy Holder's daughter.

SINÉAD: I wasn't really playing!

SHANE: Or Noddy Holder's daughter after a lot of really good plastic surgery! *KERSSHHSSSHH!*

VICKIE: But it was BP Fallon that introduced us to her. And they both had the shaved heads. And he brought her around. And she had the baby and John (Reynolds). Jake had just been born so whatever year that was (1987). What I remember most, Sinéad, is that I made you tea. Because you drank tea and you didn't drink the alcohol. I thought that was a bit strange. Usually people would come around and do a huge line and then a large whatever. But you wanted a nice cup of tea.

SHANE: Oh yeah, Charlie was there, wasn't he?

VICKIE: Charlie? Yeah, he was.

OLAF: Sinéad, didn't your record company put you under pressure to have an abortion when they discovered you were pregnant with Jake?

SINÉAD: Yeah, they did. I was 19, almost 20.

OLAF: Was it intense pressure?

SHANE: All record companies are intense!

SINÉAD: I don't know whether it was intense or not, but it's how you feel it. I certainly felt it intensely, if you know what I mean. It was interesting because me and Karl Wallinger were both having babies at the same time. But none of this happened to Karl. In those days, record companies had a doctor. If you were ill, they sent you to their doctor. And these were these rock 'n' roll doctors. I can't remember this guy's name. He had a brilliant fuckin' name. You'd probably know him, Shane. An old American guy. *(A brief head-scratching session comes up with the doctor's name).*

Anyway, they sent me to this doctor when I told them I was pregnant. And when I got there, and I was only 19 and freaked and all, this guy said to me, 'Your record company has spent one hundred thousand quid recording your record, and you owe it to them not to have the baby'. And then he tried to convince me that terrible things would happen to the baby, for example, if I went out on tour while I was pregnant, or got on an airplane or whatever, that the baby would be ill. Not that it would die, but that it would be born mentally handicapped. I swear on a stack of Bibles that that's literally what happened.

SHANE: Was that when you were making *The Lion and the Cobra*?

SINÉAD: Yeah, it was while I was making my first record. And what actually happened was that I had a producer originally on that record at the time, and I fucking hated what he was doing. So what happened was we recorded the album twice. And the first time I recorded was the hundred thousand quid that the record company had spent. But they actually pulled the album. I never told them I hated it, but they began to hate it. So they ultimately pulled it. And had I listened to this doctor guy, I would've gotten rid of my baby and, what happened was, they pulled the record anyway. And we went on to make another. I was also under pressure from other places not to have the baby. And I did actually give in. So I went to hospital not to have it, if you know what I mean. And thank God, what happened was I completely freaked-out. Just freaked-out, like! And I wouldn't let them anywhere near me. It was really funny, because they called John... and John Reynolds basically wasn't around or whatever, blah, blah, blah. So they called him and told him to come in. And the fucking social worker asked him was I on drugs, and was that why I was freaking out. Because I was on drugs? So, thank God, the social worker said something like, 'If she doesn't have this baby she's going to become a raving lunatic forever'. Of course, I'm a raving lunatic anyway *(laughs)*.

SHANE: What age were you again?

SINÉAD: I was 19 at that time, going on 20. That was around November/December and I turned 20 on the 8th of December.

SHANE: Was the age of seniority 21 then?

SINÉAD: I dunno. I haven't a clue. So I almost didn't have the baby because of it, because when you're that young and under that kinda pressure. Everybody was telling me at the same time that you're not gonna earn any money, you're gonna be fucked. I was living in a council flat at the time. So I was under a lot of pressure. But yeah, the long and short of it is that the record company had their doctor say that to me. But nobody said a word to Karl Wallinger!

SHANE: You know what it says in the constitution, yeah? I'm not gonna get involved in the arguments about gays and women and all the rest of it, but in the constitution it says... *[goes off on a rant about politicians kowtowing to the Catholic Church]*.

SINÉAD: *[Interrupting]* Actually, Shane, I've just realised something. My daughter just flashed through my mind. Sorry, I'm thinking about her, because she's gonna be home in a little while. I know you've met her a few times before, but she adores you. She's gonna totally fucking freak out when she comes in here and sees you!

SHANE: I've met her before, haven't I?

SINÉAD: Yeah, but when we came out for dinner that night, she didn't realise that you were Shane MacGowan. She'd only heard the records, but she hadn't seen you. So she was sitting at dinner all night and she didn't realise it was you. And then she said 'Who was that guy over there?' So when I told her it was Shane MacGowan, she nearly went mad. When she comes in here, she's gonna freak. But isn't that sweet? She loves Shane MacGowan and Johnny Cash. She loves all of Johnny Cash's murder songs, you know all the really dark ones? So she's at a guitar lesson now and she's learning how to play 'Folsom Prison Blues'. Ha, ha!

SHANE: But that's one of his happier songs! He kills his wife! *[laughs]* Oh no – he kills a bloke! Just to watch him die! KERSSSHHHSSSHHH!

SINÉAD: Actually, that reminds me... *[proceeds to tell a scandalous story about a certain internationally famous cult rocker]*. Anyway, at the time he was just really dicking her around. So your instinct if you love somebody is to definitely not let that person anywhere near you – or them. Do you know what I mean?

SHANE: This should be the classic interview of your fucking career, Olaf! Do ya know worra mean? *KERSSSHHHHHHSSHH!!!* You're really getting the stuff here!!! *KERSSHHHSSHHH!!!!*

SINÉAD: Actually, you'd better leave that out. That's off the record!

OLAF: Ah, don't do that to me!

VICKIE: No, you'd better not print that.

SINÉAD: Nah, there's no point causing a load of shit at this stage.

[Tape goes off briefly as Hot Press *is sworn to silence].*

SHANE: We better go back to *Theology*, yeah? It's gonna be an 11-song record, yeah? A mixture of acoustic and full band...

SINÉAD: Right *[nods]*.

SHANE: Well, it really knocked me out, yeah. I especially loved the Dublin sessions. I preferred them to the London ones. But naturally – with me being a Republican wanker! *[laughs]*. Who produced the Dublin sessions?

SINÉAD: Steve Cooney.

SHANE: I know him, actually.

SINÉAD: He played guitar on it as well. He's amazing. I love him. Yeah, I co-produced the Dublin sessions with him and Graham Bolger. But I wasn't producing the London ones. RonTom did those. Oh, hi there!

[We're interrupted by the arrival of Jake, who joins us at the table].

SHANE: So it's all ready to go, yeah? You gonna tour it?

SINÉAD: Yeah, it's coming out on June 26. And there's gonna be a tour.

SHANE: What's going on the cover?

SINÉAD: There's two different covers – there's a different one in the States than there is here. The one here is just kinda blue with a symbol on it, and it says *Theology* in this writing. And the one in the States has a photo on the cover and the title in the same writing. Nothing too wild or exciting.

SHANE: Coming from someone who's got a natural hatred of organised religion – which is fair enough, yeah? – the title *Theology* is, well, it's a *title*. You know what I mean? And then when you hear the album...

SINÉAD: I don't think it's true that I hate organised religion, though. Because there's things about it that I love. I'm in love with religion. But what I don't like about it, I suppose, is that as far as I'm concerned God and religion are two different things. I don't believe that religion believes in God, actually. And I believe that God needs to be rescued from religion. But that doesn't mean that I don't see good things about religion, i.e. the good thing I see about it is that there is a God which needs to be rescued from it.

SHANE: Do you believe you're part of God?

SINÉAD: Yeah. Absolutely.

SHANE: Then again, everything's part of God. So we have to rescue ourselves?

SINÉAD: Abso-fuckin-lutely!

SHANE: Anything else you wanna say about it?

SINÉAD: I dunno. What do you want to know?

OLAF: Tell us about the track 'Watcher Of Men'.

SINÉAD: Every line of that song is actually scripture, from the *Book Of Job* in the Old Testament. What I'm interested in about the Old Testament is how much – in the *Book Of The Prophets*, for example – how much what they're talking about reflects what's going on in our world today. And there's only one book in the Bible, in the Old Testament, that deals with the issue of death – or of life, really. And it's the only dark, negative book in the Bible, as such, that goes through all these terrible things.

It's the story of Job, who adores God or whatever. And one day the Devil goes to God and says to him, 'I'll betcha if you gave me permission to fuck this guy up, he wouldn't love you then'. And God, for some reason, is bastard enough to say, 'Yeah, okay, cool – do your worst'. So the Devil goes and fucks up Job, kills all his children, kills all his animals, covers him in boils, and ruins his fucking life entirely.

And Job spends months and months gradually getting worse. And he has all these conversations with his friends, about has he done something for which God is punishing him? So he runs the gamut of it. Really, the book deals with suicidal feelings – the feeling of not wanting to live and how life can be so hard that you don't know how to live, and you can't explain it to yourself. So it's all symbolism.

But anyway, he suffers all this shit and he's complaining to God and screaming and shouting, but he never gives up believing in God. His friends try to convince him that it must be his fault if God's done this to him. And Job, interestingly, denies that, and says he knows he hasn't done anything to be punished for. He screams and shouts at God. But at the end, what happens is that God gets pissed off with Job and says, 'Who the fuck are you to question whatever shit I decide?' So God's a bit of a bastard in it. But that's the whole answer to the question of life. And it is a wise lesson, although it's not what we all want to hear. But it's about death also. The thing is you just accept it – don't question it, don't ask about it, don't try to understand it, or even don't try to understand anything that happens beyond death. If we needed to know, we would know. That's more or less what the story says. So at the end of it all, Job just says, 'Oh, okay, I didn't understand those things. So I accept that I'm dust and ashes and I don't have a say in those things.'

SHANE: Which is very close to Zen, actually.
SINÉAD: Yeah. But it's a very dark journey that brings him to this conclusion.
SHANE: Yeah, but Job is definitely the ultimate in yang, yeah.
SINÉAD: Job is the one to read when you're suffering. There are incredible lessons in it. And again, it's not always things that you want to fucking hear. But it shows you how to manage suffering. There'd be bits that you'd reject or whatever, but there'd be bits that are powerful that would sink in. Anyway, that's that song. Every line from that song is from Job.

SHANE: I didn't know that. I mean, I know the story of Job, but I didn't realise that about the song. I think all the titles are brilliant actually. I love titles like 'The Glory Of Jah'. That's a fucking brilliant song!

SINÉAD: Every line from that is scripture as well. It comes from the *Book Of Samuel*.

OLAF: I really liked 'I Don't Know How To Love Him' as well.
SINÉAD: Well, I didn't write that. That's by Tim Rice and Andrew Lloyd

Webber. It's from *Jesus Christ Superstar*.

OLAF: Well... I'll just hang my head in shame! I genuinely didn't know that.

SHANE: *KERSSHHHSSSHHH!*

SINÉAD: You're a bit younger than all of us so maybe you just missed it *[laughs]*. We all had that soundtrack in our houses growing up. But just because I didn't write it, doesn't mean you can't ask me about it.

SHANE: It's a great track. It's the best fucking version of it that I've ever heard. Actually, I think this album is probably the best thing you've ever done. You know worra mean? At some stage of the game you just go... *[whistles]*... and you think, screw it, let's just have some fun, and I'll say exactly what I mean. And, like, whether I write it or whether I didn't, don't really matter. I've ripped loads of stuff outta the *I Ching* and stuff like that.

OLAF: How do you write songs, Sinéad?

SINÉAD: It's different every time, really.

SHANE: I don't really know how songs come to me. It's a bit like comparing people to each other or something. Sometimes I can hear a song coming through, but I don't really like it so I let it go. Mostly, I either get bloody silence or I get... *[laughs]*. Which is fine by me because I love doing covers. Doing covers is a bit of a release, innit?

SINÉAD: It can be. Definitely.

OLAF: Would you two work together again?

SHANE: Definitely *[nods]*.

SINÉAD: Oh yeah.

OLAF: 'Haunted' was a brilliant duet.

SHANE: That was a great version alright. It's funny, you talk about record company pressure. Originally I just wanted to produce her doing it, but, now, looking back, at that duet, it's good. It's a different thing, you know. Actually, what's your favourite... nah, that's a stupid bloody question! *[laughs]*

SINÉAD: No, go on. What?

SHANE: Have you got a favourite track that you've recorded? Actually, that is a ridiculous question because I couldn't answer it myself.

SINÉAD: No, it'd probably take a long time to answer because there's so many. And it changes all the time anyway.

OLAF: Did you record 'Haunted' together? As in, in the same studio at the same time?

SINÉAD: I can't remember. Did we?

SHANE: Yeah, we did. There were a couple of really great musicians there at the time. And there was a bit of a row.

SINÉAD: Was there?

SHANE: Yeah. *[Mumbles incoherently]*. Ya know worra mean, like.

SINÉAD: All I remember was rehearsing the song with you for *Top Of The Pops*. Me and you were in my dressing room rehearsing it, and you kept falling asleep. But it was really clever. I'd sing my verse and you'd be looking like you were asleep, and I'd be going, 'Shit, he's not gonna wake up'. But you'd always wake up when you had to sing your bit. It was incredible.

OLAF: You're a true professional, aren't you, Shane?

SHANE: I sing in my sleep. I talk in my sleep. That's the only joy you'll get out of me, darlin'! *[laughs]*. I even tap my foot!

SINÉAD: Actually, if you don't mind, I wouldn't mind finishing up now, because I'm kinda fucked!

OLAF: Any final words for your fans?

SINÉAD: Em... *[pauses and pulls face]*. I don't know. Actually, I don't wanna say anything to my fans. I don't wanna be all gacky and be saying things to my fans... *[adopts American accent]* like some country star, you know.

SHANE: Are you happy with the interview?

SINÉAD: I love it, yeah. I *think* ...

SHANE: *KERSSHHHSSHHH!!!*

{JUNE, 2007}

SELECTED RECORDINGS: 2000-2010

CHAPTER FOURTEEN:
Chuck Palahniuk

"The kid looks around for something that might do the job. A ballpoint pen's too big. A pencil's too big – and rough. But dripped down the side of the candle, there's a thin, smooth ridge of wax that just might work. With just the tip of one finger, this kid snaps the long ridge of wax off the candle. He rolls it smooth between the palms of his hands. Long and smooth and thin."

It's the penultimate night of the Cúirt International Festival of Literature, and American author Chuck Palahniuk is reading onstage in Galway's Town Hall Theatre. Soberly attired in a crisp white shirt and neatly pressed black trousers, and speaking in a distinctively nasal accent, he could be a middle-manager at Microsoft delivering an annual report. Except that 'Guts' – his infamous short story about masturbation gone wrong – is about as far removed from a Microsoft annual report as it's possible to get. A manual report, more like…

"Stoned and horny, he slips it down inside, deeper and deeper into the piss slit of his boner. With a good hank of the wax still poking out the top, he gets to work."

There's a full house, and just about everybody in it collectively groans in disgust. Somebody in the balcony passes out (later, I'll hear that their fall resulted in a cut forehead and a chipped tooth), and there's a brief interruption as the fainter is helped out of the theatre. The number of people who've keeled over at public readings of 'Guts' is now officially in three figures. A few moments later, Palahniuk continues, "Even now, he says those Arab guys are pretty damn smart. They've totally reinvented jacking off. Flat on his back in bed, things are getting so good, this kid can't keep track of the wax. He's one good squeeze from shooting his wad when the wax isn't sticking out anymore."

It's all a very long way from Seamus Heaney (who was standing on the same stage two nights earlier). People are shifting uncomfortably in their seats, biting their fingers, holding in their nervous giggles and horrified moans. Literary events are rarely this discomforting. Palahniuk is less than half-way through 'Guts'. Things can only get worse. "The thin wax rod, it's slipped inside. All the way inside. So deep inside he can't even feel the lump of it inside his piss tube."

More squeamish groans, more muffled shrieks of laughter. You could probably power the Town Hall for a month with the tension in the room. "From downstairs, his mom shouts it's supper time. She says to come down – *right now!*"

It all suddenly proves too much for one rapidly purpling audience member, seated about two-thirds of the way back. Middle-aged, balding, and undoubtedly a Walter Mosley fan (the LA crime novelist read first tonight), he certainly didn't pay good money for this onanistic horror show.

"THIS IS PURE SHITE!" he angrily roars, shooting up from his seat. "YOU'RE NOTHING BUT AN AMERICAN CULTURAL IMPERIALIST! WE SHOULD BE HEARING IRISH WRITERS INSTEAD OF THIS SHITE!"

Annoyed audience members attempt to hush him, but the guy's going anyway, banging past knees as he heads towards the aisle, dragging a backpack and a long coat with him, and continuing to angrily register his protest as he leaves. "PURE SHITE AMERICAN PORNOGRAPHY! YOU SHOULD BE ASHAMED!"

As the theatre staff hurriedly escort the enraged protestor to the nearest exit, an unperturbed Palahniuk leans into the mike and calls gently after him, "But... you're going to miss *the ending*." The crowd bursts into loud cheers and spontaneous applause.

Culturally Imperialistic American Pornographer: One.

Disgruntled Balding Irish Crank: Nil.

Rewind about six hours. *Hot Press* is being introduced to the author in the lobby of the Galway Radisson. Palahniuk (pronounced *'Paul-Ah-Nick'*) looks nothing at all like the man I'd expected to meet. All the dust-jacket photographs I've seen were of an intense, brooding, long-haired biker type. But he's obviously had a haircut, and left his leathers back home in Portland.

As the *Guardian's* Bob Flynn quietly comments, the 44-year-old looks a lot like David Byrne. Actually, he looks like a David Byrne stalker. Abnormally normal. His handshake is firm, but not especially friendly, and his eyes are elsewhere. Maybe it's just jetlag, but my first impressions are that he'd really rather be doing something else. He's disinterested, like the aloof older brother of the girl you brought to your Debs. But then, as I'm already aware, he has pretty good reasons to distrust journalists. This is a shame, because I really want him to like me.

Although I was aware that the movie *Fight Club* had been based on his novel, I first discovered his work when I picked up a battered copy of *Invisible Monsters* in a Thai guesthouse last year. A wildly imaginative, sophisticatedly druggy, and weirdly sexual story about a beautiful fashion model who gets her face blown off in a drive-by shooting, I was instantly hooked. I'd just gone through an intense J.G. Ballard phase, and Palahniuk's sparse, satirical prose was the perfect antidote – 'same, same, but different' (as they're fond of saying in Southeast Asia). Having devoured *Invisible Monsters* in two sittings, I immediately went looking for more.

Fortunately, he's popular with young western backpackers. Most second-hand bookstores in Thailand had at least a few of his books. Within a couple of weeks, I'd read almost all of his published novels – *Choke, Diary, Lullaby, Survivor,* and *Fight Club*. I actually enjoyed *Fight Club* the least, but only because I'd already seen the movie.

When I tell him all this, he simply nods and smiles. I offer to buy him a drink, and he requests a bottle of mineral water. He's obviously not the hard-partying type. Before I go to the bar, in mild desperation, I present him with the copy of *Palace of Wisdom* that I'd planned on giving him afterwards, in the hope that my book of collected interviews will impress him enough to open up to me. It seems to work. When I return from the bar, he's reading through it and smiling. "Wow!" he says, "you've met Michel Houellebecq. What's he like?"

We waste precious minutes of interview time discussing the works of Houellebecq and DBC Pierre (both of whom he greatly admires). Aware that Palahniuk spent much of his youth living in a Burbank, Washington, trailer park, I ask if he read much as a child, and hit the record button.

"I did, yeah," he nods. "But it took me forever to learn how to read. I was a really slow kid for reading and writing. And I think that's why I attached to it so much – because when I finally got it, there was so much joy that I wasn't the idiot of my family any more. So that's why I got stuck on books."

Were your sisters and brother academic?

"They were all bright. They were all the valedictorian of their class. I wasn't, but they all were. But, in my family, it was very important to my folks that we all studied."

His favourite childhood read was Jack London's classic *Call of the Wild*. It was the novel that inspired him to want to become a journalist in later life.

"My younger brother and I both loved that book so much that I really thought that being an adult was just gonna be just one glorious adventure. So I figured that if I became a journalist I could do that. Everyday would be something different. And it'd be meeting interesting people all the time. And I just didn't anticipate how poorly journalism would pay. And I didn't anticipate that it would require me to go to school board meetings or city council zoning meetings. So I only did it for around six months after college."

Of course, not too many kids from Washington trailer parks study anything at college (unless it's at the McDonald's-owned Hamburger University). He bristles slightly when I mention the words "poor white trash," but acknowledges that the description is probably accurate.

"I definitely would *[describe it as that]*. My little brother's done really well. He's an engineer for Chevron and he lives in South Africa. Both my sisters have done really well. And one day, one of my sisters made a mistake talking to my mother of saying, 'We haven't done really bad for poor white trash'. And my mother was so hurt by hearing us referred to as 'poor white trash' that it's been a sore point in our family ever since. My grandparents got the first tombstone that anyone in my family's ever had because of *Fight Club* money. It was the first time that someone in my family could afford a luxury like a tombstone. It was really nice."

His parents, Carol and Fred Palahniuk, separated and divorced when he was 13, leaving Chuck and his three siblings to live, on and off, with their maternal grandparents at their cattle ranch in eastern Washington. Did the stigma of coming from a broken (mobile) home make you a weirdo or an outsider in high school?

"I was a little bit, but I was more of a working kid. I got out and I got a job when I was 14, and then I worked throughout the rest of high school. Sometimes we stayed with my grandparents, but mostly I lived with mom, and visited dad. My father had a new marriage every two years – like clockwork."

Sounds like one of the characters in your books!

"Or most of my peers!" he laughs. "You know, I still remember my friend Cindy at a toga party 20 or 25 years ago, when we were really drunk, and we were sitting in her basement. She was really drunk and she was leaning on me and she went, 'My mom, let me tell you about my mom – my mom gets married *a lot*'. And it was such a perfect line for my entire generation. And it went into *Invisible Monsters*. Our parents got married as a hobby."

When Chuck turned 18, he was taken aside by his father and let in on a dark Palahniuk family secret. He wrote about it in 'Consolation Prizes', the final essay in his excellent 2004 journalism collection *Non-Fiction*: "My father was four in 1943 when he hid under the bed as his parents fought, and his 12 brothers and sisters ran into the woods. Then his mother was dead, and his father stomped around the house looking for him, calling for him, still carrying the shotgun."

To make matters just that little bit weirder, he and his siblings had often spent their summers sleeping in the actual 'murder room' of the old family house in Idaho. That disquieting realisation aside, his father's revelation explained a lot to him. "I think in one way it meant that my father didn't really have any... sort of... parenting. My father pretty much had to make it up. I think that's why he was such a poor father, he'd never been given any kind of effective model for what to do."

He takes a sip of water and nervously twists the tarnished ring on his finger – it's his late father's wedding band. "But they did their best. For really poor people who had very little guidance of their own, I think they did really well. Like, most of the people I went to school with, my mom was always sending me obituaries. They're all dead or in prison, you know."

A solid student, Palahniuk graduated from the University of Oregon's School of Journalism in 1986, and then relocated to Portland. He worked for a local newspaper for about six months, but finding the daily grind of hackwork too imposing, he began working as a diesel mechanic instead.

"I wasn't making good money in journalism. So to pay off my student loan and to get a new car – because my car was just a piece of shit – I started at Freightliner. I lied. I made a fake resume that said I'd been a teen mechanic, a diesel truck technician, and I got an apprenticeship on the assembly line. And I did that for several years. And then I became a service documentation specialist. I was still a mechanic, but I wrote about what I did as well. And I got shipped around the country to do recall procedures – to work on trucks that'd been recalled."

Was there some subconscious reason for making the move from being a trained journalist to a diesel mechanic?

"Just lack of funds," he shrugs. "You know, once I started drawing a journeyman's wage, there was no way I was gonna leave that money behind and go back into a market where I was going to be five, six, ten years older than all of my entry-level peers."

Hilariously, he wasn't the only journalist getting his hands dirty at Freightliner. "The assembly line was filled with guys who had journalism degrees!" he laughs. "We used to joke about it. I remember one guy, Ken, once said that they should teach welding in journalism school, because if you know welding you get an extra $2 an hour – the welding differential. And there were a lot of guys who had just started to do that for a couple of years ... and then stayed until they were 65."

Although he still occasionally did a little freelance journalism, he actually stayed at Freightliner until his writing career began to properly take off. This took well over a decade: he spent most of his 20s working on the line.

"I didn't read anything between high school and turning 30," he admits. "You know, there was always something better to do than reading. I couldn't find a single book that really interested me. I watched TV constantly. I didn't start reading or writing until I was 30. Everything was better than books."

He blames this intellectual apathy on his chronic marijuana and television habits (both of which he's since kicked). "Oh my god – marijuana was my *entire* twenties," he recalls. "Even in high school. But I didn't really start writing until after I gave up dope. I could do journalism on marijuana; if I had to go to an event and cover it, I could do that. I couldn't keyboard very well, though! But giving up television and giving up marijuana really happened at about the time I started writing."

Perhaps unsurprisingly, at some point in his stoner late-twenties, Chuck began to feel that there was something missing from his life. Raised a Catholic, and wanting to do something more spiritually satisfying than fixing diesel engines, he volunteered to work for a homeless shelter.

"I was doing that because I hated my life so much," he explains. "I was just so miserable. And I started going to a church. I thought, 'I'll go to church and see if it makes me happy'. They had a 'giving tree' in my church at Christmas, and you had to pull an ornament off, and it was a kindness you would do for somebody else. And my kindness was to take a hospice patient on a 'date' – quote unquote – and it ended up being this hospice where really young charity cases go to die of hepatitis or HIV or whatever. But the only thing I could do was drive them – I didn't have any nursing skills or cooking skills or anything like that. And so I would drive them to whatever they wanted to do before they died. And I would end up taking them to their support groups. And I would end up sitting in on all of these support groups full of people dying. I felt so inauthentic sitting there."

Kind of, 'Ha, ha, you're dying – and I'm not!'

"*Exactly!*" he guffaws. "Ha, ha! But you can't really say that. You really can't say: 'Just go on with your dying, I'm just here for the free coffee!'"

The experience of holidaying in other people's misery totally cured his spiritual malaise, and lifted him out of the funk of depression in which he'd been wallowing in.

"I felt *sooo* good after those groups. I came out of those groups thinking, 'I'm $17,000 in debt, I've got a shitty car, I've got a job I hate – but, goddammit, I'm not *dying*. I am not one of those dying people'. And then I started sort of fictionalising it in my head, making up a story about somebody who just goes to those groups to feel better. And that became a short story that eventually became part of *Fight Club*."

He also became a member of an anarchic group called the Cacophony Society in his twenties, and is still a regular participant in their mischievous activities. These include the annual 'Santa Rampage' in Portland (a prank/alcohol-fuelled public Christmas party where everyone descends on the town wearing a Santa costume).

Such antics would later form the inspiration for *Fight Club's* 'Project Mayhem'.

"Somebody brought me a flyer for an underground party when I worked at Freightliner. It was called 'Voodoo Wedding' and it was just this big tropical-themed rave. And at one point they started throwing raw chicken entrails out over the dancefloor, and people just freaked and screamed and slipped and fell down and fought to get away from these chicken entrails. And I just had a blast. It was the most fun I'd ever had at a party. And after that I became part of the Cacophony Society."

Still bored, in his early thirties, he began attending a creative writing workshop, run by author Tom Spanbauer. He wound up discovering a hitherto hidden talent. "Every Thursday night I'd go to Tom's house and have red wine with a bunch of people I liked, and we all read our work. And it kept me working because every week I had to bring something. My friend Monica is a really great writer, so I had to bring something better than Monica."

Were you the class star from the beginning?

"No, Monica was really good too. Sometimes Suzy would bring in something absolutely incredible, or Rick would."

Have Monica, Suzy or Rick been published?

"No, they haven't published," he admits. "Monica has got a book coming out next year. I'm taking her on my tour next year, because I really like her work and I hope she gets a good reception."

He tours a lot these days – reading in bookstores, theatres, libraries, nightclubs or wherever. He says it's important to him to go out and meet his readers.

"I'd never been to a reading until I started doing them. It's really important for me to demonstrate to young people that they can do this. That our culture is something that we generate ourselves, that human beings do this. Because, with my upbringing, I just thought that everything was decided in New York and sent out to the world. I didn't really realise that *people* decided. I never knew I had that kind of power. And so, in a way, I wanna just physically be there to prove that human beings do this."

So are you an altruist?

"No, I'm basically just a bored person who wants to have that life full of ongoing adventures that I wanted to have as a little kid."

You've written in *Non-Fiction* about the loneliness of the novelist's life – spending your entire life jerking off in front of a computer screen in a darkened room.

"Yeah. Wow! I managed to successfully sidestep having an entire life. Good for me! But I don't want that. I'd much rather be out at parties listening to people. Because this – this – part of my job is really, really draining."

Much of Chuck's raw material comes directly from the mouths of strangers he encounters at signings or readings. "It's typically at events that people will come up and tell me incredible stories – stories that will become the next book or whatever. A lot of it is research, a lot of it is socialising and a lot of it is... testing. Like, I'll take something like 'Guts' on the road and I'll read it slightly differently in every market to find out where the laugh comes, what I can change to heighten the tension. It's same as doing vaudeville, where you sort of perfect a little act."

So do you see yourself as a performance artist?

"Only a performance artist because Tom Spanbauer insisted that we read our work out loud. And Tom's idea was that it's gotta do its job in seven to 10 minutes, and it's gotta do its job out loud, and when you read out loud, you instantly find out where it fails and where it succeeds. So it was just a practise that we all got into."

Backtrack to the early 1990s: before he was even dreaming about going on book tours, Palahniuk discovered that although he had a gift for fiction writing, success didn't happen overnight. His first book, *If You Lived Here, You'd Be Home Already*, remains unpublished.

"It was just awful – *awful*," he says, shaking his head. "The only part that survived, that I used in *Fight Club*, is Marla's speech about the condom being the glass slipper of our generation. You put it on, you dance all night with a stranger, you throw it away – the condom, not the stranger. That's the only tiny part of that whole 700-page novel that survived."

His next attempt was *Invisible Monsters*, which was rejected by numerous publishers for being too disturbing. "It was rejected after being *almost* accepted by a dozen different houses. It was such a long sort of flirtation, with no fuck at the end. It was just so irritating."

He says he wrote *Fight Club* as a form of revenge – wanting to disturb one particular publisher even more than he had with *Invisible Monsters*. In the book, an unnamed narrator addicted to therapy groups meets a mysterious, charismatic and nihilistic stranger, and together they set up an underground network of bare-knuckle fight clubs, before getting further organised and waging war on corporate America.

A revised and expanded version of a short story he'd first published in the compilation *Pursuit of Happiness* (the story became Chapter Six of the novel), to his great surprise, it was instantly accepted. "In 1995 I sent the manuscript in, and an agent accepted it. It sold right away. I was really surprised."

And presumably delighted?

"You know, I was so high, I wish I could've bottled or somehow preserved it. I was just so incredibly happy and high for two or three days. And I then realised that the advance was incredibly low."

How much was it?

"It was $6,000. It's the kind of advance that they call 'kiss-off money'. Because most of the people at the publishing house don't want to acquire this book, but they don't wanna piss off the editor who does wanna acquire it, so they offer money so low that they're hoping the writer walks away. But my agent had sent a manuscript copy to a movie scout named Raymond Bongiovanni in New York, and Raymond really, really liked it. And at the same time, I didn't realise that David Fincher had seen it in galley, and taken it to Brad Pitt. And by that point, Raymond had already gotten Twentieth Century Fox to option it by the winter of 1995 going into '96."

Strangely enough, it was actually Bongiovanni's death that gave birth to the movie. "And then Raymond died – he died of AIDS – and at his funeral it was all of these very influential people. And his obituary in *Variety* said at the very end, 'The last wish of Raymond Bongiovanni was that the gritty Chuck Palahniuk novel

Fight Club become a movie'. And it was just incredible. They even talked about *Fight Club* in his *eulogy*. And my agent called me from the funeral and said, 'You could not get better publicity than this'. And the whole thing was so gruesome and so sad – but also sort of funny. But that's what got it started."

In the autumn of 1999, David Fincher's controversial film version of *Fight Club* – starring Brad Pitt, Edward Norton and Helena Bonham Carter – was released. While it was widely critically acclaimed, media mogul Rupert Murdoch (the man whose $30 million paid for it) apparently wasn't very happy. "No, Murdoch didn't like it," Palahniuk says, "but his son apparently really loved it. That's what I was told by some people."

The movie shot straight to No.1 in the US box office in its first week of release, but it died soon afterwards.

"It *tanked!*" he laughs. "I still remember one of the producers calling me the very first weekend, and he was hysterical, just going, 'It's tanking! It's *TANKING!*' I was going, 'Shut the fuck up – I don't need to hear that!' But, luckily, it wound up being a huge DVD hit."

1999 was also the year in which terrible personal tragedy struck. Several months before *Fight Club's* release, Chuck's father, Fred Palahniuk, had answered a lonely hearts ad (under the title 'Kismet') and started to date a woman named Donna Fontaine. She had recently put her ex-husband, Dale Shackelford, in prison for sexual abuse, and Shackelford had vowed to kill her as soon as he was released. He made good on his threat. Late one night at the end of May, 1999, Fred and Donna were returning to her home in Kendrick, Idaho, when Shackelford ambushed them. He shot them both, then dragged their bodies into the house, before setting it alight. Chuck went to the coroner's office alone to identify his father's burnt corpse.

"None of my siblings would come with me, which was really irritating," he recalls, twisting the wedding ring. "I took his hand and moved it, and it was definitely him."

In the spring of 2001, Shackelford was found guilty on two counts of first-degree murder and sentenced to death. Chuck had personally requested that his father's killer receive the ultimate penalty. "They asked me what I would prefer," he recounts. "They asked all of the nearest relatives what they'd prefer – and at the time I said I would prefer the death penalty."

Did your brother and sisters agree? "They didn't even respond, they were so torn-up. I think my little sister went to the trial with me, but I can't remember if she stated her preference."

Is Shackelford still in prison?

"He will be forever and ever. The appeals process is gonna take at least 25 or 30 years, so it's almost a moot point."

Were you a supporter of capital punishment before that?

"I'd never given it a thought until I sat down with the medical examiner for that jurisdiction. And he brought out a thick folder and he said, 'I'm not supposed to show you this, but these are all the crimes this man has committed since he was seven-years-old. These are all of the people he's put in hospital, these are all the lives he's destroyed'. And after I'd seen this enormous amount of misery that this man had generated – since he was *seven* – I thought, maybe in this case we should resolve this man's life."

Had you met your father's new girlfriend?

"I'd talked to her over the phone. Just a couple of times. But that was the extent of it."

In the wake of his father's murder, Chuck Palahniuk began working on a new novel called *Lullaby*, in which an investigative journalist discovers an ancient African culling poem that kills anybody who hears it spoken aloud. First, though, he released *Choke* (a satire about sex-addiction and how to make money from the Heimlich Manoeuvre), which in 2001 became his first major *New York Times* best seller. He'd now moved from being a cult figure to a mainstream literary celebrity.

Fame can have its drawbacks, as he discovered when he was interviewed by *Entertainment Weekly* journalist Karen Valby in 2003. During the course of the interview, Chuck admitted off-the-record that he was living with his long-term boyfriend (it had previously been assumed by many newspapers that he was married to a woman). As he tells it, Valby began taunting him with a series of telephone calls, telling him she was going to 'out' him in her article. In response, Chuck put an angry audio recording on his website, not only revealing that he's gay, but also making negative comments about Valby. When her interview finally appeared, though, it made no mention of his sexuality, aside from describing him as unmarried. The recording was swiftly removed from the site, but the whole incident still rankles.

"I thought that she had been very coy about her anger. And the article didn't mention the fact that she had called me repeatedly through the tour that year, sort of taunting me about what she was going to write. And there was so much left unsaid that, in my frustration, I just wanted people to somehow understand the enormous game that was being played."

Although some people accused him of being embarrassed about his homosexuality, he says he has no regrets.

"It was just as well," he sighs. "She wasn't the only person playing this game and I was getting this kind of passive-aggressive bullshit from so many people that I wanted to resolve this. My sexuality is not a big deal to me, you know."

What does Chuck think of mega-selling books like *The Da Vinci Code*?

"If they get people to read, they get people to read. So I can't really slam them. Harry Potter gets people to read."

Have you read any of the Harry Potter books?

"I tend to read shorter things like short stories," he says. "I have a real limited attention span. But I still think it's great that so many kids are reading because of things like Harry Potter."

Palahniuk is famous for diligently responding to every single fan letter he receives – often sending small joke-shop gifts (like plastic severed fingers or fake vomit) with his replies. Is that not becoming a burden at this point?

"You know, it was until I moved to a system of windows. When I know I'm gonna have a block of time, I can announce that as a mailing window, so that I know that I can answer all of the mail that I receive during that designated time. If the mail is just sort of trickling in, a few letters a day, it can take over. This way it all comes in at once, and I can be really good about responding to everything."

Do you have time to critique every story that someone sends to you?

"Not really. And also legally I've been warned not to – liability wise. But I always try and at least write back."

Of course, while fake plastic vomit is pretty cheap, it can still get expensive to send out one per reply. *The Observer's* Sean O'Hagan, who visited Palahniuk in Portland in 2005, reported witnessing the writer spending $25,000 on replying to 1,000 fan letters (enclosing boxed furry toys with each letter). Chuck isn't worried, though. After all, it's only money – and he's got plenty of it these days.

Cúirt organiser Siobhán Calpin comes over and asks me to wrap it up. So, with just a couple of minutes of Chucktime left, I ask are there any other movie versions of his novels on the cards. It turns out that almost all of them are currently in development.

"*Choke* has been cast. It was supposed to have started production by now, but there were some problems. Susan Sarandon's playing the mother, and they had Ryan Gosling playing the male lead, but he dropped out. *Lullaby* just got optioned by a German director. *Diary* – they have a screenplay and an Icelandic director.

"What else? Oh – *Invisible Monsters* is optioned. The writer/director team that made *Constantine* last year have *Survivor*.."

His most recent novel (actually, more a series of interconnected short stories – including 'Guts') is *Haunted*, published last year to less than ecstatic reviews. What's coming next?

"Just before I left to come here, I turned in next year's book," he tells me. "And it's a book called *Rant*. And it's a big biography – written in the style of an oral biography, where you interview hundreds of people and then you parse the interviews together topically. And so it's borrowing that non-fiction form to tell a biography of a fake person. It's probably the closest thing to *Fight Club* that I've ever done."

Would you ever consider doing a memoir?

"No, because it would be so boring," he smiles. "When you read the stories that I write, you're really seeing maybe the best anecdotes of a thousand people crammed together. You're seeing the best of the best that I could find in the world to present. And a memoir would just be sort of one fairly banal, poor white thing after another. Who wants to read anecdotes about me watching *Gilligan's Island* every afternoon of my childhood?"

Calpin returns to say that time's definitely up. As I gather my stuff, Chuck asks me to sign his copy of *Palace of Wisdom*, while he signs my copy of *Non-Fiction*. As we each inscribe the other's book, I ask will he be reading 'Guts' in the Town Hall later tonight.

"I'm not sure," he says, stroking his chin. "'Guts' is a joy to read – it is a joy. I can go up there completely wasted and tired and angry, but reading that story is just so much fun. At the same time, I'm reading with Walter Mosley later so it kind of depends on what the audience looks like. I don't wanna offend Mosley's audience with something that's too much. I'll probably do something else. What do you think?"

"I think you should definitely read 'Guts,'" I tell him. "I'd say they'll love it."

{MAY, 2006}

SELECTED RECORDINGS: 2000-2010

CHAPTER FIFTEEN:
Dolly Parton

As she strides confidently across the luxuriously carpeted reception lounge of the Shelbourne Hotel's vast (and vastly expensive) Princess Grace Suite, the first thing that strikes me about Dolly Parton is how aptly named she is. Sugar, spice and all things silicone, the legendary country and western singer actually looks like a doll, albeit more like the kind you'd find in an upmarket sex shop than in Toys 'R' Us. From across the room, she's the living embodiment of all that Taliban fighters expect to find ready and waiting for them in the heavenly afterlife.

A high-heeled, peroxide pixie with perfect teeth, torpedo breasts and an hourglass figure, she looks like a million dollars (despite the fact that her gold sequined dress only cost something in the region of thirty grand). What she definitely doesn't look is 56 years of age. At least, not until she gets close enough for you to note the thickness of the make-up. Even so, she'd easily pass for well-maintained early forties. And as the old saying goes, you still wouldn't turf her out of bed for eating crisps.

As she proffers a perfectly manicured hand, I compliment her on her youthful appearance, remarking that she looks exactly as I remembered her from her 1982 movie *The Best Little Whorehouse In Texas*. I'm being more polite than truthful, but the compliment works wonders.

"Well, I've been around for a long time, but I'm pretty well preserved," she admits, with a beam so wide you could happily hang yourself off it. "I'm a cartoon anyway and cartoons never age. It's like Mickey Mouse never ages, Minnie Mouse never ages – so hopefully I never will."

Having said that, after four decades of fame, she's no longer a spring chicken. Despite my protests, I've only been granted a miserly 30 minutes in her company so, even before we've hit the couch, I've already asked if it bothers her that she's no longer the prettiest C&W chick on the block?

"No, not really because I really have been very fortunate," she says, in her treacly Tennessean drawl. "You've gotta look at it like it is. I've been in business for 40 years. I've won everything you can win, I've had hit records, I've got to travel, I've made good money. I appreciate that very much. So I would never begrudge other people. I still don't feel like I'm done, though. I truly am an artist, and my music is still my number one."

But don't you also have a thriving business empire to run?

"Well, I'm not doing it for money," she says, looking a touch offended. "It doesn't make any difference how much money I make because of all my other businesses. I'm not doing it for that. Thank God I've been fortunate. I don't mean this in a vain way either, what I'm about to say. I have joked about it, I've said that I had to get rich in order to sing like I was poor again. But I count my blessings more than I count my money.

"My music still burns in me," she continues, earnestly. "I never stopped writing, I never stopped doing any of that. Money will come if you do something good enough or if you stay at it, but I don't begrudge the young people. I'm not done yet. I don't care if I'm 100, I don't care if I'm 70, I don't care if I'm 60, I don't care if I'm 56 or however damned old I am – it's 56, I think! But it's like: I don't feel any different than I did when I left the Smoky Mountains and went to Nashville. I *feel* young, I feel excited about the business, I feel excited about my new dreams, I feel excited about the things I still wanna accomplish, I still *can* accomplish. So I'm still out there. I'm still an active person."

She sure is. In fact, Dolly Parton has been pretty active musically since the late '50s, when – having been spotted performing on a local TV station – the pretty and precocious 14-year-old daughter of impoverished Tennessee farmers (she's the fourth of 12 children) first signed to Mercury Records. Her 1962 debut *It's Sure Gonna Hurt* lived up to its title and completely bombed, but somebody somewhere twigged her obvious potential and it wasn't long before she was wowing national audiences on *The Porter Wagoner Show*. After a few successful years dueting with Wagoner, she quit and moved to Nashville.

The usual highs and lows of C&W life followed, you might say, but by the early '70s she was a regular visitor to the Country Top Ten with hits like 'Jolene' and 'Coat Of Many Colours'. She was also much in demand as a lyricist, with artists like Emmylou Harris, Olivia Newton John and Linda Ronstadt all covering her songs. In 1977, her cover of the Barry Mann/ Cynthia Weil song 'Here You Come Again' was a crossover smash, reaching high in the pop charts on both sides of the Atlantic, and making her an international superstar in the process.

A reasonably successful string of movies in the '80s – not to mention No.1 chart hits like 'Islands In The Stream' and 'Nine To Five' – gave her career momentum and despite a serious slowdown in the '90s (though the royalties from Whitney Houston's version of her song 'I Will Always Love You' probably kept the bank manager at bay) she's still going strong. Although she doesn't chart as regularly as she used to, nowadays she's considered a bona-fide icon and is recognised just about everywhere she goes on the planet. She practically got mobbed on Grafton Street in the centre of Dublin this morning; she cheerfully admits that she wouldn't want it any other way.

"I'd be disappointed if I went somewhere and nobody noticed me," she laughs.

Here today to do some interviews and TV appearances to promote her new album *Halos & Horns* (which we'll get to in a moment), she laments the fact that the last time she visited these shores was way back in 1984. "That's too long," she sighs. "I love Ireland and I love the Irish people. I'm part-Irish so this is kinda like coming home."

Olaf and Martin McDonagh

Shane, Sinéad and Olaf

Sinéad O'Connor & Shane MacGowan

Olaf and Chuck Palahniuk

SELECTED RECORDINGS: 2000-2010

Dolly Parton and Olaf

Jonathan Rhys-Myers

SELECTED RECORDINGS: 2000-2010

Mike Scott

Damien Rice

Tommy Tiernan and Olaf

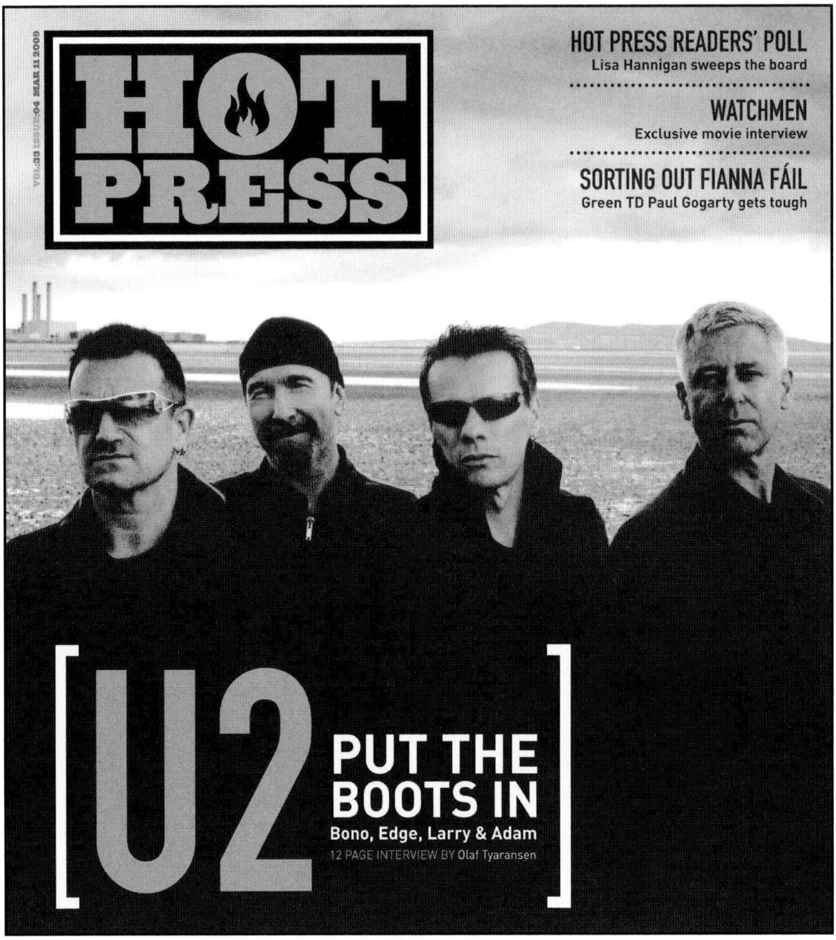

SELECTED RECORDINGS: 2000-2010

Bono, The Edge, Larry Mullen Jr and Adam Clayton on the cover of *Hot Press*

Bono and Olaf

Is it true that you're also part-Cherokee Indian?

"Yeah," she nods. "There's some Cherokee Indian blood in my mother's family. It was an illegitimate thing, so I mean it's not really in our genealogy. But my grandfather had told us many years ago – because my mother's people are very dark and we were always going, 'Where'd this come from? We're Irish and English and Scottish!' Well, there was the girl that the grandpa loved, and all that, who was Cherokee Indian. So anyway, somewhere down the road we've got some Cherokee – but mostly we're Irish. My father's people were Irish-Scottish and my mother's people were English-American, so we're a real mixture of everything."

A Dolly-mixture even! She probably does it with all the male journalists she meets, but when Dolly Parton is practically sitting in your lap, playfully examining the ring on your finger and huskily remarking on how *"purr-dey"* she finds you, it's hard not to be affected by it. Especially when her intoxicating perfume is getting you higher than heroin, and if you were willing to do the prison time you could actually reach out and touch a pair of magnificent breasts that you've been fantasising about ever since you were old enough to fantasise. All of which, in an awful-pun kind of way, brings me to uncomfortably shift my position on the couch and ask her about, em, Dollywood (that's the one in Tennessee, mind, not the one in my trousers).

"Dollywood is now in its 17th season," she says proudly. "And for those of your readers who won't know what it is, it's a theme park back home in Tennessee. Right now we're spread out over 150 acres but we have as much land as we need, and every year we develop some more parts to the park. And it's a family park. We have all the music and things like that."

Dollywood isn't just about music though. "We try to preserve our Smoky Mountain heritage," she explains. "We have an active sawmill, we make our own breads, a lot of our own foods, and all that kinda stuff. But we have all the music of the world, and we bring people from all over the world. In fact, we have a Festival Of Nations. We have our Irish groups as well: every year since we started it Irish groups have been coming to Dollywood. They love it – we really especially like them."

Would you ever think of tackling any traditional Irish songs yourself?

"Yes, absolutely. I hope to do some great Irish albums in the future. One of my big dreams is to come here and stay for a while and find some songs. It's in my DNA, the home of my soul. So I definitely am gonna do some Irish – some true Irish stuff – in the future."

When I ask her which Irish artists she admires, she's particularly gushing about Sinéad O'Connor.

"Oh she's got a fantastic new album out. I think she's going on the show I'm going on tonight. But I was listening to Sinéad's new album – somebody sent it over because she was going on the show – and it's fantastic. I love that Irish music. She's a great artist. I don't know her personally so I have no comment on any of that *(I hadn't said anything! – OT)*. But I think she's wonderful, I love her singing."

Going back to Dollywood for a moment, are you very involved in it personally?

"Yes I am," she affirms. "In fact, I wouldn't put my name on anything that I wasn't gonna be involved in. I'm just not one of those kinds of people. It's very important to me that things be of a certain quality, if I'm gonna be out promoting it and trying to earn people's money. But we do a lot of great work through the foundation there at Dollywood – we help with the health and education of the county, especially with the children. We have the Dollywood Foundation Imagination Library, where we give every child that's born in the county a book from the day they're born, once a month, until they start kindergarten. It's kinda like a head start, to teach children how to learn to love books and how to read – and even a lot of the parents don't know how to read that well so it really kinda gives them a little family moment. There's a lot of poor and underprivileged people in our part of the country. So it's a way to help.

"Not only do we have our amusement areas at the park – it's a theme park – we have a lot of wonderful programmes and things that go on there as well."

Of course, you may already be familiar with the delights of Dollywood from the special C4 show Graham Norton did from there last year. "That was fun!" she squeals. "I enjoyed working with him. He was so fun. We were just so compatible the way our little energies worked together."

As a gay icon, do you get on with gay men generally? "I have a lot of gay fans and a lot of gay friends. I have a huge gay following – male and female. But it didn't matter if Graham was gay or not, he's still silly and fun and magical. Our personalities really gelled."

Talk turns to the subject of her new album, *Halos & Horns*, a record which she claims came about entirely by accident, when the song demos she was producing went much better than expected. "I didn't intend to produce a record," she says. "I was just producing these song demos. But it started sounding so good that I was getting really excited. I thought, 'I don't need to clutter this up or add any other people'. I told Steve (Buckingham – her regular producer), 'This stuff I'm doing is turning out really good'. He said, 'Just go with it'. I decided I wanted to use everybody from up home, or at least fresh people. There was nothing heavy or hard about it. I just went in with the pickers and we all kicked ideas around. That's how you produce great records anyway – let talented people do what they do. It's fairly 'live', because I'm not the kind of singer who can start and stop and go back and get the same feeling. I just had a big time doing this."

Although it's mostly a collection of folk and bluegrass songs, the album closes with a remarkable cover of Led Zeppelin's 'Stairway To Heaven'. "It's getting a lot of attention," she grins. "In fact, we're gonna be doing it in our concerts when we come here, we've worked it up as an encore 'cos people wanna hear it. But I just love the song and my husband loves the song, and since I'm doing a lot of this bluegrass stuff and I had great success with the song 'Shine' – which we won a Grammy for and which was another song from the rock field – so I thought I'm gonna tackle it. What's the worst they can do – just won't like it?"

Have Page and Plant heard it?

"Yes and they loved it. Robert's been out on tour so he's been doing a lot of interviews. And he seems to make mention of it a lot – I guess because people are asking him about it – and he says something different every time, but he seems to like it. He says he really likes what I did with it, and that makes me feel good."

Another track 'Hello God' is obviously her response to the tragic events of 9/11: *"This old world has gone to pieces/ Can we fix it, is there time?/ Hate and violence just increases/ We're so selfish, cruel and blind."*

"I'm gonna perform that on the CMA award show, with a big choir and all," she enthuses. "They thought it would be a good song to do, instead of doing all the usual patriotic stuff. As a writer and an emotional person, you write about things that you feel. And I was also trying to write about the feelings of other people who maybe aren't able to write them down."

Did 9/11 give you a sense of, 'What the hell am I doing with my life'?

"Well, it did. I think that's what it did more than anything else with everybody. It just made us all know how small life really is, how fragile we really are, and how anything can happen in the blink of an eye to change everything. And then it makes you think, 'Oh my god – we were so spoilt to think that nothing could ever happen to us!' And it did! And wow! Then you start thinking about your family, then you start thinking about your soul, you start thinking about your religion and your faith. And is there a God? And if there is then…? And that's kinda what 'Hello God' is about. Hello God, are you out there? Are you listening? Or have we done pissed around so bad and so long that you ain't even hearing us anymore? Now of course, we wanna run to you and have you fix it!"

And what does Dolly Parton think about her president's war on terrorism?

"Oh, don't start asking me a bunch of political questions!" she laughs, playfully slapping my hand. "I'm not gonna go there! I'm a singer, I'm a writer. I'm not gonna get into all that. I definitely have my opinions and they're very strong, but I don't voice them publicly because one thing gets taken out of context, and suddenly you're about that. Believe me, I ain't smart enough nor good enough to know what one should do."

But although you play the dumb blonde, you're so obviously not… (I gush).

"Well one of my first hit records was called 'Dumb Blonde' and that's kind of followed me around over the years," she smiles. "But the song says just because I'm blonde, don't think I'm dumb, because this dumb blonde ain't nobody's fool. But I'm sure I'm a fool sometimes but I'm not fool enough to talk politics … so what else you got?"

The album also features 'What A Heartache' – a song that first appeared on the *Rhinestone* movie soundtrack in 1984 (she also starred in the film). The movie bombed, but the song's actually not bad. I ask her how serious she is about her acting career?

"It's really more of a sideline," she says. "I enjoy it but it has to be just the right thing, something I would enjoy doing. And I'm not getting offered a lot of the great scripts now. Same as like with the country music field – you reach a certain age and you're no longer 'new country' and you're not gonna be played on the radio, the new artists are. So then you find a way, like I'm doing now, to still get your music out to a crowd that appreciates what the music's for. Same with the movies. I still would like to do the movies, but it's not my first love. The music is my first love."

When I mention another album track 'These Old Bones', we get on to the subject of graveyards. I've read somewhere that Dolly has been writing songs in graveyards for years. Is it true?

"I love 'em!" she laughs. "In fact, I just found some old graveyards where I'm gonna go to do my video for 'These Old Bones'. They're quiet and peaceful and beautiful and they're well kept. And I also make up stories about all the people under the tombstones, what their life was like. So they give me great ideas for stories."

And what would you like written on your own tombstone?

"Em…," Dolly scrunches her features. *"You think she's here – but she ain't!"*

Behind every great woman lies a great man, and the man behind Dolly Parton is her husband of nearly 40 years – a former asphalt contractor named Carl Dean. In true C&W style, they met in a laundrette on her very first day in Nashville.

"We've been together 38 years and we've been married 36," she says. "We never had children of our own but we raised five of my younger brothers and sisters that lived with us, we sent them to school and all that."

How does a marriage between a cultural icon and an asphalt contractor survive that long? "It's a good question. I think part of it is because we're not together all the time – I travel a lot. Another reason is because we're not in the same business, and he doesn't try and meddle in what I do. He was in asphalt paving for a long time and now he buys property and cleans it off. He's a heavy equipment kind of guy and he just kinda does his own thing. But we're good friends and he's secure in who he is, I'm secure in who I am, and we just have enough stuff that we enjoy that we have in common that makes it great, and enough stuff that's not in common to make it interesting."

Of course, just because Dolly's wearing a wedding band, it doesn't mean she doesn't flirt or hasn't had extra-marital relationships in the past. At least, not if her lyrics can be believed. I mention her controversial '70s song 'Bargain Store': *"My life is like unto a bargain store/ And I might just have what you're looking for/ If you don't mind the fact that the merchandise is used/ But with a little mendin' it can be as good as new."* Many C&W radio stations actually banned the track when it was first released.

"They wouldn't even play it, yeah, because of what it said," she recalls. "But you know what? I've lived a lot in my time. I said I was married, I didn't say that I was dead. It's like one of those things. Just cause I'm married doesn't mean that I don't flirt or tease or whatever. But that song is so true of everybody. Most of my heartache songs have not been brought on by my husband. He's been kinder to me than all the other men."

Despite this, she's insistent that when it comes to preserving good marital relationships, honesty isn't always the best policy.

"My first country hit was called 'Just Because I'm A Woman' and when it was written my husband and I had been married for about a year, and we were just as happy as we could be," she recalls, laughing. "And I just felt compelled to be totally honest with him and tell him everything. So I told him some stuff that he wished I hadn't told him, and I wished I hadn't told him – I wish to this day that I'd never told him. I was just trying to be honest about it. It was the only time in our whole marriage that there was like a little cold spot. But it was like one of those things that I wanted to kill myself – because I thought I was doing a good thing just having this totally open relationship, which had nothing to do with any other ones, but it was just that I was feeling that because I did love him so much, I just wanted to come clean about some… other stuff. So believe me – you can write this on paper – if you're out there, do not tell shit you don't need to be tellin'. Because it'll come back to haunt you!"

Not only has Dolly's marriage survived throughout her showbiz career, she also seems to have successfully avoided the pitfalls of drink and drugs.

"Well, I just have a good time doing what I do. I didn't say I hadn't done any of that stuff. It's just that I've never had a problem with it. Anything I do I try to do in moderation… or in great secrecy . I've gotta be very discreet! But no, I've never had a problem with any of that. I'm just very anchored, very serious about my work and very anchored in my spiritual life…"

The record company man reappears, accompanied by our infuriated photographer Mick Quinn (who's been given just a couple of minutes to get his shots). To my great disappointment, I realise that the interview is basically over but, as she ever-so-professionally pouts for his camera, I manage to get in one last question.

Does Dolly Parton have a motto in life?

"Yeah, do everything – all the time," she laughs, as she poses. Then she looks over at me and winks conspiratorially. "And do *everyone!*"

{NOVEMBER, 2002}

SELECTED RECORDINGS: 2000-2010

CHAPTER SIXTEEN:
Jonathan Rhys-Myers

If fidgeting was an Olympic sport then Jonathan Rhys-Myers could effortlessly win gold for Ireland. The 23-year-old Dublin-born/Cork-bred actor just can't seem to sit still for a moment. Throughout our interview, he changes his position more often than a Flood Tribunal witness, constantly shifting in his chair, picking at his chicken sandwich, lighting Marlboros, flicking his hair, and fiddling with his mobile phone.

He doesn't look directly at you either, his eyes seeming to evasively flick every which way except at the person he's talking to. It's somewhat disconcerting for a while, but eventually I realise that he's not being rude. It's simply that, like many young actors, he's restlessness personified – a strikingly handsome, five-foot-something frame of typical thespian insecurity.

No wonder he's constantly moving. Although Rhys-Myers has now appeared in nineteen different movies, he's far from being in a position to rest on his laurels – and he knows it. His star is definitely on the rise, but it's not yet shooting. Until recently, he was best known for his role as the young assassin in Neil Jordan's *Michael Collins*. It was just a small part, but his looks made an impact with casting agents, and gradually his career began to snowball. He subsequently played a series of increasingly prominent roles in films like *The Loss Of Sexual Innocence*, *Velvet Goldmine*, *Titus Andronicus*, and the forthcoming *Prozac Nation*, as well as playing the sly Steerpike in the television series *Gormenghast*. Not formally trained as an actor, critics generally agree that, while he's far from flawless, he's steadily getting there. He doesn't demur, but his ambition and passion for his chosen craft is obvious. Having worked alongside the likes of Ewan McGregor, Anthony Hopkins, Rupert Everett, Minnie Driver and Christina Ricci, Rhys-Myers seems well on the way to making a major impact in the world of movie-making. For the moment, however, he comes across as someone with an awful lot to prove.

OLAF TYARANSEN: I understand you had a serious heart condition when you were an infant.

JONATHAN RHYS-MYERS: Yes. I had a weak heart and very weak kidneys, so I was kept for seven months in St. James's Hospital, Dublin, where I was born. I was in an incubator. Then I was in Dublin for another year-and-a-half, and then we went to Cork city. I shouldn't be smoking, really, you know *(lights one cigarette from the butt of another).*

Is that something that still affects you?
No. It hasn't occurred. At the same time you want to watch it.
What kind of upbringing did you have?
Definitely working-class Irish. I went to a State school, the whole ball-game. I knew what 'not-having' was, but *everybody* didn't have in the situation I was in. What my neighbours didn't have, I didn't have. And so I naturally didn't think of it as too rough a thing. It was only as I got older that I realised how underprivileged it was. When I started to get a little bit more privileged and able to get more things, I thought, 'God almighty, how did I live when I was a kid?' Actually I had everything I needed, in truth.
Your father left your mother when you were four?
Yes.
You've got three younger brothers. What do they do?
They're rock musicians. They've got a rock band. They live in Jersey, and they tour around the islands. They're incredibly fucking brilliant. And the thing is, it's not even a biased opinion, because I don't like their kind of music. I'm not into their music at all; I'm into a completely different kind of thing. But I recognise who's brilliant and who's not. And they're good. They're incredibly tight for their age.
You've got an incredibly posh accent. Did you always talk like that?
When I was a kid I used to talk with a Cork accent *(said in a comically strong Cork accent)*.
So did you deliberately refine your accent to do movies?
I started talking like this from about 17, when I started really getting into acting. I also started hanging around with a different type of person. I hung around with people who talked like this all the time… so I faked it.
Is it true that you were a bit of a troublemaker as a child?
Well, I was a *child*. I don't think there's any children that aren't troublemakers. Some kids get away with it, and some don't. I was one of those kids that never got away with it. My trouble always shone *(laughs)*. It outshone the others! I got thrown out of school aged fifteen, a very bad mistake. It was a monastery school in Cork. I suppose it wasn't their fault. I wasn't a terribly interested student. But it's very difficult to get a 15-year-old to sit down and learn something they don't particularly want to learn. Why would they? It's like I'm learning more from NWA than this geography class!
Was music always a big thing for you?
Music was always *huge* for me. I've related to music. Of course, everybody does. I probably thought it was a unique thing as a kid. It was like, 'Oh my god, I've got a song for every situation I've been in'. That's the way it is. But it was always instrumental music that kept up memories for me, rather than lyrics.
You sang a couple of tracks on the *Velvet Goldmine* soundtrack. Is that something you'd like to do again?
Yeah, of course. *Velvet Goldmine* was going to be wonderful if I could have had David Bowie's music, because everybody would have recognized it. I never really wanted to try and play Bowie. I just tried to play a rock artist who was an icon. It's very difficult to play an icon because they're ethereal and not real. So I had to

play the character as if *I* was not real, and try to detract myself from it as if I was a machine. Plus I couldn't use Bowie's music. So I was using music written by Grant Lee Buffalo and Michael Stipe, and Thom Yorke got involved with it – and it was incredibly brilliant stuff, but at the same time it wasn't the hits of the '70s, which I should've been singing. That would have made the character more believable – if I was standing up there singing 'Ziggy Stardust' instead of singing 'Tumbling Down'. A couple of in-people would have been into Cockney Rebel, but the mass audience wouldn't have.

What was your situation after you got expelled from school?
I tried to go to other schools but they weren't prepared to take a kid who couldn't behave and had been kicked out of a State school. They were rather dubious about that, and I suppose I didn't try as hard as I would now. But I'm a different age now, and I've copped myself on a bit more. I don't think it was an incredibly good move to get kicked out of school. It sounds cool, but I got very lucky. I went on the hop a lot because I wasn't happy being there. I wasn't happy with my life – either in school, at home, or with my friends. I was always a loner.

So did you just aimlessly bum around for a while?
I used to hang around the pool hall with my friend, Gordon McGregor. These guys came in one day, and asked if I wanted to go to an audition for *War Of The Buttons*. They came up to me and asked me, and I said, '*fuck off!*' They said, 'Come on – *please*'. So they brought me down to Skibbereen to meet John Roberts, and I liked him a lot. I spent a weekend there, and then I went home, and then they brought me back and auditioned me again. I nearly fucked it up because I got a phone call on the Monday night to come down Tuesday morning. I was so excited that I phoned my friend Gerry, and asked him to come over, and I stayed up till 8 o'clock in the morning and slept in till 11 o'clock! I fucked up the audition. I was an eejit, and that's why I lost that film. Apparently they thought I should have been in *The Outsiders* rather than *War Of The Buttons*. So I was a little bit too street-wise and mature for them, at that point anyway. I was very disgusted. I felt like a complete failure. I was completely self-pitying.

Is being from Cork important to you?
Hugely, yes. I don't spend much time there now, but I love it. Wonderful people. When I was growing up I never thought it was a shitty town, shitty people, I need to get away from it. I *never* thought that. People are shitty wherever you go *(laughs)*. What I wanted was their respect. No matter where they're from, no matter who it is. It could be a beggar in the street or the king of the world. I still want their respect equally. And I want to be able to do the same. I want to be able to give the same warmth and respect to a beggar as I give to a king. And I suppose I wanted to be rich because I wasn't.

Are you rich now?
I haven't got paid that much money for the films I've done. I'm not a millionaire or anything like that. But I bought my mother a house in Glanmire in Cork last year, and I was quite happy about doing that. I got her a little car and stuff, and now she's working for the first time in years, and she's very, very happy and independent, and she's got a new lease of life. Life really does begin at 40.

Is money important to you?
As important as it is to someone who is young and who grew up without it. I'd want to take care of myself. I'd like to be able to buy a house for myself and my girlfriend – to live in the countryside. But there's not lots of things I want. I don't want a fast fucking car. I don't want to go to expensive restaurants. I don't want clothes, and to date supermodels. I don't have to buy Tiffany diamonds for my girlfriend. Money is important because I'd like to get paid for what I do. But also it seems to be a sort of status symbol. So, yes, I'd love someone to pay me a million for a film – *joyous!* Of course I would, who wouldn't?

Obviously nobody's yet offered you that kind of fee...
My agent says they're running out of reasons to not cast me in these big films. I thought, for years, 'I don't look the way they want me to look'. And I've got over that. Then I thought, 'I'm not acting the way they want me to act'. And so I'm constantly going to be fighting with that, my whole life. So it's basically me getting in there, and seducing them into giving me the part. That's quite difficult because I'm not American, and so, before I go in for an audition, I have to make myself American.

How's your American accent?
It's alright now *(in flawless American accent).* I just did *Magnificent Ambersons.* I played someone from Indianapolis. So I'm going to go over there with that mid-American accent and 'ah shucks' attitude.

Do you have an interest in Irish politics?
I have an interest in Irish politics, but more the politics of the early 1920s – Michael Collins's era. Me being the man who shot him! You want to know the man you're going to kill. Any good samurai is going to check out his opponent, isn't he?

Is your Irishness important to you?
It's incredibly important. It's a wonderful country to be from. I say that when I go to Los Angeles, and I try to do auditions, that I've got to become American. I don't mind that. I liked growing up in Ireland. I don't think I'd have liked to have grown up in the US. Plus, it's given an antiquity to my soul. I come from a place that's got an awful lot of soul, history, culture, and a lot of magic about it. I like being Irish.

Do you find that there's a lot of begrudgery in Ireland?
No. *The Magnificent Ambersons* was the nineteenth film I made. And I thought, 'Oh god, I've made 19 films; shouldn't I be getting paid a lot of money?' Then I thought to myself, 'Well, I've never made a film that's made an awful lot of money'. I've never been in a successful box-office hit. It would be marvellous. I said to my friend, John Paul, when I first got into acting, 'Do you think I'll make it?' He said, 'No – I think you'll be a good actor, but I don't think you'll make it like Tom Cruise or anything like that'. And I was going, 'You're meant to be my mate, you're meant to say, *'Take on the world, man!' (laughs)* That's Ireland!

Who's your role model as an actor?
Nijinsky gives me more inspiration as an actor than anyone else. But I do think Peter O'Toole is extraordinary.

Are you quite a distracted person?
Yes, hyperactive I suppose.

You don't make very much eye contact. You look around a lot.
I do *(looking away)*. Sometimes then I'll just be in your face all the time. People do find me a bit too intense. I've had this problem when I've gone to auditions in the US. I'm far too intense.

Are you quite a dramatic person?
Yes, I'm a very dramatic person. I've got an awful lot of energy. I'm very hyperactive. And that comes out as being very dramatic. Even in the roles I play, people think I'm a very dramatic actor, almost operatic. Like driving a car is an opera, especially in Dublin. I can be scandalously dramatic.

Do you have many close friends?
Not many. I have some, and the ones I have are incredibly good friends. I've got one friend I've had about 10 years. I've got another friend, Gordon McGregor, who I haven't seen for ages, but he's one of my closest friends and always will be, regardless. Two of my brothers are very close friends, but I don't see them very often. But it's a blood-love and so they'll always be there. My girlfriend's my friend. Her sister's my friend.

Are you enjoying your life at the moment?
Sometimes I enjoy it, sometimes I don't. But I'm into self-discovery, and I don't think anyone who's into self-discovery is happy. It's not going to be what you expect it to be. There's that element of it. But at the same time, you get what you can out of it. I'm trying to be a great artist, and by trying to be a great artist you have to look at all the beautiful things, and you have to look at all the horrible things, and then find the beauty in them. It's very difficult to do. To become comfortable with horrible things means you're finding the natural beauty in them.

What are you doing work-wise at the moment?
I've just finished a film recently, but today I've been screentesting for Neil Jordan's film. It's magnificent. Neil is one of my favourite directors. I haven't got the part yet. I'm waiting for him to give me the part. If he does, I'll do it and put everything into it, and if he doesn't, I'll still love him as much as I do now. He gave me my second role, which was in *Michael Collins*. That was brilliant. The part was quite small, but in the eventual film it showed out a lot more. It was very good for me. There's something about him that is very artistic. He's someone I can look up to. I want his approval. There's a couple of directors whose approval I really want. It's not like I want millions of dollars and everyone screaming my name all the time. What I want is the support of people to help me achieve wonderful things in film.

You're extremely ambitious, aren't you?
Very. I was always hungry. I knew I was going to be unique in some way. How unique I don't know. I knew I was never going to have a normal job, a normal life. Some people never get roses thrown at them, but they never get sand kicked in their face either. I've had roses, and I've had sand kicked in my face.

What was the sand kicked in your face?
Rejection. Everything I've been rejected for, I've been really, really hurt by.

How about women?

I've had a very hard time with women. But I've made that hard time myself. I'm trying to understand women. But I can never truly understand them. The only thing I can do is accept. They're completely different creatures, and they've got a different way of thinking. If you accept them rather than try to understand them then you'll have a better time. A lizard can't understand what a bird feels like, and a bird can't understand what a lizard feels like.

Are you in a serious romantic relationship at the moment?

I'm in love with this girl called Chacha. She's the most beautiful woman in Ireland, one of the most beautiful women in the world. I'm very much in love with her, and very lucky to have her.

Is that a long-term thing?

I hope so. We've been going out for fifteen months now.

Are you looking for some kind of stability in your life?

No, I'm looking for a partner. I'm looking for a Don Quixote to my... what was his name? I call myself the Don Quixote because I know if I call her the other character, she'd fucking brain me!

You were with someone else before her, weren't you?

Toni Collete. She did *Sixth Sense, Muriel's Wedding.* I met her on the set of *Velvet Goldmine,* and we were playing man and wife... and then became such.

Do you find those on-set situations happen often?

No. You have to pretend that you're in love with the person if you need to be. And so immediately you feel something for them, but it doesn't necessarily mean it's love. You're just much more affectionate to them because in your mind you're more affectionate to them.

Would you sacrifice your relationship for a good role?

I'd sacrifice *myself* for a great role! I'd rather have ten minutes of an extraordinary unique life than 100 years of a happy, boring one. For me happiness all the time would be boring. I like a bit of failure. I've gone for a lot of auditions and been rejected, and I've been really hurt at the time, but then an actor called James Conwell – who was in *General's Daughter* and *LA Confidential* – turned to me and said there's only lessons in failure, so the more you fail the more you learn. Failure isn't being knocked down.

Does your job constantly put you in odd situations?

I'm constantly in odd situations. One week, I was in *six* different countries in one week! I woke up and had to ask what language did they speak? That's strange, but at the same time you choose it. I feel as though I've been in guerrilla warfare for about the last four years. It's very tiring. You're fighting a war, basically. And you're the only army you have that you can control, and you can't control what the enemy is going to do. And your enemies constantly change.

What's been your best role to date?

I don't know.

What's been your worst?

They've all had difficult things, and they've all had great things, every part I've played.

Do you get emotionally involved as an actor?
Of course I do.

So when you did *Gormenghast*, did you become a sly little fucker?
No, I became more of a little fucker doing *The Magnificent Ambersons*. Because in *Gormenghast*, he was made rotten by something that was done to him as a child. And so as he grows up, he doesn't grow up. Because you can't grow up in a place that never changes. That was the whole point of *Gormenghast* – to try not to grow up, just to try to become more cynical as the film went on. In *The Magnificent Ambersons*, I played a character who was born with absolutely everything, and was a spoilt bastard. I became a little bit of a shit sometimes.

Do you behave yourself generally?
Yes, I do behave. But sometimes I misbehave. I don't go to clubs and insult people. I don't go to press conferences and say 'blah, blah, blah'. I haven't got a big head in that sense. I've never walked into a place and said, 'don't you know who I am?' I've never actually used my name to get into a club or anything. I'd never do that.

What's your take on recreational drugs?
Basically, there's no good in them. There can't be. It's like drink is a drug, and smoking is a drug. It gives you an immediate hit, and it feels fine, but then it starves you. So it only makes you worse. I know some people who take drugs, and they're so clever that they'll take it and get what they want out of it and then they'll put it away. But most people can't do that. They'll take it, and then life seems dull without it, and then they'll take it more and more, and then life becomes dull, and the drug becomes dull. I've never been into drugs. I've never been offered them.

Oh, come on! *Never?*
Alright, I took a line in Mexico. I thought that's it, I'm on holiday backpacking in Mexico, and nobody knows. But it wasn't very good. I don't think it totally affected me. I think it was probably 25% sugarcane, 15% soda powder, and maybe 3% coca. I've just never got into drugs in a big way. The temptation is always there. I smoke so many cigarettes, but I don't drink.

Where do you see yourself in five years time?
That's a difficult question to answer. I know where I'd *like* to see myself, but where I see myself, I'm not sure. On top of the world, of course! Let's put it this way, I'd like to give a great performance at least once for every one of the next five years. I'd love to give an outstanding performance in one film every year.

Do you accept that sometimes you don't?
Em... (*wince*). I try my best all the time.

Do you find that acting has encouraged you to explore yourself, as an artist?
Every creative thing encourages another creative thing. It's a cog.

Are you as 'on' when you wake up in the morning as you seem to be now?
Yes. I can't take my mind off anything. My mind is always full of ideas. I still want to take on the world – *today!* And it won't stop. But at the same time, I'm lazy. I'm 23 now, so I've got to start growing up. Mozart was writing symphonies by the time he was 10 years old.

Still, you're pretty young...

I don't know. I worked with a director, and I was due to go to this press conference, and I woke up at 8 o'clock in the morning and had to be there for twenty past. So I put on my clothes, and I brushed my long hair through my fingers, and walked out. And he said to me, 'You'll get away with this for just two more years, you know'. And I said, 'what?' And he said, 'Just coming to a press conference in the clothes you're wearing, and not combing your hair. You won't get away with it forever. From about 24-25, watch yourself, because you'll have to start behaving then, wearing good suits'.

What do you want to come across in this interview?

That I'm not constantly depressed and negative.

You don't strike me as being either.

I have done in other articles. I'd say, 'I've done all this, I've done the troubled youth, the manic depression youth puts you through'. There are parts to me that people haven't seen.

Do you feel lucky?

Yes, hugely lucky and, in another way, hugely unlucky. That's because you want more. I expect so much of myself. People keep saying, 'you're not doing badly'. But if you say that to yourself, you rest on your laurels. Getting to the top is like the sparring round. Once you're at the top, you start fighting like a dog to stay there.

Do you feel you're at the top now?

No *(laughs)*.

Are you the jealous type?

Yes – of whoever gets the part. No particular actor. I wanted *All The Pretty Horses*. I was on the set in Missouri playing a bushwhacker and all these wranglers came up to me and said, 'I heard you were up for *All The Pretty Horses*. You're fucking perfect!' And I met Billy Bob and he said I was a good actor. Matt Damon got it, and I was a bit jealous. I really like Matt Damon, but I don't like him as John Grady Cole. It's too fucking obvious.

Why do you act?

Because I can do nothing else that pays me as much, that makes me feel as important in the world and that I can somehow achieve the greatness in life that I want. It's like sex, it's the closest thing to the divine you can be. You can say, 'Why do you act when you never wanted to become an actor anyway?' Well, I act because I'm told I'm good at it. Plus I've never actually trained so I'm sure when I was doing *Velvet Goldmine* and that sort of stuff, I was probably one of the only Irish actors who was doing that at my age, who had started doing that. And now there's myself, Stuart Townsend, Colin Farrell. There's three of us. But I still haven't given a really great performance yet. I feel it has to come.

{NOVEMBER, 2000}

CHAPTER SEVENTEEN:
Mike Scott

Musical maverick Mike Scott is still living in a hippy-happy state of marital bliss in a spiritual community on the North East coast of his native Scotland. While this is undoubtedly fine and dandy for the Waterboy-in-chief, it's not such good news for your *Hot Press* reporter.

For reasons not really worth detailing here (save to say that there's an unhelpful, self-important little man in the Galway Fasttrack office whom I'd happily *shoot*), I didn't get my hands on an advance copy of *Book Of Lightning* – The Waterboys' first studio album in seven years – until shortly before this interview.

Two quick listens had led me to the erroneous conclusion that this was another *Bring 'Em All In* (his hugely confessional 1995 solo album detailing the break-up of his first marriage). Lyrics like, *"She tried to hold me/ She tried to hold me/ She didn't know/ That love is letting go,"* seemed to hint at trouble in his house of love.

Elsewhere, his mournful delivery of the lines, *"It's a strange arrangement/ I don't claim to understand it/ I know I created it/ But I never planned it,"* sounded like divorce-talk – to my ears, at least. Needless to say, I was wrong. Sometimes a song is just a song.

Recorded in London last autumn, *Book Of Lightning* was produced by Mike Scott himself and Philip Tennant (who last worked with The Waterboys on *Fisherman's Blues* and is currently managing the band). A natural successor to their classics, *This Is The Sea, Fisherman's Blues* and *A Rock In The Weary Land*, the new offering features the distinctive electric fiddling of long-term Waterboy Steve Wickham.

The rest of the line-up is a mix of the old and the new, featuring regular keyboardist Richard Naiff, Louisiana-born drummer Brady Blade, London drummer Jeremy Stacey, bassman Mark Smith, guitar stylist Leo Abrahams, and long-time Waterboys alumni Roddy Lorimer (trumpet), guitarist Chris Bruce, and the wonderfully named Thighpaulsandra (keyboards). Together, they've created a real electrical storm of a record, not so much a giant leap forward as an amalgamation of all the best bits of the Waterboys impressive and eclectic musical CV.

As it happens, I knew him a little, back when he was living in Galway in the late 1980s. I was a barman in the Warwick Hotel, and Scott and his band of merry men would occasionally drink there. He hasn't touched a drop of alcohol in many years, but tells me he remembers those Warwick nights well. We're meeting in his room in Dublin's Conrad Hotel. Undoubtedly it's the booze-free lifestyle but, at

48, he's looking remarkably fresh-faced and healthy. He may have left the 'Big Music' behind some years ago, but the big hair remains. It's streaked with Druidic grey, but his eyes are bright and alert.

OLAF TYARANSEN: So is *Book Of Lightning* another Mike Scott break-up album?

MIKE SCOTT: Oh, do you think so (*pulls mock-shocked face*)? I hadn't thought of it like that!

I'm just looking at the track listing – 'Love Will Shoot You Down', 'Nobody's Baby Anymore', 'She Tried To Hold Me', 'Strange Arrangement'.

It's not a relationship song, 'Strange Arrangement', but it could be. Well, you obviously took it that way. But it's not an autobiographical song. I would describe it as a figurative song. It's not like a still-life, it's more of an impressionistic song. It's about a guy who has probably got a bit of me in him, who has made compromises, and finds himself *becalmed* in his life.

That one aside, are many of your songs autobiographical?

A lot of them are, yeah, but certainly not all of them. There are some autobiographical ones on this album, but not all my songs are. Often, I just write something, and I don't know who or what they're about. They're just songs.

Do they *come* to you?

Yeah. Sparked perhaps by a title or a phrase or I might just be strumming a guitar and something jumps into my mind.

Do you always carry a notebook?

I always have paper and a pen. I don't actually carry a notebook, but I'll always have a sheet of paper in my pocket. I'll write stuff down and, when I get home, I'll download it from there into a book.

Some songwriters spend years crafting and rewriting lyrics until they're happy, while others dash off fully finished songs in a matter of minutes. Which kind are you?

I work both ways. I've written songs that took as long to write as it takes me to actually sing them. And I've written some songs that have taken me 20 years, working on them on and off. In fact, there's a couple of them on this record. The last track 'The Man With The Wind At His Heels', I began writing that at the beginning of 1986, when I first moved to Dublin. I remember it was one of the constellation of songs that was around the band at that moment in time. But I was never happy with the lyrics. Over the years, I kept going back to the song, changing a word here or a line there. But I was never quite satisfied with it. But on this album, I finally got it. So I recorded it, after almost 21 years.

I took that as the end of a cycle of break-up songs on this album, with the character washing his hands and walking away at the end...

Aha! Well, it's fine to interpret it like that, but it wasn't intended like that *(laughs)*.

Shit! There goes half my questions! Do you always know what your songs are about?

Yeah. Often I do. But sometimes I don't, Olaf. 'The Man With The Wind At His Heels' began or actually came from a phrase. I love the title. I have to say that it was stolen – or *borrowed (laughs)*. It was used by the poet Paul Verlaine – one of the very super hip French poets of the 19th century – to describe the poet Arthur Rimbaud. He called him the man with the wind at his heels because he could never stand still. And I just loved that phrase. And when I began writing the song, I just thought, 'Well okay, there's a day to be a merchant, there's a day to be a commentator and there's a day to keep the home fires burning, but there's also a day to have the wind at your heels'. A day when you're moving so fast, nobody can catch you. Which is perhaps the way I was living at the time I began writing the song. And then certain things that I've been observing in the last year or so – in the political life of Britain. Especially Mr. Blair and Mr. Blunkett – that wonderful clown, David Blunkett. And they came into the song. The misfortunes that were befalling them helped me find the last couple of lines to finish the song. And the line, "*the clown in his winter mind with his loathsome ordeal,*" is about David Blunkett. This guy who had a sort of moral superiority that was completely blown by the things that happened to him and by the way he responded to them, which I thought was fairly undignified.

Do you remember Blunkett's response to a prison riot? He reportedly told the prison officers to mow the rioters down with machine gun fire!

Yeah! How about that? Could be a little power crazed *(laughs)*.

Have you seen that episode of *Father Ted* where Graham Norton murders 'The Whole Of The Moon'?

It was wonderful! I loved it!

I presume they had to ask your permission to use the song?

No they didn't, no. I wouldn't have objected anyway, I would've said, 'Yeah!'. I loved it. I also loved when he (Norton) was singing 'Dirty Old Town' with a finger in his ear. Brilliant!

Where are you based these days?

I live in Findhorn *(a spiritual New Age community based on the coast of north-East Scotland)*. My wife and I bought a house there in 2002. She used to be a member of the community there and she used to lead holistic workshops. She was a group leader. And she wanted to get back into that. We'd been in London for six or seven years together, and we were ready to leave. And for once in my life, there was nowhere I was burning to be. There was no new place I was trying to get to. So I just said, 'Okay, if you wanna go to Findhorn, let's go back'. And it's great. Although we're ready to leave now. Time for something new again.

Do you have any kids?

No, none.

Was that a conscious decision?

No, it's just the way it worked out.

It probably wouldn't have been easy with your wandering lifestyle.

Yeah, I'm glad I haven't had kids – for that reason.

Going back to the new album, the title *Book Of Lightning* is quite biblical sounding.

Do you think so? *(horrified look)* Gosh! I never thought of that. If I'd thought of that, I wouldn't have used it! Ooohh, that's horrible! Oh God! I see what you mean, though. It's like the *Book Of Jeremiah* or something. Oh God! You know, it was just a phrase that I had up my sleeve. I needed a snappy title for the album. Actually, I wrote a little short story for the sleeve for the CD booklet for when the album comes out that includes the phrase 'book of lightning'. That should put some flesh on the bone, as it were. But other than being a title that I felt suited the album, there's no masterplan linking it to the songs.

Do you write much fiction?
I do write a bit, yeah. I haven't published anything yet, though, except for some nonsense on the internet.

Have you ever considered writing a memoir or an autobiography?
I've thought of it. Or maybe just using some episodes from my life as material for a book. But the idea hasn't landed yet. I've got some things written that could be ready to publish. I'm slowly working up to it, but I haven't set on a course of action yet.

I noticed that there's lots of weather imagery scattered throughout the songs.
Yeah, weather imagery *(nods)*. I just like that. I like music to sound like the weather. When I made the *This Is The Sea* record, the beginning of 'Don't Bang The Drum' with the trumpet intro and that *(hums opening of song)* rumbling guitar sounds to me like an approaching storm. And then the storm breaks when the band kicks in. So I love that. And when the trumpets come in on 'The Whole Of The Moon', for example, it's like a sudden sunburst with the clouds parting and the sun streaming through. The elements... yeah.

Are the lyrics as important to you as the music?
Oh absolutely. I wouldn't say either is more important, but one feeds the other.

In the past, you've recorded a couple of songs of just one or two lines, repeated like a mantra...
Well, there's a deliberate reason for that. It's so there's no escape from the idea that I'm sending out in the two lines. *'I'm gonna look twice at you/ until I see the Christ in you'* (from *Universal Hall's* 'The Christ In You'). I don't want the listener to escape that idea so I keep hammering it home again and again. So the listener has to respond to that idea – they've no choice. It was a phase I went through of these little mantra type songs.

Have you ever tried Buddhism?
I've done some Buddhism meditations, and there's something clear and honourable and straightforward about Buddhism that I like a lot. But it's never attracted me to become a practitioner. Although the Dalai Lama would be one of my heroes. And I know lots of Buddhists at Findhorn.

Are you a vegetarian?
Vegetarian – but I eat fish.

Is that a long-standing thing?
From the early '90s.

Didn't you give up booze in the early '90s?
I did, yeah. And smoking. Still off.

So what's your poison these days?

Coffee *(takes an exaggerated sip)*. Ah... deadly!

Presumably you spike your coffee with Findhorn's finest shrooms from time to time?

No. I've never taken hallucinogenic mushrooms in my life. I've never taken acid.

Really? I would've thought that experimenting with consciousness expanding drugs would have been a part of your spiritual questing at some stage?

No, you see I don't actually agree with using drugs for spiritual questing. I think they're only applicable when they're used in controlled circumstances by native communities who know from centuries of experience how to process the results. Like the American Indians with peyote, for example. But I think in Western culture, using drugs as a way to open your consciousness is a shortcut that doesn't work. Because opening the consciousness needs to be accompanied by the appropriate lessons. Otherwise the consciousness doesn't stay open. So people who took acid in the '60s, for example, yes, they had a massive consciousness expansion, but they didn't know how to process it. That's why you've got all these drug casualties. I'm not interested in shortcuts, I'm only interested in the real stuff. I'm only interested in actually earning the expansion of consciousness by the life lessons that I go through.

What's your channel to God, then? Abstinence? Music?

I'm trying not to see God as a separate thing. Certainly music, and absorption in music, is a way of having a spiritual experience for me, and always has been – without me thinking of it as a spiritual experience. Anyone who absorbs themselves in their work can have a spiritual experience doing it. And there's nothing other-worldly about it. It's not something you can only have on the top of a mountain. You can have it right where you are. It can be everyday. And should be. We are spiritual beings, it's a part of our genetic make-up. So to answer your question, I try not to think of God as something separate and out there. I think God's inside everyone. And it's not a case of separation.

Somebody once said that we're not human beings on a spiritual journey, we're spiritual beings on a human journey.

Yeah, and I agree with that. It's nice, isn't it?

I wanted to ask you about your memories of Mic Christopher *(Irish singer-songwriter who died following a fall in Groningen, Holland, while supporting the Waterboys on their 2001 European tour)*. **Were you aware that he became posthumously famous over here?**

Mic? Had he become famous in Ireland?

Yeah, Guinness used one of his songs in an ad that ran for months.

Which song? Was it 'Heyday'? That was a great song!

How well did you know him?

I hung out with him a little bit on the tour. A tour isn't a great place for getting to know someone because we're all hurtling around under a lot of pressure. But I caught his show a few times. I actually picked him to do the support. I think Glen Hansard sent me a letter that said, *'How about my mate Mick?'* And someone sent me his EP. I thought it was deadly. It was one the one with 'Heyday' on it, and 'Looking For Jude'. I thought those were great songs from a great singer. I remember I had dinner with him on the night that he went out and fell down the steps or whatever it was. I hung out with him one day in Bristol, I remember. That was quite good fun. But I hardly knew him. He was in his coma for several weeks of that tour. As a band, in The Waterboys, we – there's a term we use in Findhorn – we kind of *'held'* him. We held him in our communal or our group awareness. And every night after the show, we'd come together as a band and we'd invoke the energy that we'd generated with the audience during the show and we'd send it to Mic. It didn't work. Or maybe it worked, but he had another destiny.

Are you a believer in destiny?

Actually, no, I'm not a believer in destiny *(shakes head)*. I believe we have free will and we can choose our road. Maybe I should have used another word. He'd a different destination. Maybe it was just his time.

Not to harp on the subject of death, but you knew Nikki Sudden well, didn't you?

Twenty-five years ago. I played on his album *Bible Belt* in 1982. I played on three or four tracks. I produced and co-wrote one track, and played lead guitar on it, and I played piano on a few others. We were big mates for about a year when I was living in London. And then we lost touch, and I didn't see him for years and years. And then last year he got back in touch with me – by the magic of email. He was writing his autobiography and he wanted to check some facts with me. And I have this annoyingly accurate memory, especially for dates and years, so I was able to correct some things for him.

Were you shocked when you heard that he'd died?

I don't think I was that shocked, because Nikki lived that hedonistic lifestyle. He lived by it and, although I'm not sure it's that clear how he died, perhaps he died from it too. Although it's the way he would've wanted to go – after a gig in New York City! I was very grateful I got to be in touch with him shortly before he died, especially in such a cordial way. It was a really loving email correspondence.

It was a coincidence him getting back in touch just before he died.

A similar thing happened with Kevin Wilkinson. He was the Waterboys' original drummer. And he killed himself in 1999. Just shortly before that, we played together again. And I was so glad to be reunited with him and get the chance to play with him again before he popped off. That was very shocking, that he killed himself. In fact, I was due to do a session with him, and his sister – who I'd never met – phoned me up and said, 'I'm Kevin Wilkinson's sister'. I was wondering why she was ringing me and I knew immediately that something terrible had happened. And it had.

Have you seen many rock 'n' roll casualties over the years? Do you hang out in those circles much?

No, I plough my own strange furrow *(smiles)*.

You've managed to stay out of the tabloids and gossip columns, despite your fame and success.

I'm an odd combination. I like dressing flash, and I like going on stage and throwing shapes, but I'm also very private. I'm a very shy person.

Do you get recognised much when you're out and about?

I actually quite enjoy being recognised on the street. Generally, people are really nice. I was in Venice on holiday and a Corkman came up and asked me for my autograph. A Cork accent addressing me in an alleyway in Venice. That was very nice, and he was so charming. So it's cool.

You described Dublin as *"a city full of ghosts"* on Bring 'Em All In.

Do you know, it was to me then – but, boy, I love being back in Dublin. Every time! It's just great!

I was chatting with musician Vinnie Kilduff last night, and he told me that when he toured with The Waterboys you all used to play literally everywhere – airports, buses, hotel rooms. Do you still do that?

We do it a bit. But there aren't so many trad players in the band these days. There's Wickham, and I'll play my guitar anywhere *(nods over at guitar leaning against the bed)*. So there's two of us. But during that marvellous raggle-taggle golden age, there was Vinnie, there was Sharon Shannon, Colin Blakey – it really was like a rolling session.

Would you be into those days coming again?

Oh I would, yeah! Wickham and I have this long-standing plan to do a Rolling Thunder type tour, and get all our friends who're in bands to do a revue-sized show. Get Sharon Shannon on the bill, and so on. Steve Earle was another name we thought of. But just to get something like that on tour and then we all play together at the end. Get that spirit going again. We'll do it one day.

How does it feel to be back with a major label?

Good. I liked being on my own label too. There was a lot of freedom in it. Although, even on a major label, I'm used to doing my own thing anyway.

Is it true that releasing *A Rock In The Weary Land* almost broke you financially a few years back?

Well, I put a lot of money into the *A Rock In The Weary Land* album. I paid for that recording myself. But then that went with a major label, too. I don't think of myself as wealthy.

But you've done some major deals in your time?

Well, the big record deal that I did was the Geffen one in 1991 or 1992 or whenever that was *(for a reported $2 million)*. Although, there's a funny story about that. I did the *Dream Harder* album, which was a Waterboys album, and then I made the *Bring 'Em All In* record. And I knew I wanted that to be a Mike Scott album. It was a one-man album, it didn't feel right to put it out under the Waterboys' name.

It was a very personal album as well...

Yeah, I thought it was appropriate to stand under the name Mike Scott. But Geffen didn't want me to do that. And I had to take a cut in my advances of a million dollars to get them to put it out under my name. And then I actually bought the record back from them as well. First, I took a cut and then I bought the record back. My lawyer was working very hard at the time *(laughs)*.

Going back further, you've had your starving artist days.

Yeah, sure. I had to sell my record collection to make the next gig. I remember being on tour with my old band Another Pretty Face in 1980. We got the support tour with Stiff Little Fingers, but we lost our record deal. I remember that the first gig of the tour was in Liverpool. And we'd just enough money to pay for the petrol to get to Liverpool. The next day, we had to drive to Bournemouth. And we had no money, so we had to sell one of the amps to put gas in the van. I laugh now, but it wasn't funny at the time. We all smelt bad as well. Nobody had any money for laundry, and our socks were humming up the van something awful. Stiff Little Fingers rescued us. They gave us back our tour support. I'll never forget that. Good lads! First thing we did was we went to a bank in Bristol, got some cash out and did our laundry *(laughs)*.

Do you rate any of the current crop of new Irish bands?

I'm friends with a lot of Irish musicians and I stay in touch with them because they're my mates. As for new bands, I'm probably out of touch. I liked David Kitt when he came along. I loved that first album. I played that until the CD wore through. But apart from that, I'd probably be out of touch.

Who are you listening to generally?

The Stones, Sly and the Family Stone, Marvin Gaye, Kate Bush, The Beatles – these are the things in iTunes that I listen to again and again. Odd things like Steve Reich. Hank Williams. Oh, I recently discovered a terrific British singer-songwriter called Freddie Stevenson. Really, really good. He plays with The Only Ones – 'Another Girl, Another Planet' – do you remember that song? They were a terrific band in the late '70s and their guitar player plays with this Freddie Stevenson guy. I've discovered a lot of musicians through MySpace. I love MySpace. It's great for networking. Great for finding players. I've even found players for the Waterboys' album through it. I found a great drummer.

Are you a techno-savvy kind of person?

Not particularly, but I love email. And I love iTunes.

What are your thoughts on free downloads?

I think it's good to have an energy exchange. People are going to get the music, so it'd be nice if they give some energy the other way. But, you know, like most musicians, the thing that we want is for people to hear the music and respond to it. We want people to love our music like we loved music when we first got into it – or even now. So financial reward is a secondary consideration – for me, certainly. At the same time, without getting some financial income from my songwriting or from my records, I wouldn't be able to live. I'd have to get a day job, and then I wouldn't be able to make records and I wouldn't be able to go touring. So there needs to be that as well. Something I do like with YouTube and MySpace is the frontier spirit. My record company will probably be really pissed off with me for saying this, and I know they've got issues with MySpace. I'm with Universal and there's something going on with MySpace just now. But I do love that we can put up videos on MySpace and I don't have to ask anybody's permission or deal with any of the publishing. I can just stick it up there. It's brilliant.

Going back to the new album, is there a theme or is it simply a collection of new songs?

I didn't set out to make an album with a theme, but when I look at the album and

I scan my eyes over the track list, I realise there is a theme. And it's a theme of how deeds are connected to comeuppances, or actions are connected to reactions.

Reaping what you sow?

It's exactly that. And the characters in 'Love Will Shoot You Down' and 'The Man With The Wind At His Heels' are people who've put some chains of circumstances into action and it comes back to them, and they have to pay for it. So it's very much a karmic thing. Also, it's dealing with judgement. I began writing 'Everybody Takes A Tumble' in 1986. I could've put it on *Fisherman's Blues*. We never recorded it because I didn't have the lyrics finished. Finally, twenty years later, I finished the lyrics. And I put it into the live set and it worked out so well, we recorded it for the album. And I was listening to it recently, because I had to edit it for a single. And I was saying, 'how am I gonna edit this? It's seven minutes long!' I tried all these variations and I couldn't get it right. And then suddenly I realised that if I take this bit out and stick that bit there, I'd get it right. And when I finally had the single edited, I listened to the lyric and I thought, 'at last, I know what this is about!' I'd never known what the song was about.

Which was?

The guy in the first two verses, he's new into town, and he's saying, 'You'd better not mess with me because I'm bad news and you're gonna come a cropper if you mess with me'. And then in the third verse, the perspective widens: *"The devil drives a hard bargain/ preacher burns his hands."* We're looking not just at the narrator, but we're looking at the wider scale of things. And innocence is gone: *"Huck Finn just went out for sticks/ and he ain't coming back."* We're in deep waters. And then in the last verse: *"Sinead O'Connor is guest of honour/And The Blades are gonna play..."* Yeah, the month I came to Ireland, that's the scene in Dublin. Phil was MIA. The day I arrived in Dublin to live, he (Phil Lynott) died the same day. It was on the news on the radio when I was driving in, in the taxi from the airport, with Wickham. But the last verse we're in a judgement-free zone. I can't really put it into words, but I understand the song now. It's like: nobody should be judged. It doesn't matter what mistakes we make, we're all really doing the best we can with what we've got at the time. Even people who do terrible things. According to their own life, they actually think they're doing the right thing.

Which brings us back to the likes of Bush and Blair...

Yeah. They certainly think they're doing the right thing. We may not, but they do. It might be based on fear or it might be based on misconceptions, but they think they're doing something honourable.

Are you politically involved in any way?

Oh God, no! I was a member of the Labour Party in 1983 for a year. Paid my subscription, never went to a meeting.

Do you play many benefits or support any charities?

We played some gigs for Greenpeace; we even played on the Greenpeace boat once, in Dublin, back in '87. I was very thrilled with that because we got Greenpeace on the front page of the *Irish Independent* – or the *Irish Times*, I can't remember which one it was – but it was the first time Greenpeace ever made the front page of an Irish newspaper. Back then in '87, Greenpeace was a cult thing.

It wasn't part of everyday terminology. We even got Paul McGuinness and Bono down to that gig watching us, and turned them on to Greenpeace. And the next thing you know, apart from Amnesty International – which U2 were hip to very early, and a good thing too – but the next thing you know they're supporting Greenpeace. So it was great. Good that we played that gig.

Are you still in touch with Bono?

No, not for a long time. We were in touch about 10 years ago.

What do you think of his current activities?

I respect what he does. I'd probably agree with what he does more than I might agree with Bush and Blair. And I think the way he carries himself is very good. I think somewhere in the early '90s, he discovered the key was to make himself look silly with the funny glasses and so on. And that bought him the right to be as serious as he needed to be on the issues. Before he discovered how to be a clown as well, he was open to charges of being too earnest. He discovered this balance, and I think that served him very well. And he knows it.

How do you think you're perceived? There are elements of self-loathing on previous albums...

Oh no. I really appreciate myself!

Have you always done so?

No. The hard times I had inside myself, would've been in the mid-'80s.

Because of artistic frustration or lack of success?

Oh God, no. My parents split up when I was 10 years old. And my dad left home without explaining. He never took me aside and said, 'You know I love you but I've got to leave home. And it's not to do with you, it's to do with your mum and me'. I never had that conversation with my father. And all kids who find themselves in a situation like that, not having the maturity or the experience to process the events, but still having to deal with it emotionally, come up with misconceptions such as, 'It must be my fault'. And I was no exception to that. And even though I couldn't articulate to myself that I was feeling it was my fault, those were my feelings. And so for a long time, I wondered, 'Well, what's wrong with me that my dad leaves home?' And it took me a long time to realise that was a part of my psychological make-up, and then to start healing it. And I don't think it was until the late '80s or early '90s – and especially when I started learning to observe myself through processes like meditation – that I really started working on this. And realising that, you know, I'm just a regular guy, and actually I'm a great guy, and I should appreciate myself because there's lots of wonderful things about me. Just like there's lots of wonderful things about everyone. And in the centre, I'm made of love. Just like every single human being – their centre is made of love. And I learned that somewhere along the line, and the world looked very different to me after that.

So you're very much at peace with yourself?

Well, there's still plenty in the world that cheeses me off. I know enough to know that, whatever the appearance of the world, everything's really okay. And everything is working to some plan bigger than I can see. But I don't know enough not to get pissed off about things. So I will get pissed off about Bush and Blair or invading Iraq illegally or whatever.

When was the last time you threw a punch?

That's a lovely question *(long pause)*. Ha, ha! I *love* that question. I'm just trying to think. I can remember one, but I'm trying to think if there's another one. It was the late '80s – but I'm not gonna tell you who or why!

Are you a pacifist generally?

No, I'm not actually. I believe in being robust with people that are behaving badly. I believe in not letting bullies bully, and not letting abusers abuse. But I also believe in taking a wide view of things and trying not to be judgemental. Paedophiles is an interesting one. It's a big issue, something that's come to the surface in the last 10 or 15 years. I know it's been a big thing in Ireland, too. It's a big thing in Britain. I have no direct experience of it, which may disqualify me from having an opinion, and that's fine. But I also have a thought about it. I think probably most paedophiles were abused as children. And that when someone abuses a child, they're creating potentially a new paedophile. And to deal with paedophiles, we have to look at that. And it requires a very wide understanding. I think really to deal with paedophiles we have to suspend judgement and stop thinking of them as monsters, and maybe think of them as little children who got fucked-up by someone else. It's a self-perpetuating chain. And as long as we classify them as monsters, we're not actually dealing with the root cause.

Pete Townshend got into trouble over that issue ...

He did, yeah. Now, he claims to have been abused himself and he was on the internet, he says, researching it. And I'd be inclined to believe him. I think Townshend's a real honest guy.

What are your thoughts on Saddam Hussein being hung on the internet?

Well, first of all, I think he should've been tried in an international court, in the Hague – a crimes against humanity tribunal. International eyes on it, and an international court. Not an Iraqi court. I also think he should've been tried for a much wider catalogue of crimes, rather than the specific Kurdish massacre that he was tried for. And I've seen some speculation that he was tried for only that because, if he was tried for other things, it would've brought up things that perhaps the Americans and the British – who armed him – don't really want to put the spotlight on. As for hanging him, well, maybe a Hague war crimes court would've come up with a different solution. Maybe they'd have put him in jail, which I personally would've been more comfortable with. And there's another issue about whether Britain should've supported him being hanged. Or rather, while we didn't support it – we didn't protest it either. We don't hang people any more. So there's perhaps a double standard at work. As for it being on the internet, it was just pathetic that that was allowed to happen.

When you say 'we', are you being nationalistic? Do you see yourself as British or as Scottish or as a planetary citizen?

I'm all of them. I'm a citizen of the world, but I'm British and I'm Scottish as well. I see no reason not to be all of those things.

Do you have a personal motto for life?

I've got lots of guiding principles. Do unto others as you'd have them do unto you. I believe in the law of karma. The universe is like a great mirror. Everything you do comes back in exact degree. Might not come back in exact kind, but it comes back in exact quality and degree.

Everything?

Everything. Because ultimately, there is only one. The universe is one. I believe that's the secret at the end of all religions. There is only one consciousness and our separation is a handy illusion that let's us get through our day alright. And everything we do truly we're doing to ourselves because there is only one of us. And that's why it comes back on us exactly, because we're doing it to ourselves - or to our self.

{MARCH, 2007}

CHAPTER EIGHTEEN:
Damien Rice

"*Tell it like you still believe that the end of a century/ brings a change for you and me.*" – 'Amie', from *O*

There's no denying that the end of the 20th century brought some serious changes to Damien Rice's life. Towards the conclusion of this rare and unexpectedly confessional interview, *Hot Press* asks the reluctant star what has been his personal high point of the Noughties. Given that the past decade has seen the Kildare singer-songwriter selling truckloads of albums, repeatedly touring the globe, hearing his songs soundtrack hit movies, being romantically linked with an A-list Hollywood actress, and performing with the likes of Christy Moore and Leonard Cohen ("a wonderful, wonderful, wonderful, wonderful, gracious, eloquent man"), Rice must be spoilt for choice of momentous moments. But he doesn't hesitate before answering: "Meeting Lisa Hannigan."

The lowest point?

He smiles, wistfully: "Lisa Hannigan not wanting to talk to me anymore."

And what are his hopes and ambitions for the coming decade?

Rice closes his eyes and thinks for a moment, before answering softly: "Just to be kind." He shrugs his shoulders: "I mean, I'm pretty clear at this point, looking back, that I was a *complete* asshole on many occasions. Like, *very* clear."

Rewind ninety minutes or so. Rice walks into the bar of a Dublin city-centre hotel to do his first proper press interview in almost three years. There's absolutely no swagger about the man. With his shock of unkempt hair, garish patchwork shirt and holey sweater, the lightly bearded 35-year-old (he'll turn 36 in a few days) looks more like an impoverished eco-warrior than an internationally famous, and possibly even wealthy, musician. He seems in good form, greeting publicist Dan Oggly with a hug, and your correspondent with a firm and friendly handshake. "We met in Manhattan a few years ago," I remind him. "Yeah, I remember," he says. "Backstage in Joe's Pub."

Deciding that the bar is too noisy for recording purposes, we walk to the nearby Central Hotel. Along the way, Rice enthuses about a global warming lecture he recently attended. Ten minutes later, we're safely ensconced in a quiet and dimly lit room off the Central's upstairs Library Bar. The singer sips from a glass of still water and tells Oggly that there's no need to wait for him. "This could take a little while," he says.

It's a strange scenario. There's something unusual and impressive in Rice's resolve. A notoriously reticent interviewee, he doesn't have a new album or tour to promote. Aside from promotional duties related to a couple of Burmese benefit gigs, he hasn't spoken on the record to a journalist in at least three years. When his long-awaited second album, *9*, was released in 2006, he declined to do any press interviews at all – much to the reported chagrin of his record label. However, the singer responded positively to a *Hot Press* request to talk about the decade currently drawing to a close. And so it seems appropriate to start at the very beginning: where were you, Damien Rice, at millennium midnight?

"I was in Dublin, Stillorgan, with a friend or two at some other friend of theirs' party in their parents' house around a bunch of people I didn't really know, so it was kind of surreal," he recalls. "Because you know, you have that big build up of, *'What are we going to do for the millennium?'* And in a way it was kind of the weirdest New Year's I'd ever had, because I hadn't planned anything because I was trying to wait until the *best* option came up, and then, you know… nothing much did!"

At the time, Rice had just recently turned 26. Where was his head at then?

"I'm so blurry with the past," he admits. "The memory I have of the time was being very free but a little naïve and earnest, you know. Probably comparable to the college student who doesn't have any responsibilities yet, but doesn't really know how that might change them when the responsibilities hit."

Although he'd dropped out of an engineering degree at Trinity some years earlier, Rice hadn't been idle. He'd spent much of the mid-to-late 90s fronting Juniper, the rock band he'd formed while still at Salesian College secondary school in Celbridge with friends Paul Noonan, Dominic Philips and Brian Crosby. The band had signed a six-album deal with Polygram in 1997, but disagreements about their musical direction led to Rice departing the fold at the end of 1998 (Juniper eventually morphed into Bell X1). Disillusioned with the music business, he moved to Tuscany in the spring of 1999 and became a farmer for six months.

"I planted things to eat," he recalls. "I used to be fascinated because with my lettuce plants I could pick off a couple of leaves – I wouldn't have to take the plant up, I'd just pull off a couple of leaves – and then, in Italy, because the sun is so strong and the soil is so good a few days later those leaves would be back. You know, so you could constantly just *trim*."

Man can't live on lettuce alone, though, and towards the end of 1999, he returned to Ireland with the intention of giving music another shot. He'd been working on some songs during his time in Tuscany, and in early 2000 he set to work demoing them in Dublin. While many of the songs eventually ended up on debut album *O*, he says he can no longer relate to the headspace he was in when he wrote them.

"I had this sense about me at the time, and so if somebody did me wrong in a relationship then it was like, *'Grrrr!'* You know, I'd pick up the guitar and I'd write about it, and it was fairly… you know, I look back at a lot of the songs that I wrote in that whole period and a lot of them ended up on the record. When I look objectively at the song and the person who wrote it, they are nearly all coming from the point of view of victim-hood. You know, *'How could you do that to me?'* And I just don't really relate to that any more."

Having grown up with two sisters (one older, one younger), he tells me that he was always good with women. "I was fabulous (with women). In one way. In that I had a lot of female friends, but that ended up being tricky in relationships as well – because I had so many female friends. I got on really well with women."

Were you a player?

"No. Well… define 'player'."

Were you a 'notches on the bedpost' kind of guy?

"Not at all, no!" he laughs, looking aghast. "No, I was more of a relationship kind of person, yeah. I would go from one relationship into another."

A serial monogamist.

"Right," he nods. "Yeah, a little bit more like that… with an enthusiastic eye for beauty. I was easily distracted, but slow to get involved as well."

But presumably quite intense once you were involved?

"Yes, *very!*" he guffaws. "*Incredibly*, yeah. But then, isn't it hard to gauge what you do relative to somebody else. I mean, I'm saying, *'Yes, very!'* because people told me I was very intense, but I don't know that I was intense. Just people said, *'Oh, you're very intense.'*"

He first met the beautiful and waifish Lisa Hannigan at a gig in Whelan's in September 1999 (she'd just moved from her native Meath to study art history at Trinity). Sharing similar musical tastes and a whimsical sense of humour, they soon became firm friends and she began helping him with the recordings – providing a fragile and ethereal vocal foil to Rice's bittersweet lyrics.

"She very quickly became my favourite human being," he says, unselfconsciously.

Back when Juniper had been offered a record deal, Rice had contacted his second cousin David Arnold for advice on the music business. "My grandmother, when she heard I was recording, told me about this second cousin I had who was a film composer. I just called him for advice on something, and we got on really well, and then he said, 'Keep in touch'."

Sometime in 2000, as the songs for *O* began coming together, Rice did just that. "Basically I had recorded a couple of demos and I sent them to David – because he was curious about what I was doing – I sent them over to him. And he said, 'Well, if you want, I can get you some recording equipment'. And so he did, he bought me a couple of mics and some pre-amps, and gave me a couple of grand just for expenses, and off I went."

Now that he had a mobile studio, Rice set about recording the songs properly. "We recorded all over the place. That's the only thing I remember, which I really liked: I was really particular at the time about where to record things. Like, I knew I wanted to record 'Eskimo' in my friend's apartment in Paris because they loved the song so much. So I took my little mobile studio and went to Paris. I went through the metro with all of these microphone stands hanging off me and recording gear, sweating by the time I got to their house, and just recorded it there, and then came home. You know, so it was recorded in lots of bits and places, but basically houses, places I was living or friends' houses around the place. Dublin, mostly."

Did you have any sense then of just how powerful the album was going to be?

"No, not at all. And, it's so funny, even going, 'No, not at all,' almost means that I'm agreeing with you that it was powerful. I don't, 'cos I don't even have a notion about it being anything except that at the time I felt like I was just making one record, that I just wanted to get this out of my system, make a record and then leave it at that, you know."

What, make one album and then finish with music forever?

"Yeah, just leave the music – just make one record and be done with it. Because I felt like I didn't fit within the music scene. And, at the time, I remember noticing that the bigger songs didn't work because I was recording at home in bedrooms and stuff – big songs didn't sound good on the little studio. So the songs that came up as sounding good were all these slow, acoustic, mellow songs. One day I remember I was sitting with Lisa and I discovered this new thing on the little recorder – because it was an 8-track thing that I did it on. I discovered a new function on it where you could play one song after another. So I lined up a bunch of songs, pressed play, and myself and Lisa sat in the garden and listened, you know. We were chatting with a friend or something, I remember not paying that much attention to it, but just realising that I had really enjoyed listening back to what had been coming out of the speakers, and I wasn't paying that much attention. And that was the first moment that I realised, *'Oh, we have a record'*."

This works.

"Yeah, *'This works'*. And I remember being nearly finished so many times. I don't know how many album completion celebration shows we had in the Temple Bar Music Centre *(laughs)*. And eventually, the only song that was actually finished was 'The Blower's Daughter' so we put that out as a single in September/October, something like that, and then the album came out in February afterwards."

Released on Rice's own independent label DRM, the raw, angry and bittersweet *O* was released on the first day of February, 2002. To everyone's surprise, it immediately debuted at No 7 in the Irish charts. It came out in the UK four months later, and in the US the following year. To date, the album has sold well over two million copies worldwide. Given that there was no record label creaming off the profits, it made Rice a very wealthy man. The singer still seems somewhat bemused at *O's* massive success.

"Well yeah, obviously it went a lot bigger than any of us had thought. Because I do remember a funny scenario where I was trying to figure out a payment for the band, you know, and I said to them, *'Do you want to get a percentage, or do you want to get payment?'* And so we sat down and tried to calculate how many copies we thought we'd sell. So we tried to figure out if I paid them £100 a song, or something, would that be fair. And Shane (Fitzsimons), the bass player, who had been used to doing sessions for a number of different bands around Dublin, he said, 'I'll take the money' *(laughs)*. And I was like, 'Okay'. And then everyone else went on the percentage, and it was very funny… but we put him on a percentage later on, as a token gesture. It was funny. So, nobody had any idea."

What were your feelings at the time, watching your little indie album go multi-platinum?

"I was so busy at the time I wasn't really thinking about it. I was so busy because I was the record label at the time, I was my manager at the time, I was doing everything from organising the in-stores around the country to calling the CD manufacturer to make sure there were enough albums, you know."

Was there a lot of high emotion?

"You know what, it was a lovely time because it was just exciting. The band got on really well at the time. It was new to us all. We had all put a lot of time into it. It started flowering, and we just got to play shows, and it just started building. And when it started building then people started being able to get a bit of money out of it, so people were able to give up their pub gigs and stuff. And that felt really… everybody started getting really excited about the idea that they could perhaps make a living out of playing music.

"And it was a beautiful feeling. *Really* exciting, you know. Even though I didn't realise at the time what was to come, and had I, I might have prepared myself better, but I couldn't. From what I remember, it was brilliant *(laughs)!* But I could be just having these fond memories; I have the tendency to forget bad memories."

Within about 18 months, Rice was being widely touted as the first Irish musical success story of the Noughties. Pretty soon, he had a manager, foreign record labels, and a permanently full tour diary. Not that he necessarily welcomed these developments with open arms.

"I didn't really want a manager, and I didn't want a record label. I just didn't want any of that. But when I first did the couple of shows in the UK I had a few promoters approach me, and I didn't know who was the best. And then KCRW started playing it in America, and once KCRW started playing it, it started going into Hollywood. And then it just started spreading and spreading – and spreading."

His first sour experience came when his new UK label requested remixes of 'The Blower's Daughter' and 'Cannonball'. "They came to me and said, 'Are you open to people doing remixes of your songs?' And I thought, 'Cool'. To me, a remix was a really artistic interesting take on the song, you know. And I was like, 'Yeah, absolutely'. So they sent me back some remix from somebody in the States, and I was like, 'This is terrible. It just sounds cheesy'. So then, they said, 'Oh we'll try somebody else … we'll try somebody else'. After about ten different remixes of different songs, I was like, 'This is awful. Can you just *stop* this? Who is paying for this?' You know, probably *me*. So I was like, *'Stop!'*

"And I remember my management at the time going, 'Will you just give us something that we can get on radio, because we just can't sell this unless we can get it on radio'. And I remember at the time I wrote a contract with them, and I said, 'Okay, if you never mention the word 'remix' to me again, then I will let you use this one remix'. And so myself and my manager wrote a little contract. And so they used the 'Cannonball' remix. But I remember there was a bit of fighting, you know, it took a bit of clashing before getting to a comfortable place with that, because it drove me nuts. I felt like, 'Why are people trying to change this? What's wrong? Trying to sell it? Sell *what*? *Why?*' That just wasn't in my… to me it had already sold more than I had ever dreamt it would sell. And so I didn't have a concept of beyond 5,000."

How many albums had you sold by then?

"At that point it was probably a couple of hundred thousand. So that was the first time that… *(pauses)*. I remember at the time the band were really with me, and it was me and the band against the management and the label. There was a bit of that going on. But then slowly over time, then, I guess the management learned how to work with me, and me with them. We just learned to be clear with each other, I suppose. And then the band problems started happening after that, you know."

What were the band problems?

Rice shifts uncomfortably in his chair and grimaces. "It's a very tender subject. Okay, so… hmmm. I'm trying to remember where they first… I think where a lot of it stemmed from was myself and Lisa were very, very, very, very, very close."

So you were actually in a relationship?

"Yeah."

When did that begin?

"That had just kind of happened through the making of O. And so the record felt like a record of creativity and love, and just that whole sense of like coming together with a bunch of people – and in particular then with Lisa. We just worked *really* well together. I loved her taste. Whenever I'd do something and she'd comment on it, most of the time I'd just completely agree. We just were very, very compatible; in the studio, on the stage. But when that relationship changed it just made it very difficult because we never had the space from each other to get used to the change."

Needless to say, there were many pressures on the couple's relationship. Having toured the world pretty much non-stop for three years, the label began pestering Rice for a follow-up album. He and Lisa began to seriously fight during the recording of 9.

"As I said, I had only planned to make one record, so then at the end of the three-year touring period since O had come out and – we were nearly four years, actually, and then we took a break, and then naturally everybody is going, 'Another record?' And in my head I was like – I had written a few new songs and stuff, but I was like, I hadn't recorded in such a long time I didn't really know what I wanted to do. But we booked a few sessions, you know, here and there, we did this, we went to a little house somewhere in the country and tried a few things out. And none of it worked to my satisfaction. None of it was good enough. It was good, but it wasn't good *enough*. So after time with me kind of not being happy with what we were doing that made me a bit frustrated, and then the band got frustrated because they thought, 'When are we going to make another record? When are you going to finish?' There was a sense of, 'You are never going to finish'."

Coming under increasing pressure from the label, his band, and his fanbase, Rice reluctantly capitulated and more or less threw the second album together.

"I just kind of got bullish about it then, and just finished the things, like, *'What song do you like?' 'Okay, this one'. 'What do you like?' 'This'*. And so there was just this thing of like one person liked this song, one person thought we should do this. So I just listened to everybody in a way. The guy from the label liked one song, the manager liked another song, and we just did these songs, put them down. And then it was like, *'Okay, everybody, you said I wouldn't finish the record. There you go, the record's finished'*. There was a little bit of that to it."

He gets visibly agitated at the memory.

"It was a bit childish, but it was also a bit desperate. It was that I was desperate to hold onto people's love, you know? I was going, 'Don't think I'm bad' or 'Look – here's an album. There it is. Is everybody happy? Now we can go on tour! We can make some more money, and everybody can pay their mortgages, and everybody can be happy where we can go and work, you know, you don't have to sit around and wait for me'. You know? And, of course, now I regret that because I would take half of the songs that are on *9* off. I just don't think it's as good a record as it could be."

I listened to it twice last night. It's a very good album.

"Yeah, but just skip – skip – skip – skip. There's a couple of songs that there's no – it's like, why did I put that song on?"

Is that why you refused to do any press interviews to promote the album?

"Yeah. I was a bit angry. Yeah. And just a bit… I had become quite self-obsessed because I had been on tour for – I wasn't used to this thing where all these people around me were working for me, so if Damien wanted anything, then Damien got it. And if Damien this then Damien that… it was just like that very much. And after a while of that, it's very uncomfortable. You try to keep your feet on the ground, but at the same time the whole thing was just going, going, going. And I had just been so busy, I had gotten to the point where I don't want to talk about myself anymore."

Had you done a lot of press for *O*?

"Not that much, no. Like, I never had a gruelling schedule because *O* was over such a long period of time. It started in Ireland, and then it went to England the next year. And then later on that year it went on to the States, and then we came back to England, and then it grew, so it was very spread out. A lot of people who would put out a record would do most of their press in the first couple of weeks or months of the release, you know. I did it over four years. When *9* was released I found it really difficult to deal with being what people wanted me to be."

What did you feel they wanted you to be?

"A musician who is super-happy to go out and promote himself and his music, and sell his music to the world, you know. And be a bigger musician, and more famous, you know, and more money. And the more money I got, the more uncomfortable I got. The more fame that came along the more uncomfortable I became, and I am not famous! I mean, I can walk around anywhere. I'd be at one of my own shows watching the opening act and have a conversation with somebody about Damien Rice because they don't recognise me. But even still, even with the little bit that I had it was uncomfortable. It was just uncomfortable, like the idea of signing an autograph to me, is just uncomfortable. I just don't get it! I'm like, *'I'm not that guy. Sorry'*. I'm just not that guy."

Who are you then, Damien?

"I'm not the guy that wants to be famous and make loads of money and sell loads of records, I'm not *that* guy. I don't want that. I just want to be true. I want to be… I want to serve music. I want to be honest. I want to write stuff that's honest, that inspires, that people can take comfort from, or fuck with, or, you know, whatever.

And so any of the things that were the classic things you are asked to do on the road, which is like, meet-and-greets with people, and signings, and photo-shoots, and interviews, it's just not me. It didn't seem genuine. And I knew that I was in the headspace at the time that if people started asking me questions I would just be a real... *(pauses)*. I wouldn't be polite. I knew I wasn't in a polite phase at the time, and I didn't want to insult anybody so I thought it better not to do things."

Were you drinking heavily at the time?

"No. I don't really drink, I don't really do drugs."

Do you find that you obsess much about things?

"I obsess, yeah, I process. Yeah... *(draws deep exaggerated breath)*. I do that a lot. And probably how I escape is I vented a lot on stage, and again, going back to being an asshole with the people that I love the most."

By the time the *9* European tour began (the album was released to mixed but generally positive reviews in November 2006), he and Hannigan's relationship was more or less totally on the rocks.

"I can't remember, because it was a little on-and-off and on-and-off, it was like a classic scenario of... like, we were in each other's company all the time, working together, resting together. You know, and then when we came off the tour we were hanging out together, so it was just like full-on all the time. And so it was on-and-off as well. So that just created a natural discomfort for the other band members. Whenever there was any fire with myself and Lisa, everybody felt this."

Things came to a head before a show in Munich at the end of March 2007. Following a heated argument backstage, Rice reportedly fired her minutes before they were due to perform (he released a tersely-worded press statement the following day announcing that their creative partnership had run its course). So what actually happened?

He takes a sip of water before replying: "Her and I just weren't getting on, and I wanted everybody to get on again. I was such an idealist in a way that I just wanted everybody to be happy. I wanted to please everybody. Her and I weren't getting on, there were certain issues, so I called a band meeting and said, 'Let's have a band meeting, let's sort this out', because I'm a big sorter-out-er.

"But then I think a lot of the band had grown kind of tired of, 'Oh God, another meeting to sort some shit out', you know. And even though I didn't like having the meetings, I felt better sorting the thing out than leaving it lie. And so that was all good, but then we had the meeting and I felt that... I just felt that Lisa didn't contribute to the meeting at all and just... and I had held the meeting so that she could say whatever she wanted to change, or whatever.

"So I went into her dressing room before the show, just after the meeting, and asked her what was wrong, why didn't she contribute to the meeting? And she said that, *'Well what's the point? You are just going to do what you want anyway'*. At which point I just lost my head. I lost my head, you know."

He shakes his head, regretfully.

"Instead of, you know, whether she was right or wrong there was probably an element of truth in what she said because at the end of the day I had to make – there had to be one of us who made the decision. And, inevitably, it was me at the end of the day. That's just… But at the same time, you know, I felt like I was very open, but the problem I had at the time was just this explosive head, where I just COULDN'T HANDLE ANOTHER FUCKING PROBLEM! You know? It was that energy. It was like, *'WHAT IS WRONG, NOW?'* You know? *'WHO IS NOT PLEASED NOW?'* It was *that* energy in me at the time. So I just had an allergic reaction to it, if there was something wrong with somebody. It just drove me nuts.

"And, of course, when I went nuts then people went, *'Oh my God, what is wrong with him? He is such an asshole'.* So I just lost the head with Lisa that night, and just shouted at her and sent her home, said I was sick of working with her, which, of course, now I realise it was just frustrated love. I mean, I loved her and just didn't know how to be around her and… just be friends, you know. Just be friendly. So, again it was a very sort of sad situation."

How was the show that night?

"Terrible," he laughs. "The worst one on the tour, probably, you know. It was awful, yeah. The band were uncomfortable, everybody was uncomfortable, I was uncomfortable. The audience, then, were just uncomfortable."

Although the couple had had many arguments before, this one was different.

"Whenever it happened before, Lisa just left the tour," he explains. "It happened numerous times, her and I would just get to an explosive place, and we just needed space. Like I said, we never had space. We never had the space to get over things. We never had the space to be away from each other and just appreciate each other and learn how to be friends. And so, that night the frustration just came out kind of uncontrollably. Lost my head, as usual. Overreacted to something, as usual, but after the show I was very calm again. Very, very calm.

"Lisa was the one who was mad after the show. I told her clearly that I loved her and, *'Let's just take some space. We are not getting on right now'.* And I just wanted to save our friendship rather than fighting every day on tour, and end up hating each other at the end of it. Because it was a long tour we had ahead of us. But she didn't respond to any of that, and hasn't spoken to me since. So …"

The *9* tour came to a close six months later, in November 2007. At the end of that month, Rice attended a nine-day seminar at something he calls "The School" in Los Angeles. He'd gone for counselling before, but this was something different: "I don't want to talk too much about it, but it was like a school for questioning your thinking. Like, a nine-day school, and it was just the most incredible thing I've ever done, and I came out of that just totally different. Let's just say I went in the door cynical, frustrated, feeling like a victim to the things that had happened to me, even though I had been so fortunate in so many ways. A classic scenario for me would be somebody that I didn't know going, 'Oh, congratulations on all the success. It's so brilliant, you must be so happy!' And I was miserable, you know, and didn't really know why, and didn't really know what to do about it.

"So, basically I went in the door feeling like I was a victim to whatever had happened in my life. And then I played the victim because I didn't know what to do about it. I didn't know how to feel better, I didn't know how to be better, I didn't know how not to be angry, I just didn't know how to be the guy that I felt I was before it all happened. And I came out the door of the school completely transformed, so clear that I had brought it all on myself, that I had done it all. That I was responsible for, essentially, pretty much everything, and could have changed it at any moment had I really wanted to.

"And I just took responsibility, came out the door with responsibility for absolutely everything I had done, and with a very clear mind. A very clear mind. And, yeah, just came out changed, but at that point it was… that bit too late."

Did you try to contact Lisa when you came out?

"Yeah, yeah. Yes, I mean, tried. Attempted, but…" *(shrugs helplessly)*.

Hell hath no fury, I joke.

"Yeah," he laughs. "And not so much, because I didn't want to bug her. I got a pretty clear message that she didn't want to… she hadn't replied to any of the texts or emails, or whatever. I knew she was angry so I didn't want to call her and put her under pressure, so I just sent her another email, and then something else, and then invited her to come back and do whatever shows she wanted to do on the tour, whether she wanted to do Marlay Park or the New York stuff, just come in for the big shows so that we didn't have to spend too much time together. You know, I just put it out there through my manager because it was the only way to contact her at the time. But just, you know, pick and choose, cherry-pick basically, was the term I used. *'Just cherry-pick'*. If there is something, *anything*, that you want to do, we all love you and we'd love to have you back.

"But I think she had just drawn a line, you know," he continues. . "She'd had enough, and so she drew a line, and she quit smoking and she quit me, you know. And… I get it. You know, I get it. And I don't, because I'm different, because there's nobody that I can think of that I wouldn't want to speak to, that I've ever met, no matter whatever I've thought they've done to me or not, you know. I'm always open to conversation, but everybody's different, and that's brilliant."

I'm getting the vibe that you're still very much in love with her.

"I love her," he declares. "I love her so much, you know. And I love her so much that I love that she hasn't spoken to me – because even in that I have learned so much over the last two years. I have learned to appreciate the friends that I do have, and not to fuck up anymore. And, you know, thanks to Lisa's resilience, her and I are not fighting any more, so that's a positive thing."

You had a much publicised relationship with actress Renée Zellweger a couple of years back. Was that part of what pissed her off?

"Oh, we're getting personal now, aren't we?" he laughs. "Here's the thing, I mean, I know you've spoken to Lisa so you know what she's like as a character, I just happen to be in a really open space right now, and at the same time I want to be very respectful to Lisa. I hope you understand."

I do. So anyway… Renée Zellweger?

"Renée happened before the big troubles," he says, waving his hand dismissively. "It was just… I had relationships, Lisa had relationships. We were still on tour with each other and having different relationships, and… it was difficult. It was difficult because we got on stage every night and sang songs that were about each other."

Of course, Hannigan has since gone on to have her own hugely successful solo career. Has Rice listened to *Sea Sew*?

"Yeah, yeah."

Are some of the songs about you, do you think?

"Well, you know, that's not for me to say," he shrugs. "And how can you ever really know, because even if somebody tells you, how can you know they're telling the truth? You know, I didn't write it."

Incidentally, are you in a relationship at the moment?

"A romantic relationship? Oh my God, no! That's one thing I'm quite clear about at the moment – that's not for me right now at all."

But enough of Rice's romantic woes. Talk turns to money. Although *9* didn't sell anything like *O*, presumably he can afford to never have to work again?

"I'm very good at surviving off nothing," he says. "I was very good at living off nothing. And I probably have enough now that, if I invested it wisely enough, I could take out a little nothingness every week to live off. But money has never been my motivation, so therefore I wouldn't sit on my ass just because I have money, because I never wanted it, you know, never cared about it."

Well, you must have quite a lot of it at this point!

"Yeah, which I stress about because if the dollar starts devaluing and I have money in dollars! It's like, whatever."

He tells me that there's a part of him that actually misses being broke. He comes from a working class family, but money was always far more important to his parents than it was to him.

"Money was important to my dad; well, not that money was (important to him) – my dad was looking for us to get financial security as, I suppose any father would, but I, being that little bit rebellious, then went for the opposite. The fact that I was arty-farty, and had no money… *(laughs)*.

"But at the beginning, the fact that I had ten years of what he would call poverty, you know, I kind of loved it. I got a thrill out of that. Because I still did the things I wanted to do. If I wanted to go to Europe I found some way of scrounging enough money together to get a bus to London, and London to Paris, and Paris to… And I did it that way, played on the streets or whatever. I found a way. I just found a way.

"And, you know, I think we glorify money in some ways. Like, when I would go to Europe I had no money so therefore I had a genuine integrity when I met somebody on the street from playing, so happy to stay in their house because I had no money to stay anywhere else. Or staying in a youth hostel where you'd meet tons of interesting people; whereas now I just stay in a hotel where you meet nobody except the receptionist. And it's hard for me to go and stay in a hostel now because I feel like I'm forcing it. It feels contrived. Or to try to meet somebody on the street, because it's like I don't *need* to play on the street. I *needed* to back then."

Aside from your house, what's the most expensive thing you've bought for yourself?

"I bought a sailing boat."

What? Like a yacht?

"I wouldn't call it a yacht," he smiles. "I mean, you can sleep on it. I guess some people might call it a yacht, but it's not like a… you know, I'm new to sailing and all that, so it's an old banger, really is what I got. If this was somebody's first car, it would be the equivalent of buying some old Datsun or Volvo, or something. You know what I mean? Not a vintage thing, but it was really cheap from that point of view compared to what boats normally cost, because it had already done all its depreciation. But, it's brilliant. I love it."

Where do you sail?

"Mostly around Dublin Bay, and I went down to Wicklow, stayed overnight there and came back up, that kind of thing. So, just getting used to that. And then eventually I'd like to do a tour in the Mediterranean on the sailboat. I absolutely love the water, and my head goes into a really nice space when I'm out there. And I love the idea of touring like that in the future, as well. We had a chat before coming in here – global warming, all that kind of stuff that's going on at the moment, and has been going on for a while, or whatever, and I'd just like to be… I'm not into the do-gooder side of things, you know. If I want to go and do a sailboat tour around Europe, I just see it as an intelligent thing to do; you save on fuel, you get to be outdoors…"

You're late for all your gigs!

"You're late for all your gigs!" he laughs. "And it will force me to have dates more spread out so it will be less intense, so therefore each show, to me, will be that bit more special. You won't make as much money, but then, that's not my motivation, you know. It makes total sense to me, it's not that I'm trying to do good. You know, what, to me, sounds more inspiring, exciting, interesting: go around on a tour bus, or go around on a sailboat? It's like, go around on a sailboat! Without a doubt."

Are you happy at the moment?

"Very… in three-quarters of me. Very happy. Very happy, very clear, very relaxed. And there's just one little part of me that's a little agitated, and it's the part of like, you know when I get this knock (*triple taps the table*) from whomever, management, or whomever, it's like, 'When are you doing another record?' It's like, 'Aaaagh!' You know, it's that. I mean, I love… I have fallen back in love with music, and I feel like my relationship – because I have taken this time off – it feels a lot healthier. I feel a lot lighter, and I'm not writing about the same things anymore. It's just coming from a different place, it's not coming from a victim place anymore."

Are you writing a new record, then?

"You see, there you go, you just said the words, '*new record*'. I happen to be writing at the moment, yeah, I'm writing. I'm probably in the studio most days doing bits and pieces."

A moment later, he admits that he is actually working on a new album: "This one I have been working on, which has been with a bunch of friends – actors, musicians, other artistic friends from around the world – and it's all collaborations, every song is a collaboration, so I have been co-writing with lots of different people. And then getting different singers, and musicians to play on the songs.

"The whole idea of that album is to just give something back, you know, to just do something good with it, because most of my friends that I'm working with – a lot of them tour a lot, or travel a lot, or they're actors, so, you know, I just thought, *'Hey, do you want to do something?'* It was this simple idea of doing something creative, or using what it is you do to do something to give back."

Ultimately, though, his musical career isn't the first thing on his mind. There is something that is far more important to him. Far more important indeed. We have come full circle ...

"I would give away all of the music success, all the songs, and the whole experience to still have Lisa in my life. Like *that!*" he tells me, snapping his fingers. "No question."

{DECEMBER, 2009}

SELECTED RECORDINGS: 2000-2010

CHAPTER NINETEEN:
Tommy Tiernan

The unfortunately acronymed Thomas William Anthony Tiernan – or 'TWAT', as his beautiful blonde wife Yvonne jokingly informs me – needs no introduction in these pages. Nor in muddy Stradbally. It's the second afternoon of 2009's Electric Picnic, and all is good. The moment Ireland's undisputed High King of Comedy walks onstage in the *Hot Press* Chatroom for a public interview in advance of tonight's headlining show in the Comedy Tent, the audience bursts into spontaneous, rapturous applause. There are several shrieks of, "We love you, Tommy!" They clearly do.

"It's like a press conference or something," Tiernan quips, as he sits behind his microphone. Speaking in a plummy BBC voice, the grey-bearded, 40-year-old controversialist gravely intones, "this country is now at war with Germany." The crowd are in stitches before we've even begun. They remain that way throughout.

OLAF TYARANSEN: Okay, I'd just like to open by congratulating you on your recent marriage.
TOMMY TIERNAN: Thank you very much *(wild applause from audience)*. Ha! Why does everybody clap when somebody else gets married? Do ye think you're *safer?* Yeah, I'm married a month today.
Congratulations!
Thank you very much. So far, so good. If the rest of my life is like the first month then I would heartily recommend it.
What I want to know is how did you find a priest who was willing to marry the two of you?
He was an old, old man. No, except the priest, actually was interesting. Do you remember – I don't know if you remember this – but in the '80s in Ireland, folk masses were springing up like rashes. They had guitars and sandwiches – *(sings)* *"He is risen from the dead..."* and they all kind of floated around in this kind of... without substance world. And the priest was a family friend of my wife's, and he originated in one of those folk groups, and he's now in his early forties, and there'd be a heft of us who'd be there or thereabouts. You know, and we might grow beards and listen to Jim Morrison or whatever, and this man has avoided all that. He listens to Cliff Richard and Val Doonican, and I don't think he has ever had to shave in his life. And he forgot half the mass because Gay Byrne came to

the wedding *(audience whoops and cheers).* Yeah, and you know Gay Byrne is like the Mount Rushmore of Ireland. But the priest didn't know he was coming to the wedding. And the priest was up on the altar doing his stuff, and he saw Gay Byrne in the audience – and he *fuckin' lost the plot!* He started forgetting bits. My brother was supposed to do Prayers of the Faithful, and the priest forgot about it! A friend of ours was supposed to sing the 'Our Father', and had been practicing for ages. There's a great tradition of the 'Our Father' being sung in Irish, Liam Ó Maonlaí does a great version of it... *(sings) 'Ár nAthair, atá ar Neamh, go naofar d'ainm, go dtagaidh do ríochhhht.'* It's fantastic, fuckin' soulful stuff. My friend was all set for this, and in the back of the church practicing, 'Chhhhh... chhhh... chhhh'. And the priest just fuckin'[goes], "*Gay Byrne!* What the *fuck* am I going to do?! What the *fuck?!*" So that's the priest we got, anyway.

Do you get many priests coming to your live shows and feeling the need to go over and say, "I'm a priest but I still like you," kind of thing?

Ah no, not really. The heat of that is kind of gone. Nowadays it'd be more... what year is this? 2009. I think, maybe 10 or 15 years ago the church thing had more weight, you know. I think they have been sidelined now. I think a priest trying to gain the moral high ground now is, eh... I don't think they've got the ability to do that anymore. So, I don't really get priests anymore. Not really. I get old women.

Old women?

This old woman in a bookshop came up to me, and she had the softest hands that I've ever felt – these lovely, beautiful, child-woman hands, and she said, "Tommy Tiernan, I love you." And very few people tell me that they love me and say my full name. It's a thing that affects me, you know. She says, "Tommy Tiernan, I love you." And lovely soft, lamb hands, and she said, "but would you ever keep your mouth shut!"

I think we should all say that, "Tommy Tiernan, I love you." One, two, three...
AUDIENCE: *"Tommy Tiernan, I love you!"*

And I thank you very much. I don't take that personally, but I will deliver the message to Tommy Tiernan when I see him. He will be moved.

What's your take on the recent blasphemy law?

Ah, my God, you'd wonder what people are thinking about when they spend time on something like that, you know. Eddie Izzard has a great take on it: 'Blas fo' me, blas fo' you, blas fo' everybody'. Blas, is that the Irish for 'taste'? Does anybody speak Irish here? Blas? Taste? Maybe it isn't. I don't know. I don't really have a take. It wouldn't concern me. I'd get more concerned about something like Brian Cowen referring to the Irish people as a brand. When Brian Cowen spoke to his Árd Fheis the whole fuckin' country was watching that because here we were on a very interesting part of a fuckin' magnificent journey, which is the journey back into an Ireland where money isn't the most important thing. And the politicians and all the economists were panicking because they don't have the vision to lead us into that country, or when we're there they don't know how to mind us. And Brian Cowen got up and he said, "Ireland is a great brand." And I thought, for the leader of our country to see us in purely economical terms is fucking blindness to a degree that the man should be sent to prison. We should adopt Chinese gulags.

Old Ireland, in order to be the King of Old Ireland you had to pass many tests, and one of them was you had to be able to walk naked to Tara. And not just naked in your body, naked in your mind, naked in your soul. And you are saying to people, "This is who I am, completely vulnerable and uncovered, but I am still fit to lead you." And Brian Cowen, they're just so... Would you say to Bobby Sands that he was a great brand? Would you say to a young itinerant girl, running down the hill on a summer's evening, her freckles moving back towards the back of her head with the speed, would you say you are a great [brand]? It's blindness of an alarming degree. An alarming degree. And I would get more concerned about that than, you know, a blasphemy thing, which is like something out of a Monty Python sketch, really. It's not relevant.

Actually, Tommy, all I'll say to you there is that I was actually at that Fianna Fáil Árd Fheis, and he didn't say 'brand', he said *'land'*.

He said 'land'? *(puzzled)*

"Ireland is a great *land*." *(Audience cheers)*

Well, that's fair enough. That's fair enough. In some other dimension, he said, 'brand'. In the dimension I'm in, right now.

Actually, I'm lying. I wasn't really there.

Well, you were ... in another dimension.

Onwards. Your comedic colleague, Andrew Maxwell, recently got very drunk before a show. Now, I actually like Andrew, he's a good guy, but...

But why this trial, then, Olaf? Why would you bring it up in front of all these people unless you want to pass some kind of judgement on him? If you like him, let it go, let's move on to the next question *(audience cheers)*.

No! No! No!

As a friend of mine said, "May Jesus who died on the cross have no hard feelings against you."

Okay, I shall move on.

Ha! That got you back for 'land'.

It ain't over yet. You recently entered the *Guinness Book of Records* for... (longest continuous stand-up performance)

That was before I was married, now, and my wife didn't mind... there's a joke there for anybody who wants to take it on. I took the book out for a few drinks beforehand, I didn't just plough into it. I took it from behind. Ha, ha! Go on, sorry.

I think I saw you when you were about 18 hours in, or something like that. You were still quite lucid.

I saw your silhouette. I saw you 'cos you came in about 10 or 11 o'clock. I remember that, yeah. I do remember it. One of the interesting things about that was that we did it in a place – those of you who know Galway – in a place called Nun's Island. And in Nun's Island there is an Order of Poor Clares. They're nuns who, more or less, take a vow of silence. And they spend all their time praying, sending out love. They believe that they... they believe in the power of prayer, so they believe if they sit in a room in Galway, and, you know, send – I was going to say via Bluetooth – but via Blue Nun – they send love out, you know. *"I love*

Galway, I love Galway. May Jesus who died on the cross have no hard feelings against Galway." It's almost Rastafarian: "Ah send out pure love ta Galway!" And they're doing this all the time, but they do it in silence. So, next door to me you had these nuns who were being very careful, and not speaking, and it was marking the time that Christ spent in the tomb *(Tommy's world record was set during the Easter weekend – OT)*. And it was love, and they were sending out love, and they didn't speak at all. Love. And it all was honourable. And love. And next door to them there was me going, *"Eat me balls! Eat me balls!"* Different kind of love. That was interesting for me that those two things were going on within a couple of hundred yards of each other.

The last time I interviewed you, you were doing the American thing, trying to crack America, and then you kind of changed your mind, and said, 'No, fuck that, I'm just going to just concentrate on being the best Irish comedian there is', and dealing with Irish people and Irish ways and laws or whatever, but you seem to have changed your mind again since.

No, I think what happened was I decided that any notion of trying to crack America is useless and you have to enjoy… we all know people whose goal drives them so much that they are past the goal. It's not fun. It's not really a life at all, you know. So, I guess I still go to America. I did a big tour with Dylan Moran and Ardal O'Hanlon in the spring of this year. We are going back to do the west coast now in a couple of weeks, and it's great fun doing it with them, and I'm still doing American TV and all that, but I don't have this idea of cracking America anymore. You know, it's blind, it's silly, you know. So, I just try and do things that I enjoy. And I think in a sense, as well, for a comedian, you do have a kind of responsibility not to take your own career seriously. That you need to do things that are funny because you are not supposed to take… isn't it kind of odd when you see somebody who presents themselves on stage and says, "Here I am and my job is not to take anything too seriously, but that *CUNT* went four minutes over his time and is eating into my space!" So, I think you have to do funny things. So, one of the things I am trying to do is just to do that, just to do interesting work.

I see you're about to do a 'world tour' of Mayo.

Yeah! F.A.K.T. *Fact!* Which starts in two weeks time, I swear to God. We are doing Westport to Kiltimagh. We are dipping into Roscommon for a little bit of Ballaghadereen but you'd forgive us that. So, we are doing eight gigs. What I have done is we picked a couple of counties and we'll do a world tour – counties that interest me. So I'm doing Mayo, I'm going to do Donegal. And then in January or February next year, I'm going to do Offaly, I'm going to do a world fuckin' tour of Offaly! I had my stag night… I had my stag night in Bannagher, and it was fuckin' amazing. There was people – they've never seen the ocean but they know how to have a bit of craic. So, it's that idea. It's the idea of Ireland being an amazing place, you know.

Apparently, it's a great brand.

Ha! There you go. The serpent has bit its tail!

Okay. I'm going to move it over to the floor in one second, but just one final question. When was the last time you cried?

Now, you won't believe this. You won't believe this. But I actually cried so much last night...

When the Electric Picnic bars closed at ten o'clock?

Ah hey, I'm free from that yolk. My friend Hector's 40th birthday party was last night, and I danced there until about two o'clock in the morning. Now, I had to give up at two because you can't dance all night on tea and Fanta. And I went back to my... I'm staying in a hotel and I put on my MP3 player and I played songs that made me cry, and it was...

What kind of songs?

[Sings] "I try to say goodbye and I choke/ Try to walk away and I stumble/ Though I try to hide it/ It's clear my world crumbles when you're not near..." I cried to that. I cried to, what is it, the big weepy one of Tom Waits ... "Come on up to the house, when you... you can't come in, won't you come on up to the house." So I wept last night.

Okay, we have a roving microphone, I believe, so does anyone have any questions for Tommy?

"The world is not my home..."

Quick! He's singing! Questions? Somebody, please?

Audience Member: Did you see Cowen on Ryan Tubridy (*Tubridy's* Late Late debut was the previous night – *OT*) **last night?**

No, I didn't see Brian Cowen on Ryan Tubridy last night, but rumour has it that Ryan teared him a new arsehole, which is a big surprise to everybody. It's a bit like finding out that Kermit the Frog is a serial killer. But, no, I didn't see it, no.

[African] Audience Member: I have heard about you. I am seeing you for the first time. What is your star sign?

Now, the only way I'm going to be able to understand what you're saying is if I listen in your accent. Have you ever noticed that, that if somebody's talking in an accent you don't understand, you have to listen in the accent. *(Adopts deep African accent)* So... *fah-ya ah-heed ma fren', and ah will liss-an.*

(Audience quietens nervously).

Now, hang on, before you speak, have you noticed how tense everybody in the room got? And me and you are just having a bit of craic! And I might know this cunt. This might be a plant we've set up just to freak you fuckers out. And I soon as I start going, "*Weel, wat haff you gat to say?*" ye are all going, 'What the fuck is going on here?' Hang on, if he was from Cork and I started impersonating his accent, would there be tension in the room? No, there wouldn't, so shut the fuck up! Your question, sir?

Audience Member: I have heard a lot about you and I know you are very famous, and I am seeing you for the first time. So, I am very curious, I want to know your star sign.

My star sign? Ah am born un-dah da sagn of Geminah. Ha, ha! Oh, you're a bunch of cowardy cunts, the lot of ye! You're a bunch of cowardy cunts! I am Gemini, my friend.

Audience Member: [Dublin accent]: I saw an interview with you...

Oi saw an intear-ve-ew wit you! Oh ye're all laughing now. Oh, this is okay? Oh yeah, taking the piss out of the Dub. Oi saw an intear-ve-ew wit you!

Audience Member: Do you really feel like you killed Father Ted?
Do I really feel like I killed him? That's a true story.
Olaf: Yeah, Tommy did kill Father Ted.
I made that fucker dance too much. It's a true story, yeah.
Olaf: Tell the story.
Tell it again? Okay, this is a true story. I was in the very, very last episode of *Father Ted*, and I played Father Kevin, the depressed priest. And there was a scene in it – Ted gets news he's going to America and he is – *Los Angeles* – and he thinks it's going to be Hollywood and Sharon Stone. It's actually the projects or whatever the fuck. But he doesn't know that yet, so he is all excited about going and he's putting on this – I'm in his sitting room, and he's putting on this disco music, and it's, [theme from *Shaft*] *"Who's the private dick..."* All this mad stuff. And I'm trying to have a conversation with him about how sad I am. And we are shooting it over and over again, because I keep fucking up the lines, and the director says, 'Dermot, I'm sorry we have to do that again'. And Dermot (Morgan) says, "Ah no, really?" I said sorry. My first time, you know, I was nervous. Being in the sitting room on Craggy Island, it's like finding yourself in the Rover's Return or something. So, I kept fucking it up and doing it wrong and Dermot is dancing and going, "I can't fucking dance anymore, Jesus, me heart!" And, "Please Dermot, one more time, please." "Fuck! Jesus! Heart!" And, "Do it one more time," and Dermot danced, and 24 hours later, may Jesus who died on the cross have no hard feelings against him, the man passed on to the next dimension, and God be good to him.

And three or four days later the funeral was on, and it was very sad, and, as you know in all funerals, you know, especially Irish funerals, it's like people – it's all about weeping but you need a bit of fresh air as well, so you're weeping and you are crying and you're moaning and mourning, and then you need to kind of go for fresh air and then go back into the weeping and the moaning. And we all know sometimes the sex you have after a funeral is fuckin' fantastic, because both of you are on the edge of life – "I don't want to die!" "And I don't want to die!" And then, sometimes the laugh that you can have at a funeral is fantastic as well, because it's all about just getting a bit of air so you can go back under and swim in the grief again, and moaning and crying and weeping, and the coffin is being brought up out of the church, and everybody is sad and there are children and Chris de Burgh, and it's very, very sad. And as the coffin is going past a member of the cast of *Father Ted* turned to me and said, "You killed Father Ted!"

Okay, any more questions?
Audience Member: Tommy, I seen you in Letterkenny a couple of times and they were great gigs and you talked about having drunken sex. now that you're off alcohol, what's it like to have sex sober?
Okay, sure. Let's dance with that for a few minutes. Well, the... when you give up drink initially, it's fantastic, you have a... it's like the horn that the Angel Gabriel was blowing into Heaven. It's fantastic, it's like... it'd remind you of being sixteen, you'd ride all night. As Christy Moore said, "There'd be spunk flyin' all over the place." *(Audience collectively groans)* You'd just be good for any amount of drillin'. And now I'm... eh ... I...yeah, now I... it's different now. It's been five years since I

stopped drinking and the, kind of, the morning horn glory is gone. I'm still capable of an erection, but it's just that I can hear a creak when it comes up.

Audience: *Uggghhh!*

A very good friend of mine said that the whole object of sex, he thinks, is to be able to find somebody with whom you can go to the limits of your passion and still feel comfortable. That's an amazing thing... the limits of your passion, and still feel comfortable. Imagine doing that sober. The *limits of your passion*. And I think, in a sense, all of us are kind of afraid of the limits of our passion. Why? Because we reckon, and we're probably right, it has something to do with our *arse*. And we didn't think we were that type of person, did we? Oh no, we're those dirty people!

Olaf: Actually, the last time I interviewed you for *Hot Press*, you admitted to sticking something up your arse. It was a silver dildo, wasn't it?

It was a silver dildo, yeah. Ha, ha! It nearly broke me back. Yeah, I put a dildo up my arse once. You have to try these things. I tensed up everywhere apart from my arse. I must have had some kind of thought process, "If that clenches you're fucked, you might never get it out!" My back went rigid, and oh, it was awful. Fucking awful experience!

Olaf: You're the Richard Gere of Ireland.

I had my face down on the pillow, like that, and it was happening, and do you know when you are very weak, but you have to communicate essential information?

Olaf: Oh, hang on - you had help with this?

Oh... my wife.

Olaf: Will somebody please call *The Sun*?

I was there, "Take it out. Take it out. I think my back has snapped. Please take it out."

Olaf: We're going to go for another question, because Tommy is getting excited here.

Audience Member: What's the best heckle, and which comedian do you admire most at the moment, or someone you'd go and listen to?

David O Doherty is fantastic, isn't he? Neil Delamere is great. There's any amount of them are brilliant. Dara [O'Briain] – he's English, though. Hey look, you can't be too sincere, now, in all fairness. Any of them, really. No surprises, really in terms of people. I like most of them, you know. And what was the other question? The best heckle? I should remember these more. The best heckle I ever had was actually a line that a fella helped me with. I was doing a show in New York, and it was a late show, it started at about 12 o'clock at night and there was a couple of drunken Irish in the front row, from Monaghan or something like that.

Audience Member [presumably from Monaghan]: *Yeeeeaaaahh!*

Ha, ha! If Hitler had hated the Irish, I tell ya, Anne Frank wouldn't have stood a chance of fuckin' hiding anywhere because all the Nazis would have to do is call out the names of Irish places and an Irish person would scream out, "*Yeeeaaahh!*" Then, "Fuck, sorry Anne. He said Monaghan. I couldn't help meself. We're all going to die now. Go on, Monaghan, ye fucker ye!" Anyway, there was a load of drunken boys from Monaghan there, and there was a bit of the show I was doing about encouraging my father – my father was having sex with my mother, and I was in the next room, and it was going on cos they were hammered, and it was like hour after hour of *[bedsprings going]* 'eee ... eee ... eee ... eee ... eee.' I had fuckin soccer the next morning and... I just wanted them to hurry up and get it over with so I...

Olaf: Whipped out the silver dildo!

And the Monaghan boys were there. And I was there imagining myself shouting to my father, "Go on, Daddy! Go on, Daddy!" And this Monaghan lad shouts out, "Drive her like you *stole* her!" So – 'Drive her like you stole her'. I have always wanted to... this sentence, to me, is funny, right. And I don't know... it's a sex sentence. And I'm trying to imagine a situation where it would happen, and would it be a compliment or not? A guy is having sex with a girl and it's all very, you know, she's not, you know... She turns to him and says, "Jesus Christ, you're riding me like a Guard!" Ha, ha! Anyway, that sentence interests me, and I made it up myself, it hasn't happened or anything. What would you do if someone said to you that you were riding them like a Guard? Anyway, sorry.

We have time for one more question. Tommy is playing tonight in the Comedy Tent, I presume, at 8 o'clock.

At 8 o' clock, yeah.

So, one more question... and it better be good.

There are two. The hat fella over there, and the green t-shirt man. Sure we'll do both of them, for the *craic*. We'll do the hat man first.

Hat Man: Where do you get your hats from? 'Cos they're all flippin' brilliant so they are!

Say that again.

Olaf: He asked where do you get your hats?

Oh, where did I get my hat?

Olaf: He gets them from The Edge.

I met the Edge once, he says, "I like your hat." I said, "Thanks!" *[pregnant silence... laughter]* The Edge gets his hats specially fuckin' made. He said to me, "My hat – I get my hats specially made." I said, "Ah Edge, you're ridin' me like a Guard!" What kind of a man gets his hats specially made? Take a chance... go into Penneys.

Green T-shirt Man: Going by your Nazi joke and your Israeli joke... have you ever been accused of being anti-Semitic?

Have I ever been accused of being anti-Semitic? I certainly have, yeah. In America, these two people waited for me after a show. I used to do this joke along the line of... The Jews say they never killed Jesus, and the joke was I say the line, "Well, it wasn't the fuckin' Mexicans," was the joke, like. Yeah, Jewish people came up to me afterwards, and they... Have you ever seen people whose eyes are so *aflame* with *righteousness* and they never have a... The whites of their eyes are so pure and fuckin' white, they're just one-stream people, they're not people that have gaps for more than one train of thought. This one train of thought fuckin' purifies them. And these people were just saying that the Israelis are a hounded people. And god, Olaf might have more to say about that than me, but... You know, whatever, I'm not here to hound anybody, but these people come up to me afterwards and said, *[irate]* *"What you said ..."*

I tell you who I don't fuckin' like actually, just as an aside. I read something that Frankie Boyle said, he's a Scottish comedian, and he says, and it made me very angry because he said that any time he hears a comic doing a piss-take of an accent he goes up to them and tells them, "that's racist!" And I thought to myself, that kind of attitude doesn't belong on the comedic stage. Because it's all about being reckless and irresponsible and joyful, it's not about being careful and Protestant and Scottish and mannered.

It's about being fuckin'... it's trusting your own soul and allowing whatever lunacy is inside you to come out in a special protected environment where people know that nothing they say is being taken seriously. But these Jews... these fuckin' *JEW CUNTS* come up to me! *[Audience bursts into laughter and applause]*. Fuckin' Christ-killin' bastards!!! Fuckin' six million? I would have got 10 or 12 million out of that. No fuckin' problem! Fuckin' two at a time, they would have gone! Hold hands, get in there! Leave us your teeth and your glasses!!!

{SEPTEMBER, 2009}

SELECTED RECORDINGS: 2000-2010

CHAPTER TWENTY:
U2

It's not yet 9am on a bright February morning in Galway City, and Bono is putting your *Hot Press* correspondent through some serious aural torture. "Sorry, man," he apologises in that familiar cigar-smooth, Mid-Atlantic purr. "I've just got to run you through this security machine for a moment."

"AAAARRRRRGGGGHHHHHHHHH!"

Relax, folks, the U2 singer hasn't gone Guantanamo! But the screeched feedback from the two digital recorders placed around my mobile phone's loudspeaker as he runs his own through a London airport x-ray machine isn't easy on the ears. He's en route to Berlin for a midday meeting with Angela Merkel's office and, never a man to waste a precious moment of his increasingly busy days, has decided to call yours truly to clarify a few points we'd discussed in London some 60 hours earlier.

A moment later, he retrieves his phone from the other end of the scanner. "You still there?" he asks. "You've just been x-rayed... and have come up *wanting*. Your soul, Olaf, is being viewed by British security."

Bono's in good form – and not just because Merkel's government has agreed to budget another €900million in African aid for 2010. As U2 gear up to release their 12th studio album, *No Line On The Horizon*, they're seriously getting their promotional boots on. A few weeks ago U2 played at Barack Obama's inauguration. Last weekend, they performed the album's first cut 'Get On Your Boots' at the Grammys. In March they'll be doing a week-long stint as David Letterman's house band.

Before that, though, they're opening this year's televised Brit Awards at Earl's Court. So let's rewind a couple of days to the late afternoon of Tuesday, February 17th, and the moment a sleek back Mercedes pulls away from the front entrance to Claridge's Hotel. I'm sitting in the back with The Edge, fervently hoping that we get stuck in rush hour traffic. We're heading towards Earl's Court for U2's tightly scheduled soundcheck, and my interview time with the skull-capped guitarist is to be measured in miles rather than minutes. The 47-year-old is polite, softly spoken, thoughtful and articulate. He only occasionally looks across at me, talking mostly to the back of the driver's headrest.

OLAF TYARANSEN: So this is the longest-ever break between albums in U2's entire career.

THE EDGE: Yeah *(smiles)*. Unintentional, but yes.

Was that because the original Rick Rubin sessions were abandoned?

Well, we started work on music pretty much immediately after the tour. In that very casual way that we tend to after a tour, because everybody's so fried that you don't really rush back into the studio. So I was writing on my own and Bono was scribbling lyrics on his own, and slowly we started to get around to the idea of making some music. I did some work with Rick one-on-one in Los Angeles, and then we finished off a few songs which we demoed in Abbey Road in Studio 2, which was a fantastic experience.

When you say 'songs', do you mean finished tracks with lyrics?

Well, one of them was 'Window In The Sky' which was the track on the compilation that we put out (2006's *U218 Singles*). That compilation was a little bit of a distraction, but it was something that we wanted to do. It was what we call 'the truck-stop CD'. We just felt like it was missing out there in the wider world for casual fans – something on CD that was a sort of summation of what we'd done over the years. So we put that together with 'Window' as the new track, and a couple of other things that we worked on with Rick that we didn't really finish but were sounding really good. And then we did 'The Saints Are Coming' as well, which we did with Green Day for the New Orleans event for the reopening of the Superdome. So we were pretty busy with Rick doing some stuff, and it was all progressing well. We did a couple of preliminary demo sessions and there were quite a few tunes that were showing promise.

So what happened?

And then during that time we said to ourselves, *'why are we rushing here?'* We actually don't often get a chance to start making music in an atmosphere of no pressure, no expectations, no judgement – just literally for the sake of it. So we said, *'let's just take a step back and let's, out of curiosity, see what we can change about the dynamic of our song-writing. Why don't we invite Brian Eno and Danny Lanois into the process and see what happens?'* Just to see if there was a spark in that extended writing line-up, so to speak. So we did a couple of really quick sessions with them and it became very clear almost immediately that this was gonna be a very fruitful experiment.

Which spelled the end of Rick Rubin's involvement...

At that moment we decided to put the work with Rick on hold and just concentrate on where the muse seemed to be bringing us. So we laid the Rick project to one side and got into writing material with Brian and Danny. And still we maintained this idea that we don't wanna think about where it's gonna go or what's gonna happen to it – we just wanted to make music for the joy of making music. And we were finding it a very freeing experience. A liberation of a certain kind. And everyone was really into it and in such a great mood. It reminded me in many ways of early on and why we got into a band in the first place. Just that joy of playing.

Do you ever play guitar just for yourself?

Well, at home when I'm on my own, I'm writing all the time. I get a huge kick out of that. So it's not a case of playing so much as composing, but I work a lot on my own.

I was thinking more in terms of the guitar as an instrument of romance. Like, do you ever serenade the missus with it?

Occasionally, but probably not as much as I should, in truth *(laughs)*. I guess I'm more engaged by the idea of creating something than I am just playing with no agenda of any kind. But this was creating with no agenda in mind. This was just finding great ideas that we didn't necessarily have a home for, or an ambition for, but we just thought that we probably would get into more unusual territory if we didn't put a label on it. And in fact that turned out to be the truth.

We made great headway early on and we thought, *'well, we'll have the album out sometime in 2008 – maybe even early 2008'*. But the minute we started to think about a schedule for release, everything started to become much more difficult as we started to try and reel the songs in, so to speak, and put manners on them, and figure out what they were, and beat them up, and test the arrangements, and test the themes or whatever.

Surely that's just an inevitable part of the creative process?

In truth, it is just part of the process. For us, whilst on occasions we'll put out something in that raw unfinished state, we know what a finished song sounds like. We can't cod ourselves. If something doesn't have the legs, we *know*. And that's a curse and a blessing because it means that we constantly beat ourselves up, and beat up the work.

I've heard that you ultimately wound up with 50 songs. Does that mean that there's another 39 finished U2 songs in the can?

There's a ream of material that's in various states of unfinished-ness. Some ideas that we would have spent half-an-hour on have got real promise, but we haven't looked at again. Or songs we would've spent a lot of time on, that for one reason or another just didn't fit with this collection. So we'll get back to them. In some ways, we're in a very good position for a follow-up album, with so much stuff there. And a lot of quite experimental stuff as well.

How experimental did you get?

Towards the end of the process, we were trying to balance out the moods. We didn't want to make an album that was too mono-dimensional in terms of its mood and emotion. We wanted to have a contrast of light and shade within the work, and so having got a lot of more moody pieces, we held some of those back. So [for] the next release, we're not short of dark, brooding material.

You began recording the album in Fez. What attracted you to Morocco?

Well, it was a combination of just the idea that we should get out of our comfort zone and find somewhere where we wouldn't so readily repeat patterns of work and patterns of writing and approaches, because when you're suddenly in a new context, everything is fresh and you see everything in a different way. But also I think there's something that attracted us about the location of North Africa. There was a religious music festival on, which was the original reason to be there. Bono had been invited a few years running, and he was going through his schedule and he saw this invitation and said, *'You know, maybe I should go and maybe I should see if the others would like to come'*. So that was one of the original reasons why we considered it. And then to our surprise, Adam and Larry showed huge enthusiasm for the idea. They were well up for it. So we went for different reasons, but mostly a kind of instinctive sense that going somewhere different was going to be inspiring for us. And I think that turned out to be very much the case.

After Fez, you recorded in the South of France, and then for periods in New York, Dublin and London. Were you looking for a city vibe to contrast with North Africa?

Well, I think our little place in Hanover Quay is a bit limited sonically. You know, it's not a designed space, it's a found space. So we knew that for certain kind of acoustic, sonic reasons there were other studios and other rooms that would be better suited for what we were trying to do. So we looked at Olympic and we looked at Abbey Road again and we looked at various rooms in London. And we ended up choosing Olympic.

You recorded in New York as well.

Yeah. Wyclef Jean has a room there and we moved in for a couple of weeks. I don't know whether it's just the gypsy instinct we now have after touring around the world for so many years, but it does seem that if we stay anywhere for too long, everyone loses some of the inspiration and excitement. So moving around did keep the energy up, and kept everyone's focus.

Did Bono's various extracurricular activities impede the recording?

We figured it out. It's been a feature of the last few records where we know Bono's gonna not be present for periods of time during the making of the record. So we just plan around that and I use the time to work on the musical side. It actually is pretty good. It adds a different sort of rhythm to the process. But being away, I think, also helped everybody really focus on what we were doing. So being in Fez, that was the only thing we were concerned with from one end of the day to the other – making music.

Did you bring your kids over?

No, it was just the band and a couple of crew and Brian and Danny. It was very focussed.

How long was the Fez session?

It was just two weeks, but it was great. And some of the material... I remember clearly at least two or three songs being born in that location. And very quick. Like, maybe three or four hours. We'd start with one little idea – it might be a rhythm or a chord progression or a guitar or a keyboard sound – and then very quickly through a series of ideas thrown in... I think 'Unknown Caller' came together in about four hours. It was a live performance and once we had hit that arrangement, we only ever played it once. So that song, there were a couple of iterations that were different leading up to that version, but that definitive version was only ever played once. That is also true of 'No Line On The Horizon' and 'Moment Of Surrender' and 'White As Snow'. Although 'White As Snow' we had to do a little bit of editing afterwards, but basically there's four songs that were only ever performed once in their final version. Because it was that kind of a free-flowing song-writing workshop atmosphere. That's why we thought this album was gonna be easy, gonna write itself.

And then it all went pear shaped!

It's funny how the other songs just took a very long time. Because the song-writing, as it were, just wouldn't come. We needed patience. We went down a few blind alleys before we got songs like 'Get On Your Boots', 'Stand Up Comedy', 'I'll Go Crazy If I Don't Go Crazy Tonight'.

Moving away from music, as a prominent Dublin hotelier are you worried about the credit crunch?

It's very weird what's going on out there. I don't think anybody's gonna be able to escape from it. I am concerned, but at the same time I think it will eventually come back. It's really a case of *when*, not *if*. I suppose we're in a slightly better position than a lot of people in that we hadn't started work yet on the next phase of The Clarence. You know, The Clarence is still open and it will remain open in its current guise. We might start slowly sort of enacting the process of getting ready for the build, but in the interim we're quite happy to just let it run as it is.

How about the proposed U2 tower on Sir John Rogerson's Quay?

I'm pretty out of touch with that, because we're sort of the junior partner involved in that whole project. I think the issue with that, as it is with a lot of projects, is that finance has just dried up. So it's a case of waiting it out until financial conditions change and make it possible to go ahead.

Speaking of financial conditions, what do you make of bands who're practically giving their music away? Like the Radiohead experiment?

I think everyone's scrambling to find a new way that you can earn a living from making music. Certainly for artists like ourselves who have a healthy touring reputation, we're probably the best placed. But it's really tough for younger groups and bands that don't do a lot of shows live to make money. I think Radiohead were very smart and very brave to try that approach of a brand new model – the honour system. It's like the shareware system. Same concept – you get it free and you give what feels right. And I don't really know whether it was successful or not, but it's that sort of out-of-the-box thinking that's necessary, because the music industry has become a victim of its own lack of imagination with respect to the digital revolution. So if there's an original idea out there we certainly could use it *(smiles)*.

You've come up with a brand new format to release this album on, haven't you?

We're looking at a kind of a widget that would offer a much more rewarding visual coefficient to an album on a computer screen. Because there isn't really anything that takes advantage of this quite decent visual medium of the computer screen – or the TV screen in your living room if you've got your computer hooked up to it. We – and you, I'm sure – are of the generation that loved vinyl records not just because of the music, but because of the artwork and the opportunity that that sized format offered the bands and the creative team involved to do all kinds of things. The CD is not a fair swap for the beauty and the sacred quality of a great piece of vinyl. So if the computer is the future of music, let's take advantage of the screen. We haven't quite figured it out, but that's what we're looking at.

Are you looking forward to playing the Brits tomorrow night or is it frustrating to just be playing one song?

It's a little bit frustrating just doing the one song, but we haven't really played much in front of a live audience for the last few years so it's always great, particularly when you've got some new songs, to get a chance to play them live. It's funny how they take on a different personality. Like 'Get On Your Boots' – really we were trying to give it a more 21st century sound on the record, and it's sort of almost hip-hop meets early rock 'n' roll combo feel. But it's gone a little bit more to the rock 'n' roll side when we play it live. I guess the chemistry of the band is a bit more evident.

What gives you the bigger buzz – creating new music in a sunny Moroccan courtyard or playing live in front of 50,000 people?

There is something incredibly special about the interaction between U2 and the U2 audience. It's very hard to compete with that in anything else that I will ever do in my life. But in terms of just experiencing a unique thing with your friends, the fact that the creative chemistry between the band themselves is still as strong – we're actually writing material that I think is as good as anything we've written – after so many albums, and so many years, is great. And it was an amazing thrill to be in the room when some of these songs were coming together. It's a real hairs on the back of the neck moment when you're playing and suddenly something really special starts to happen in the room and everyone kinda knows it and gets it. And those magic moments, there's a lot of them captured on this record.

Has it become easier being in U2?

No. I think it's very similar to the very beginning so nothing's really changed. The spirit of the band as a creative unit is the same – it's quite intense and we put ourselves under a lot of pressure. And we never succumbed to the temptation of resting on previous achievements and thinking that we now know how to do this and, ergo, everything we do must be great. We've held onto this idea that it doesn't come easy and it demands everything you have to give. Also, there's no formula you can use. Because all our best moments seem to come at the moments when they're least expected, and they come in ways that no-one can predict. And it's about being alert to the possibility that something could just happen in the room, and even if your head is somewhere totally different, you've got to be aware that Bono's gonna do something and we'll be off. Or Adam or Larry or myself – or Brian and Danny, in this case. The most important thing is to recognise when there's something happening and be sensitive to it, and not think in any sort of formulaic way. Because we've never survived on craft. Craft is the least important part of what we've learnt over the years.

What's been the biggest mistake U2 have made in their career?

Well, there's a consistent mistake we make which is that we think things are gonna take less time than they do, but I imagine if we thought pessimistically with our schedules, we'd probably work half as hard *(laughs)*.

Well, work always expands to fill the time you've got to do it in.

Yeah. We get ourselves into this situation a lot where we're like, 'Oh wow! We've really gotta step up to the plate and we've gotta do this because there's so much happening. It's *embarrassing* not to have this album finished, we've gotta get this thing done!' So that's a natural and I think a necessary thing. It's like you guys writing. I mean, if you didn't have a deadline …

I'd rewrite forever!

You would! But our schedules are self-created. And we always seem to get that wrong. But you know in the end I don't think that's a mistake. I'll have to think about that one actually… *(pauses)*. I think maybe for a while our mistake might've been allowing a certain kind of judgement or a tone that was prevalent about our band and our work to sort of become internalised by ourselves. And not having the confidence to judge what we had done accurately and go, *'You know what, we've done some pretty good stuff over the years!'* I think we spent too much time thinking about what other people thought of our work and not enough time probably realising that our fans were right *(chuckles)*. If you know what I'm saying. And in my experience now, music fans are pretty much always right. The judgements of the cognoscenti are not necessarily that accurate. It was very sobering for me to realise that far from disco sucking, disco actually was far more interesting than a lot of rock 'n' roll of the disco era. And the genius of the Bee Gees: I'm wondering how I could have missed that at the time – but I did.

Because they weren't deemed cool.

Because they weren't cool. But it's absolutely brilliant. And the many millions of people that knew that were actually right. So *that*, we probably didn't figure out early on.

U2 have always had their media detractors, but recently it's been even more intense than usual – in Ireland, at least. I'm thinking about things like the Lola Cashman court case. Given the ridicule the band were subjected to at the time, do you now think it was a mistake to take your former stylist to court over a cowboy hat?

It's a hard call, because that was a point of principle for us. Had we known the way the whole case was going to go, we might have tried to short circuit that whole thing earlier on and gone about it a slightly different way. But it's very hard if you firmly believe that somebody has stolen your property and is selling it at Sotheby's, it's very hard to swallow that and leave it alone. It stuck in the throat. But that's water under the bridge at this point.

You've also been getting a kicking over your tax situation. Do you think you've been unfairly singled out?

I think there's a problem of scale for us in Ireland. And I think Bono's work has also cast us, and particularly him, in a certain light as far as the general public are concerned. And at times it's sort of a quite silly situation where every time there's any kind of a problem, you get the (*Dublin Northside accent*), 'Well, where's Bono now?' Ha, ha! When the East Wall was flooded – "Where's Bono now?" When Waterford Crystal are in trouble. It's just slightly out of kilter.

Do you ever get any personal grief walking around Dublin?

No. Most people know the score. They know who we are. They know that we are going to act appropriately in every aspect of what we're doing. We don't go into explanations. We don't go there. But in the end, I don't think most people think that we're squirreling money in tax havens. We're not! We're not living in Monte Carlo or Lichtenstein. We're living in Ireland, we're paying tax in Ireland. We're totally tax compliant and we always have been. Our business structures and arrangements are there because we operate in every country around the world. We play concerts all over the world, we work all over the world and we pay tax all over the world. It's just people speculating about what's what, and coming to conclusions and... *(shrugs)*. We're not willing to go there, and why should we? In the end, my feeling is that's between us and the taxman. As it should be for every single person in the country. Why should that be the subject of public debate? It shouldn't be!

What are your feelings on all of the corruption that's been uncovered by the tribunals over the last few years?

I think there's a culture of getting the job done by cutting corners in some cases, and I think we've come unstuck in a serious way because of a certain sort of looseness. Which is probably ok in certain areas, but you don't want looseness in areas like the banking sector. You just don't want that. Or in government. You don't want fuzziness, you want very clear strict straight lines. But it's very much part and parcel of the way things get done in Ireland, and you could argue that that way of doing business and that way of operating has also over the years been hugely beneficial. So it's very difficult. It seems now that every entrepreneur and every successful businessman is being viewed with total suspicion for being overly greedy and taking advantage of the boom years. Well, it's like you can't have it both ways *[laughs]*.

How do you mean?

What we need now is *jobs*. We need entrepreneurs, we need people who are willing to get out there and have ideas and do stuff. So I would be a little bit concerned now that we might swing the other way and turn the clock back to that period before there was any kind of economic prosperity on the horizon. I think we just have to keep our heads together. I mean, Ireland's been so brilliant on so many levels over the years. It's shown so much great leadership in so many areas of culture and politics – the politics particularly of the developing world or whatever. But it's not a time to panic. It's time to slowly but surely get the house in order, but I would be very much in favour of not allowing this heads on pikes mentality to prevail, because I think it's very counterproductive.

The vast and cavernous Earl's Court venue is buzzing with activity as a small army of workers prepare for tomorrow night's mega-bash. Cleaners, carpenters, technicians, soundmen, assistants, cameramen, security personnel, and the occasional celebrity scurry to and fro. Busy, busy, busy...

No more than ourselves. As soon as we arrive, The Edge is ushered off towards the stage and *Hot Press* is directed towards the band's dressing room (the Kings Of Leon are just up the corridor). Manager Paul McGuinness and publicist Regine Moylett greet me warmly, coffee me up, and take me into a small side room. No sooner have I taken my jacket off and pulled up a seat than Larry Mullen, Jr briskly walks in. Dressed entirely in black, the blonde-haired U2 stickman easily looks 10 years younger than his 47 years. He's affable, courteous and professional. However, there's a cold steeliness to Larry's eyes that suggests he'd go through you for a shortcut if you ever pissed him off.

OLAF TYARANSEN: We're under a bit of time pressure here so I'm gonna ask you to talk pretty quickly.
LARRY MULLEN, JR: *I'lltalkprettyquickly! (Laughs).* No, it's all a bit chaotic, but if there's stuff you want to clarify later I'm sure we can figure it out. But I'll talk fast.

Edge tells me that that the birds were shitting on your drums in Fez.
Yeah, they were. They wrecked my new electronic drumkit. It was just one of those great moments, you know. This idyllic place, everything is just perfect – or not perfect, but it's pretty close. From a musician's perspective, anyway. Brian Eno's on one side, you've got the rest of U2, you've got Daniel Lanois doing his thing on his guitar. The roof is open, the sun is shining. And suddenly the birds are shitting on you! So that suddenly brought us back down to reality.

Was it the legendary Joujouka drummers that attracted you to Fez?
No, not at all. The original idea was to go to this spiritual festival that goes on every year in Fez. And I was certainly interested to go along and see it, but there was talk at one stage of us performing at it. I think every time you record, you need to be placed somewhere. It just seemed like a good place for us to be. I don't really understand why – sometimes you don't.

You'd visited Morocco before, hadn't you?
Yeah, we'd been before and we liked the vibe. It's just a very interesting place. Musically its influences are Arabic, you know. There's nothing Moroccan, necessarily. Like, the drums are Egyptian. They're Egyptian drums and it's fascinating to watch – complex and all as it is. But no, it was really just to see the festival. And then to debunk there for a couple of weeks and record, as well. But the idea that there wouldn't be an idea was very much part of it. And that was what was attractive to me.

As a drummer, do you have any sort of academic interest in the history of drumming or of drumming styles?
I'm about as basic as you get as far as drums are concerned. When I started, I was a huge Gene Krupa fan because what he did sounded simple enough to me. And I liked Buddy Rich and I liked a lot of the jazz players, but I always knew that that wasn't where I was going to be. So I never studied with that in mind. When I was a kid, when I went to learn how to play, I got frustrated that I had to only learn on one drum, that I couldn't use more. I was one of those kids that got bored easily.

This was when you were in the Artane Boys Band?
I wasn't there for very long. But they wanted you to learn these things over and over again. And they were absolutely right. But I wanted to play Croke Park. I wanted it *now*. And it was the same when I was learning how to play. I wanted to be better than I actually was. I never thought I was better than I was. But I guess I missed a golden opportunity to become proficient, and I ended up with U2. So

you've gotta weigh it up! *(shrugs, laughs).*

How good a drummer are you now? Would you say that you're at the top of your game?

I would never say I was at the top of my game, not by any stretch. I think within U2 we've always worked as a team.

Even though it's your band!

I guess *(laughs).* No, I've always wanted to be part of a band. That was always the idea. So I'm a very good member of U2. I'm not sure I'm even the best drummer in U2. But that doesn't really bother me. I'm interested in being inventive and I'm interested in being creative. And I don't care what that takes. And that's not necessarily about chops. There are some extraordinary players, really great players, out there.

Do you ever throw a lyrical suggestion at Bono?

Absolutely. That's part of the rich tapestry of U2 is that there are no rules, and everybody has an opportunity to contribute on whatever level they want to. And early on in the record, I got an opportunity to go into a studio and to do my drum parts. Edge is in another part of the world, I send him those drum parts. He's got guitar parts he sends me. So we work very much like that. Not on everything, but on a lot of the stuff.

I spoke to Ronnie Vannucci from The Killers recently…

He's a great drummer!

He was telling me that the band put much of their new album together via email, just sending each other their various parts and working independently of each other. Do U2 do much of that?

It's not as set in stone as that. We use that technology if Edge is in another part of the world, as I say, and I'll be somewhere else, and we'll work together. But what we don't do is we don't go back and forth by email. I'll send the idea, Edge sends his idea, and then we'll come together as a band and thrash it out. And we know what we're talking about. So we all get a sense very early on of where the song is going. And it goes and meanders for a long period of time, and in the last two weeks of a record is when you actually realise what you have and when things start to change and move on. The things you held onto as being so important, they disappear – and that's part of the game. We don't write in a traditional fashion and we never have. We're not very good at writing in a traditional fashion.

You're a bunch of amateurs!

We are! But that's what separates us is that we are… if you want to pitch yourself against some of the greatest singer-songwriters or just songwriters, we're not songwriter-ly and if we try to be songwriter-ly what we do is we lose that thing that makes it special.

Could U2 continue without any one member?

I'm sure it could. Of course, it'd be very hard for U2 to continue without Bono, but think of Van Halen, think of AC/DC. But I don't know. Do I see myself doing this into my seventies? No, I don't. There will be a time. Whether that's on an individual basis or a band decision. But right now I just think it's very exciting to be out there making music. Making music and being creative is an incredibly amazing thing to be able to do. And the fact that people still want to hear what you do and people still want to come and see you. Why would you give that up? It's a very hard thing to give up. And it's not the money, it's not the success, it's just the challenge of being creative. Within the band, it's the creative thing that drives people. It's not being at the top of your game. Will we ever be as good as so and so? You can make all the comparisons, but I think that's an error. You can only be as good as your last record. It's a cliché, but it's true.

You recently told an interviewer that you didn't like seeing Bono palling around with people whom you consider to be war criminals, i.e. Bush and Blair. Was he upset with you?

I don't know if he was. I didn't discuss it with him. Bono is a big boy who understands that there are differences of opinion and there always have been. That's just the way it is. We've been disagreeing on everything except music for more than 30 years. There is an impression out there that U2 is some kind of corporate team – that we move together and we all agree on everything. But we don't. That's not how it works. It's important that people not understand that, but that they recognise that that is the case. That we all have a point of view and an opinion and we don't always agree. And I think the older you get the harder it is to find things that you agree on. And that's why having a creative basis is so important – because that is something that we do agree on.

Are the friendships within the band as strong as they were when you were in school?

You ask yourself that question. Are you still friends in the same way as you were with people you knew when you were 15? You grow up, you have a family, things change. You're not a gang of four guys from Dublin kicking against the world anymore. Things have changed. Friendships have changed. They've developed. They're different.

Speaking of family, you've now got three kids. Is it difficult combining a rock 'n' roll career with the responsibilities of fatherhood?

It's a real challenge, just trying to get the balance right. I haven't figured it out. I really haven't figured it out. I don't know. There's a certain amount of guilt that goes along with being away for long periods or being in the studio. You're distracted a lot of your time. Of course, your priority is your family. But this is my job, this is what I do. I've been doing it since I was a kid and I'm not qualified to do anything else. And I hope my family are resilient enough to withstand the pressures and difficulties that my life imposes on them. It's not comfortable all the time.

I guess Adam's the lucky one there.

Well, I don't know if he's lucky. I think having kids is a really lucky thing. It's certainly different: it's a lifestyle choice. He's made a different choice. But he doesn't have the complications, you're right about that. It's not as complicated.

What do you make of what's happening in Ireland at the moment?

On an economic basis? If I thought it was just an Irish phenomenon, I'd be really concerned. But I think it's a worldwide phenomenon. So everybody is going through this. What was particularly difficult for Ireland is that it was so good for so long – we couldn't be touched – and to have it go so badly wrong so quickly is a shock to everyone. I don't know. I'm not an economist. I'm not even close to an economist. I hit things for a living. But I live in Ireland and when you see what's going on... *(shakes head)*.

In fairness, it's not going to hit you that badly ...

It doesn't particularly affect me the way it's affecting other people. I'm a rich rock star. There's a lot of people really hurting out there and I'm not in that position. We tour internationally, we sell records internationally. So there is a certain amount of discomfort, I have to say. I haven't felt that before. I didn't feel it in the '80s, but I'm definitely feeling it now. There's a different mood. Rich people and successful people are all lumped in together now – and (there's a perception that) everyone's ripping everyone off. But I think that will settle down. I think it's a kneejerk reaction, and it'll find its level. Or else there'll be revolt.

There's certainly a spirit of revolution in the air.

There is revolution in the air, but the advantage we have is that the European community is a parachute. And it was a parachute in the very poor times, it was a parachute in the good times, and I think it'll be a parachute again.

I take it you'll be voting 'yes' to Lisbon in the second referendum?

I was very confused about Lisbon. I thought it was very, very badly managed. I'm bipartisan as far as politics is concerned, but I thought the government did themselves no favours. I thought they didn't explain it properly. So you ended up with extremists. So I was very confused about what was in there. I think there are probably some very good things in there, I think there are some compromises. I think there should be an opportunity to vote on it again. I know that's a hard thing for some people to swallow, but I don't think the facts were laid out clearly last time. And I think it's very unfair to expect the people to vote on something when the facts are not obvious. I mean, I think there were government ministers who hadn't even read the text of it.

Brian Cowen admitted he hadn't read it!

Well, I'm not being critical of him, but I just think there was a certain amount of complacency that happened around that time. You know, we're all on the pig's back so we can do what we want. That may have been an error.

The chickens have come home to roost.

They have – and there's no glory in it at all. There's no glory in seeing people losing their jobs, people who've never been on the dole. You know, I've been on the dole. I didn't find it humiliating, I just found it difficult going in there and... oh, I dunno. It was just a difficult thing. But I was 17 at the time and there was a certain expectation that this was going to happen. So I was prepared for it."

An assistant, the lovely Frances, knocks on the door and tells Larry it's time for his soundcheck. As he firmly shakes my hand ("Hope you got what you needed!") and prepares to go and hit things, Bono unexpectedly breezes in. I think he's just coming in to say hello, but actually the interview schedule's just been reshuffled. "There's been a change of plan," Frances informs me. "Turns out that Bono has an appointment immediately after the soundcheck so you won't be able to do your interview then. I'm afraid you'll have to do it now."

Wearing his trademark yellow Armani shades and a tan leather jacket, Bono has a long black scarf wrapped around his neck. When he greets me, his voice is lower and huskier than normal.

OLAF TYARANSEN: Have you got a cold or a problem with your throat or something?
BONO: I haven't had throat problems for years, I'm very happy to say.
Are you still smoking cigarettes?
It's easy, you know, I give them up every few months. It's one of those scenarios. But I only smoke when I'm drinking and, as you know, I don't drink very much *(wry smile)*.
Let's get straight into this. It seems that you're mostly writing from the perspectives of other characters on this album...
Well, it's not in any method acting approach or anything like that. It was just a way of getting a fresh starting place. And I'd just kind of worn out my own biography or autobiography. The last two albums were very personal. And I'm not sure if I could bare it any more, let alone anyone else. The irony is, of course, as Oscar Wilde taught us, the mask reveals the man. So you end up in fancy dress revealing your true self. You end up in these very emotional places which you shouldn't understand, but somehow do.
The closing track 'Cedars Of Lebanon' is written from the perspective of a war correspondent.
I, of course, am not a war correspondent, but I've spent a lot of time in those bars with those bravest of men and women. And I've a very deep conviction that were I not doing what I'm doing now, I'd be doing what you are. And I'd probably be writing about music and art and all my other interests, but I can imagine I'd also find myself in some very unsafe places because that's my tendency. So I've a lot of not just sympathy but *empathy* for these people. And I've met them all over – from Sarajevo to El Salvador to Addis Ababa. And they tend to be there for the highest-minded reasons, and then for other ones.
They're usually very damaged people in my experience.
Have you had a lot of experience with them?
Yes and no. I've never been a war correspondent myself, but I've met a few of them.
You've started wars! Ha, ha! You've been through your own wars and, indeed, documented them very well, I might add. But yes, I've had some extraordinary conversations late into the night. But the self-immolation, self-destruction that we see in rock 'n' roll in late night taverns is a very different thing from the kind of damage of people who have witnessed lives extinguished for no good reason. And I obviously relate to that bit of it.
What's your release from that?
It dawned on me, and it was pointed out to me by my friends, and indeed by my missus, that I never ever talk about what I've been through when I'm off in faraway places and experiencing things I'd rather not. That's a phenomenon in itself, that

you just don't want to bring it up. Though there is another phenomenon which is when the trauma really kicks in and you can't *stop* talking about it. And I've met a few like that, too. Who, at dinner, tell the most gruesome stories and don't know that you can no longer finish your meal now. So there are a few like that.

You were recently quoted as saying that your other obligations and activities outside of the band have become so demanding that your creative day now ends at midday. What time do you usually get up in the morning?

I get up at six. I was actually up at five this morning. But I'm up early when I'm working. Unless I'm out. Then I go to bed at six! But I don't go out as much as I used to, hardly at all. But if I have any moments of clarity, it's in those hours. And that's when I write and that's when I read. Now, when I saw I'm not being creative after midday, that wouldn't mean to suggest that there's nothing creative in rehearsals *(laughs)*. Or that there's nothing creative in taking care of business. I think we all know that that is very creative. It's just not *as* creative. And the stillness of the morning before kids get up is a very, very powerful moment for me. And then when they get up, I've got to take them to school, or make their breakfast at the very least, and then get back to work. And then my head gets filled with all the other ideas and I don't think as clearly as I do in the morning.

I saw you in The Clarence resident's lounge the other week. Two days later I opened a newspaper and you were over in Washington. Then I read you were in France somewhere, and the next day you turned up at an event in Dublin. Last weekend you were playing at the Grammys in LA. So my question is – exactly how many Bonos are there?

There's a factory!

You're like Saddam Hussein with all of his body doubles!

Yeah... *thanks!* For the analogy. But the band, when they saw me getting busy, opened a factory. It's just there at the back of Tallaght. And there's various different ones and they're being used for different occasions. But I think, unlike Saddam Hussein, they're hoping I get assassinated! *(laughs)*

You recently told *Q* magazine that you're in a band with three people who persecute you as a national sport. How bad does the persecution get?

It's humour, really. It's a lot of fun being in U2. Unless things are going poorly – then people tend to lose their sense of humour. But if things are going well and we're on the crest of a wave then they're really funny guys. All of them – even Larry!

Larry recently called your friend Tony Blair a war criminal. How do you feel about that?

Well, it's a very serious accusation and I wish he was joking, but I'm sure he wasn't. I think it's very hard to use those words, but I suppose we do all the time. We advance tirades against politicians and people who are in positions of power. And I guess that just goes with their job. And if you take a decision like going to war in Iraq, you know that that's about the most important decision you're ever gonna make in your life. And he's ready to be judged by that decision and he knows that some people think – including I – that it was a grand error. But, you know, I think Larry... it wasn't a surprise when I read it. It wasn't like, *'Oh, Larry thinks this!'* Of course he does! But he thinks Eamon Dunphy's a war criminal *(laughs)*.

Yourself and Paul McGuinness publicly differed on the Radiohead 'honesty box' approach recently. You were quite in favour of their experiment.

I was in favour of the instinct to find a new way of being with your audience. And I thought it was brave and courageous to try these things. I do not like the concept of giving music away free. Yet I don't think that's what they had in mind. They were swapping their music for a relationship with their website. Now, I don't know how many people continued to take it free from LimeWire, but I would consider that a bit of a betrayal – and apparently there were many hundreds of thousands who continued. And that's not good. Now, it says something quite small – just that it takes a lot of people to change a habit, and it might just be that. But it also shows a lack of respect for the band's wishes. I don't think music should be free. And I think the music business has become like lambs to the slaughter. It's very easy to say, *'what has the music business ever done for us? They overpriced their CDs in the '80s and the '90s so fuck 'em!'* But when we say the music business, we're also including artists, bands, lighting people, sound engineers, people who run rehearsal studios. And they're also gonna be out of a job, while the technologists and telecoms and whoever else walk away with the booty.

You've seen the strike in Hollywood over the digital rights by *writers*. Digital rights of the digital space, that was what that strike was about. Because they're very smart and they knew what was coming. But unfortunately the music business – and I include us in it – are not that smart. So now we're back, if we're not careful, to playing troubadours at the table in the castle of the king. We should've been sitting at that table.

Or owned the castle!

Own the castle! That's always been our modus. And decide what's for dinner. And it better not be you! *(laughs)* Which it absolutely most certainly is at the moment.

The Irish government have just reduced their promised African aid again. How do you feel about that?

Well, it's three times now over the last 18 months. And I just spent the morning with (Bishop) Desmond Tutu, and we were talking about it. It's a very difficult situation for a rich rock star to comment on. These are unimaginable circumstances that this government, and indeed every government, find themselves in. Whilst Ireland is in a bigger mess than Germany, it is a matter of great pride to the Germans – and to me who worked with them – that Angela Merkel for 2010's budget increased aid by €900million. This year. Same as she did in 2009 and same as she did in 2008, for the 2010 budget. And made a beautiful speech about this is the point to stand with the poorest of the poor. President Obama has also committed to doubling aid – originally by 2012, but certainly by the time he leaves office. How he gets there, we don't know. We've gotta trust that they'll get there. Same with this [Irish] government. They have enormous respect around the world, the Irish government.

Seriously?

Last year I think we were No. 7 on the charts of leadership on these issues.

And there's a broader conversation to be had, which is what's really happening is capitalism has gone up on trial. The project, so-called, of globalisation has gone up on trial. And there needs to be some honesty about it – both positive as well as negative.

How do you mean?

It is clear that globalisation has brought more people out of extreme poverty than any other idea in the history of civilisation. It is also clear that it started to not work for the bottom billion a few years ago, and needed to be rethought with their inclusion. Examples, the WTO (World Trade Organisation) talks breaking down and really first tier economies, second tier economies getting all the airspace, and nobody really giving a shit about the billion people living on a dollar a day. That was the first clue that globalisation wasn't working for everybody. But up until this point, you could always say that every year the middle classes were growing – look at India. Wherever you looked, it seemed like globalisation was working. And whatever happens now, the rethinking and retooling of this model had better include the majority of people who do not live in the west. Or else there will be some other kind of turbulence or revolt. This is a really important time.

What do you suggest doing?

What we would suggest in the One campaign – DATA is now folding into the One campaign – or what our brainiacs in our policy teams are saying is that this is a time in a global stimulus package to include a percentage for the developing economies. It could be 1%, it could be something small. But remember when we did Live 8, people were saying, "*$50billion? That's outrageous! $25billion for Africa by 2010? That's outrageous! These are ridiculous numbers! You and Geldof are mad!*" Well, now that you see trillion dollar packages happening, do we look greedy then? I don't think so. There needs to be new people involved in the global economy. It's good for everyone if Africa comes through. We saw what happened when India started to develop. India has a middle-class now of over 200 million people. And that's one of the reasons why there was such swagger in the City of London and on Wall Street, because Russia was coming in, blah, blah, blah. So we need Africa. It shouldn't be seen as aid, it should be seen as investment.

Finally, not to be boring on this subject because I know you're here to talk about music, but it's always after crises, and major, major catastrophes, that we reboot the thinking globally. You saw it after the First World War with the League of Nations, after the Second World War with the United Nations, the IMF, the World Bank, the Breton Woods Institute and the WTO. All those things after 9/11, the sort of Ground Zero and the second Ground Zero just up the road from each other on Wall Street, and the fallout from both of those events – geopolitical strife and economic turmoil – this is one of those moments. And I think this is a moment to re-imagine what the whole thing should look like.

What are people like Bill Gates and Warren Buffet like to deal with?

You know, as shabby a believer as I am, I am always amazed that some of the finest spirits that I've met in my life are… *(pauses)*. If you think of Bill Gates and Warren Buffet, who've combined their fortunes to really transform the world for the poorest of the poor, it's an overwhelming thing. I think it's *$60billion* they've decided to give away. It wasn't enough for Bill Gates to change the world once, he's doing it twice. And it's so far-reaching, and so beyond the concept of philanthropy. Because the really genius thing about Bill Gates is that he's applying that business *nous* and that sort of hard-headed tough mindedness that he applied to Microsoft to solving some of the world's biggest problems in global health. The rotavirus or trying to rid the world of the anopheles mosquito. I mean, it is a shock to still think that nearly 3,000 kids die every day of a mosquito bite in Africa.

How is Gates helping you directly?

He's supported me with all of my work. He gave me a million dollars in the year 2000 to help set up and formalise operations, because President Bush wouldn't be as sympathetic to the haversack brigade that I used to travel with. I would stay in the posh hotel and my people would stay in the guesthouse and use Kinko's for their office. But because the Bush administration was a lot more formal, we got what we needed to set up an office in DC, and eventually in London, and now we have one in Berlin and stuff. And Bill Gates was instrumental in financing that. He then publicly announced that it was the best million dollars he'd ever spent, and that was a huge thing for him to say. He got one thing wrong, though.

What was that?

He saw that I was getting friendly with Warren Buffet and he said, *'Bono, if you think that you'll ever get a penny out of Warren Buffet, you can forget about it. I've been trying for years. He's only going to deal with that when he's dead!'* Or something like that. And then Warren gave him all his money, but his family – through his daughter Susie – has been also helping us organise and is a strategic partner and on our board. So I've got to know Bill very well, and Warren quite well. And I'm really taken aback by them. Warren's a really funny guy. He's a comedian. In fact, I brought my kids to a dinner with him once in New York and they said, *'You know, that's the best grown-up's dinner we ever had!'* Ha, ha!

Do any wealthy Irish businessmen support your ventures?

Well at home, I don't know if they want me to say this, but I get a lot of support from Paddy McKillen, Derek Quinlan, Johnny Ronan, Sean Mulryan and Bernard McNamara. They give me lots of money every year, because they want the Irish to be represented.

Property developers?

Some of them are interested in the detail of the work, some of them less so, but I have a dinner with them once or twice a year where I turn up to tell them what I'm doing with their money. I'm usually standing up for about two minutes when they all tell me to fuck off and sit down, and put a drink in my hand *(laughs)*. And they're just the easiest people to deal with. They literally wouldn't even ask me for a ticket to a U2 show. Amazing people in terms of support. But Irish people are very good at this stuff.

We often see pictures of you with prominent politicians, religious leaders and business moguls. But what are the meetings you can't get?

It was very difficult at first to meet the Japanese Prime Minister, because they're very formal in government. But again, I think the association with Bill Gates really helps. And the fact that when we do get in the door, I know what I'm talking about.

And our team are at the cutting edge of development ideas. So usually people leave the meeting going, *'Oh, I'm glad I took that'*. But while some people can be difficult to get to, it used to be a lot harder.

Wasn't [Canadian PM] Stephen Harper quite dismissive of you last year?

Yeah, he was *(laughs)*. Apparently he'd like to meet up now. But to be fair to him, we did torture him. And we will continue to. The Canadians are the only surplus economy, and they weren't ready to make the same commitment – 2.7% by 2015 – as everyone else had done in the US. But Canada's one of my favourite places on earth, but it's in the grips of quite a conservative point of view on development. Everywhere else we've managed to work with conservatives, particularly religious conservatives, to move them on these things, but we couldn't manage to in Canada.

Are you optimistic that now that there's an African-American in the White House it'll make a massive difference to what you're attempting to do?

Yeah. Obama has some very smart people around him on these issues. What has to be done now is, and what we're working on now is, a kind of weaving together of three strands that will most preoccupy his administration. You might call them the three extremes – extreme ideology, extreme climate and extreme poverty. I'm talking about foreign policy, not what's happening in America. The weaving together of those three strands into a cohesive foreign policy will be Hillary Clinton's job. So we're talking about what we call 'the grand bargain' – which is how the developing world can benefit from a deal on climate change, for instance. Because the poorest countries played the least role in causing climate change, but they will pay the biggest price for it – in low lying areas like Bangladesh, for instance.

Have you ever attended a meeting of the Bilderberg Group? *(A highly secretive group of around 130 of the world's most influential politicians, bankers and businessmen who meet annually – OT).*

No. I've heard of them, but I've never attended. Why do you ask?

Well, as somebody who's walked the corridors of power, do you think that many of the most important decisions are made behind closed doors? In other words, that we're all being fooled by a sort of democracy for dummies?

The most shocking thing to me is the role that personal chemistry plays. That's the thing I wasn't expecting. Unlikely allies are made just because people like the look in each other's eye or they happen to make each other laugh. And entrenched positions are relaxed based on that kind of thing. I was very taken by that. The other thing I suppose I've noticed is the preposterousness of how conspiracy theorists really fundamentally don't recognise the human trait of not being able to keep a secret. You know, people can't keep a secret *(laughs)*. And everything outs in the end. And these cabals of influence, in the end, they all out each other. I suppose why I'm saying that is because I've learned that it's not so mysterious. The only frightening thing that I get is not that somebody's in charge that we don't know about – like the little old man in the *Wizard of Oz* – but the real shock is not that there are faceless people in charge that we don't know who are pulling the strings of this world. The real shock is that maybe no-one's in charge – and that things move more like the weather than we would like. And you can really see that with the markets. Having said that, though, there are systems in place, and hard-working civil servants, and in the end who's actually sitting in the Oval Office and the IFF really matters. Because they really can move the goalposts if they want to.

Back to music. 'Breathe' is currently my favourite song on the album…

Me, too! Me, too! It's great to perform it.

Lyrically it reminds me of Stipe's *E-Bow The Letter* and Dylan's *Subterranean Homesick Blues*, but also a little of one of Allen Ginsberg's raps. I remember when he visited Ireland in 1995, you two did some recording together. Was that ever used anywhere?

Were you not at the event in Liberty Hall? No, you were at the Galway reading, weren't you? The Liberty Hall thing was a great event. It was great. I remember I bought him a suit at Louis Copeland's. So he had this suit. And in fact, Ginsberg when he died, he auctioned everything he owned – every single thing he owned. Some people were shocked. Well, his friends were. It was Gavin who introduced him to me – he was a very good friend of Gavin Friday's. And he was always meticulous about everything he did. And he sold all of his stuff off for that Buddhist institute, Napa. Anyway, I looked at the stuff and I thought I'd buy one of his pens or something. And then I saw a copy of Oscar Wilde's *The Ideal Husband*, which I thought was so funny – for him, if you think about it. So I said to myself, 'I have to buy that!' Because I collect first editions. And I got it. I didn't get some of the other things I bid for – I guess the pens were very popular, and I didn't buy the suit. I bought the Uncle Sam hat and I gave it to Gavin for his 40th birthday – you know, the famous Uncle Sam hat he wore in photographs? And I got the book for me. When it came back, I opened it, and written inside was, '*To Allen Ginsberg – Love, Bono*'. Ha, ha! I'd forgotten I'd given it to him. But Ginsberg was a real maestro as well as a professor, and he was very good to me. And you're absolutely right about the lineage. Dylan will credit him. Obviously America was a big influence on *The Joshua Tree*, as was *Howl*. And because my style of singing is operatic, I use a lot of vowel sounds. Very restrictive for a writer. So sometimes it's nice to break away from that and just use a sort of scattergun. And as regards Michael Stipe – it's strange. It was his favourite. He loved that and encouraged me down that direction.

Your debut *New York Times* column read a bit like that.

It's from the same flow. Just a desire to use words that are not vowels.

How often will you be contributing to the paper?

I have one I'm working on at the moment. They'd like one a month, but if it's one every two months or one every three months, so be it. They've given me free reign. They've been very good. As I explained to them, I'm not very good with full stops or commas. And this is the *New York Times!* Actually in a way, I gave them the curveball of Frank Sinatra, thinking I'd see how far I can go and they went, 'Yep!' They made a few little nips and tucks, but that was it.

I know you didn't write the song from your own perspective, but on 'Cedars Of Lebanon' you sing the line, *"Choose your enemies carefully 'cos they will define you."* So who are your enemies?

I think in that sense that speaks for U2 because we've always picked interesting enemies. That's always what separated us. We didn't pick the obvious – the establishment, the 'man', us against them. That's so corny to me! Our band was always about there's no 'them', there's only us. The enemies are the things that are in the way of you realising your potential. They can be all kinds of things. Your vanity. They can be your demons. You've dealt with your demons, Olaf, and you've written about them very honestly. And I think that's the first way of dealing with it. I just think you've gotta be very careful with the fights you pick, because they'll take a lot out of you.

Fifteen minutes after I've interviewed Bono, myself and Regine Moylett are seated at a front row table in the near-empty hall watching the band soundcheck on the Earl's Court stage. "I can't believe they've set up all the tables 24 hours before the show," she says, disgustedly examining some dusty cutlery. "I'll be bringing a bacterial wipe tomorrow night." U2 will be opening the Brits in 24 hours time and, although they're only performing one song, the preparations are still intense. Much like the overblown start of the ZOO TV shows, they kick off with Bono standing on a platform above the rest of the band. Behind him a massive screen displays the lyrics (*"The future needs a big kiss/ Winds blow with a twist"*) and various related imagery – including a sperm fertilising an egg at one point.

They run-through 'Get On Your Boots' three or four times, playing it slightly differently each time. Eventually, Paul McGuinness – affectionately known as 'Magoo' when he's out of earshot – wanders over for a chat. Balding and be-suited, he's been the band's manager from day one. Considering they formed in 1976, this must be a rock 'n' roll world record. McGuinness refuses to divulge any concrete details about the band's forthcoming tour, except to say that they'll only be playing stadiums and will be doing something that's never been done before. "We haven't fully worked out the tour details," he explains. "The availability of certain stadiums depends entirely on the soccer leagues."

"Do you sometimes find yourself hoping a football team will lose a match just so a stadium will be available?" I ask. "That has happened in the past," he chuckles. "Many years ago, I found myself paying extremely close attention to the American ice hockey and baseball leagues for that very reason."

When the band finally wrap up on stage, their work is far from finished. I find myself waiting outside their dressing room while they repeatedly watch their performances on a TV screen. It's approaching 9pm by the time Adam Clayton is free to talk to me. Dressed in a military style grey jacket, the short-haired bass player reminds me more than a little of a life-sized Action Man (despite his slight lisp).

"Sorry, but I'm starving," he says, as Frances delivers a silver-foiled plate to our table (fish and vegetables). "I'm going to have to eat while we do this."

OLAF TYARANSEN: You guys have just watched that soundcheck several times. Do you always pay such forensic attention to detail?

ADAM CLAYTON: Well, it wasn't one run-through we were watching, it was every run-through that we did. Because with each run-through we were trying different moves with the cameras, we were adjusting the lighting and we were performing it slightly differently. Which means that, when you get to view it back, it's kind of when you get to do your work, to be honest. You view it back and you see what's working and what makes for a better show. You're working with the lighting people and the production people and the camera people. So they're trying to work out their moves, you're trying to work out your moves. Once they know what you're doing and you know what they're doing, it all comes together.

Have you played much recently?

We played the Grammys last week, but we haven't got our proper touring hats on yet. TV shows are just a different part of the brain.

You're going to be David Letterman's house band for a full week next month, aren't you?

Yeah. TV shows are different. You've gotta find a way to work with the cameras. And four years on from the last time you did it, it's difficult. Because you've gotta connect with the people in TV-land, as they call it *(laughs)*.

I've already spoken to all the other guys about Fez, but the only thing I want to ask you about it is did you buy any new carpets? Because I heard you auctioned off your old collection recently.

Ha, ha! Well, it was much excitement and much ado about nothing. I had a load of carpets that I bought years ago. They weren't particularly special, but I did sell them a while ago and I think there was a little bit of attention. But I do think it was rather a local piece *(laughs)*. I don't think anyone else was that interested in it.

Do you find that kind of media attention bothersome?

It can be. It's tricky. I don't actually read the Irish press that much. You know, Bono turns up at a nightclub, Bono turns up to meet Desmond Tutu. It's like, I don't know who reads it, but there's gotta be a point where they say, 'Okay, enough!'

You could never be accused of courting media attention…

Oh, I don't think people are all that interested in bass players. I think they're much more interested in people who say controversial things.

Which you don't tend to do.

Well, I don't know that much about politics or all that other stuff so I tend to have a much simpler outlook on it.

Every other member of the band except you has children at this stage. So are you viewed by the U2 brood as their crazy uncle?

Ha! *(Mock outrage)*. I don't know, you'd have to ask them. 'Crazy'? Hopefully not!

Do you have any desire to have children yourself?

Em … *(pauses)* I thought it was maybe something that I wanted – or maybe I thought it was something that I should have. But I think I'm over that. I quite like my life.

And how is your life outside of U2? How do you amuse yourself?

Well, U2's pretty much a fulltime thing. When it's not U2 business, so to speak, I try to stay in touch with music and art and film. I'm always listening to new stuff, going to gigs. I'm always in bookshops looking around at things. Going to the movies. I mean, there isn't much downtime. But I find probably because I am single and I am pretty mobile, that I get to a lot of different kinds of shows and that kind of thing.

You also make short films for U2.com.

Oh, that reminds me, I should've brought a camera to this! I must bring one tomorrow. But yeah, we've had this website for ages and we didn't really do much with it in terms of doing interviews or whatever. And I just saw these great cameras, these flip cameras, and I thought we should just film stuff, but not film it in an *'I'm trying to make a film'* kind of way. Like the camera might be stuck under a table or whatever. So they're rough and ready. I mean, I hope that it says as much about the person behind the camera as it does about the person in front of it. And they're edited a little bit when we put them out, they're like maybe a couple of minutes at a time, which doesn't really give you much of a feeling of the moment. Which I would prefer. I'd prefer it to run for 20 minutes, but I think people would be bored by that. They'd realise how boring making a record can be.

Your house has a pretty large garden. Are you a keen gardener?

Ha, ha! Not really. I know a little bit about it. I like the fact that you have a year to change your mind with every decision, but that's about it. *(An assistant enters the room and delivers dessert - two hempseed cakes with iced marijuana leaf designs on top)* Wow! I think that's a hash cookie!

You've been clean for about 14 years now, haven't you?

Actually, it's just over ten.

Has that been difficult or is it getting easier?

It became easier in the last two years. I think the first five or six or seven years, I really had to learn how to live in a new way. And it made it very difficult for me because I had to kind of cut myself off a bit and not go out and be quite controlling. But I'm sort of over that now so I'm now going out and having a bit more fun.

Did you have to change your circle of friends?

I didn't so much change my circle of friends, but there's a lot less people to hang out with when you're going to bed early.

Even in terms of the band – people going for a pint after the show. Do you miss that?

If people want to go for a pint after the show, I don't feel particularly left out. I think the big difference for me, and the big difference in terms of what happens when you stop drinking and drugging, is that your days become more important and your nights become less important. It's hard to imagine going to a nightclub. I mean, I have been to a couple of nightclubs recently, over Christmas and whatnot, but it just really underlined the fact that there's nothing particularly there for me. You have to be off your face to go to a nightclub *(laughs)*.

Do you have much input into the songs outside of your bass duties? Do you throw lyrical suggestions at Bono or anything?

I guess very occasionally. I think Bono really takes on absolutely the lion's share and more of the lyrics, and what he's had to do on this record and on other records is very often he'll write a draft of lyrics for the way the song is, and he'll sing them and realise that they're not working – and its not just a lyric thing, it's a melody thing or whatever. And then he'll rewrite a melody and then have to rewrite a lyric and then come back to it. So in those situations, I wouldn't really say that my contribution is lyrical, but in terms of the process of refining his work, I guess we're all editors to some extent.

In terms of the bass, are you constantly striving to improve? You studied in Jamaica at one point, didn't you?

I travel a fair bit. But usually, I have happy accidents. I'm not really a good enough musician to play what's in my head or what's on other people's records. So I tend to just try and play in an inarticulate way what I'm hearing, and something interesting comes out and then I just follow that down. I mean, I always try and do something out of my comfort zone. I try and move away from what I might have done before. On this record I made a conscious effort to kind of pull out old basses that I haven't played for a while that had a different sound or to go with different amps. But in the end, I'm not that thoughtful about it. It's like, very often the way we work is there's a moment of inspiration and a moment of magic and you kind of just have to be there to catch it. Very often Danny might say to me, '*Try this*' or '*Try that*'. Or The Edge or even Bono. In the old days, I might've said, '*No, I can do this!*' Now I go, '*Thanks very much, I'll take it*'. That's what you do. You know, little gifts come along and you kinda go, '*Oh, I can see what that will do and I'll take it*'.

Do you play any other instruments?

I can do a little guitar, and that's what I started on, but it's pretty rudimentary. Sometimes something comes out of it, but not that often. I think Edge has emerged and grown into being a very fine composer of what we do – particularly over the last couple of records. He's really honed his chops.

U2 are now into their fourth decade together. How long can you see the band continuing?

It depends on which member of the band you talk to. I sort of think well... what else would I do? I don't actually know how to do anything else. And I feel now that if you've been a part of those songs, if you have that history, I think you're entitled to play them until you die. As long as people are gonna turn up. Maybe people don't even need to turn up. If that's your life's work, if that's what you do, I think that's fine. If I lost interest in music, if I lost interest in playing and performing, maybe it'd be fine to grow rhododendrons or camellias or something. But I haven't lost it and I don't think I will lose it. Because the older you get, the more you appreciate that to have a career as long as U2 has, and to be able to stand up in front of an audience of people who're 20 or maybe even 30 years younger than you, and be relevant or entertained and connect, that's an amazing thing. I wouldn't walk away from that.

In the early days, you were a sceptic while the rest of the band were embracing Christianity. Have your thoughts on that changed? Do you believe in an afterlife?

I don't really think about afterlife. I'm more concerned with the here and now. That'll sort of take care of itself, I'm sure.

Are you a religious or spiritual person in any way?

I wouldn't say I'm religious. I'm spiritual, but it relates very much to the here and now and to the everyday.

I'm asking, really, because I'm wondering if you believed in the Alcoholics Anonymous idea of a 'higher power'?

Em... I really don't want to discuss that *(laughs)*.

Bono tells me he has trouble sleeping at night. Do you?

No, I'm very lucky that way. I found before rehab I had trouble sleeping. I was surprised to learn that alcohol adds to insomnia. I'd always thought that alcohol helps you sleep. So since I have stopped taking alcohol, my sleep has been much better. Occasionally, in stressful situations, I don't sleep. And I don't sleep very well if I'm travelling.

Are the friendships within the band still as strong as ever?

I think it's as strong. I think it's sort of stronger. I felt very much at the beginning of this project, and I think it's continued throughout this project, that when we were working up the material, people were being very generous with each other, they were being really supportive and nice. And it was because we started out the project without an agenda. You know, there was no clock ticking when we started. It was just to see if the band could step into a different area. And that different area, in a way, was performing much more within ourselves, for ourselves, than performing out there and trying to grab people's attention. And I think that spirit continued through the recording of the record. I personally feel – and it is a personal view – that there's been a shift in the band over the last couple of records. And it may be an age thing, but I think in our twenties and thirties the band was kind of restrictive. From my point of view, there was a little bit of arrogance in going, *'Oh, can't we just do it my way?'* And now I think I really have started to appreciate what everyone else does and actually go, *'You know, this is actually really good the way it is'*, and I'm able to do stuff that I couldn't have done on my own with these guys' support. And I don't know if that's what's happened for everyone, but that's certainly been my firsthand experience over the last few years.

I read an interview with Brian Eno that was done during the Olympic Studio stages of recording this album. He began drawing a complicated graph to explain to the interviewer the various gestations a U2 song goes through – from good to great to awful and back again – during the recording process. He was going to bring it into the studio to show you afterwards. Can you remember it?

Brian's always drawing little graphs about something *(laughs)*. I think he's got a very good understanding of what we go through. And he had an interesting attitude to it this time, where he started to enjoy being part of the band. He liked the fact that he could work on something in the morning with us, and by the evening it had turned into something. Brian's method of working is very much he likes to do it for a while and then move on. He likes to leave it as an unresolved piece very often. And that's not what we do.

What do you do?

We like to fully resolve something and work it through to the end. And sometimes we overwork it, but generally if we have enough time, and if we make good decisions, it always gets better. And that was a unique thing with this record.

That when we took the decision not to finish it in June or July for a November release, it really allowed us to go back to certain things. It allowed us to look at the proposed list of tracks and pull a few more back onto the record that we hadn't worked on, and take a few off. And it changed the balance of the record. It really allowed Bono to re-sing a few things and to rewrite some lyrics. So by the time we finished in December, everything was pretty well rounded on the record. Certainly this is the first record in a very long time where I've kind of gone, *'I understand and I know every decision that was made – and I back it'*.

Are U2 a democratic unit?

It's a strange kind of democracy in that some people have louder voices than others, but if three people think something's a good idea and I don't think it's a good idea… they're probably right *(laughs)*!

Interview over, meal eaten, and all good, Adam shakes my hand and warmly wishes me well. Then he rejoins Edge and Larry in the next room. They're still watching their performances and making notes. Seems like a good time to leave. "We're not quite done here," Adam explains. "This may take a little longer."

No line on the horizon… and no flies on these guys.

{MARCH, 2009}

ALSO FROM HOTPRESS BOOKS

THE STORY OF O by Olaf Tyaransen
Described as Ireland's *Catcher In The Rye*, this tale of teenage sex, drugs, rock'n'roll – and of course music – is hysterically funny and poignantly moving in equal measure.

"It's like The Secret Diary Of Adrian Mole, only with cannabis-induced hazes." *– Sunday Times.*

"Very funny and searingly honest" *– Irish Times*

SEX LINES by Olaf Tyaransen
Delving into the wonderful world of sex, Olaf attempts to find a Russian bride, is asked to be an extra on a porn movie shoot, attends a fetish spanking club and much more.

"Hysterically funny" *– Sunday Independent*

PALACE OF WISDOM by Olaf Tyaransen
The "enfant terrible" of Irish journalism is back, with a remarkable book that explores the dark and dangerous currents in which artists, celebrities, musicians, writers and politicos alike – including the author himself – are wont to swim. And sometimes drown...

U2: THREE CHORDS AND THE TRUTH
The International Bestseller Edited by Niall Stokes
Critical, entertaining, comprehensive and revealing, *U2: Three Chords And The Truth* never misses a beat as it brings you, in words and pictures, a complete portrait of U2 in the process of becoming a legend.

THEY ARE OF IRELAND by Declan Lynch
They Are Of Ireland is a hilarious who's who of famous Irish characters – and chancers – from the worlds of politics, sport, religion, the Arts, entertainment and the media. Written by Declan Lynch, one of Ireland's wittiest writers, this is a book of comic writing that actually makes you laugh out loud.

ORDERING INFO

All of the above titles are available online from
www.hotpress.com/books
Or write to Hot Press Books, 13 Trinity St., Dublin 2.

TRADE ENQUIRIES Tel: + 353 (1) 2411 500 or Fax: + 353 (1) 2411 538 or email hotpressbooks@hotpress.ie.

ALSO FROM HOTPRESS BOOKS

MY BOY: THE PHILIP LYNOTT STORY
No.1 Bestseller in Ireland
by Philomena Lynott (with Jackie Hayden)
The remarkable story of Philip Lynott, the black Irish street poet and rock legend, *My Boy* is not only an intimate and revealing portrait of an Irish icon, but an immensely moving account of a mother's devotion to her beloved son through the good times and the bad.

BEYOND BELIEF
No.2 Bestseller in Ireland by Liam Fay
Liam Fay has won a national journalism award for his brilliant and hilarious investigation into the wild side of faith in Ireland. Uproarious, revealing and thought-provoking, *Beyond Belief* is a triumph.

McCANN: WAR AND PEACE IN NORTHERN IRELAND
by Eamonn McCann
Published to coincide with the 30th anniversary of the Civil Rights movement, in which the author played a prominent part, *McCann: War And Peace In Northern Ireland* is essential reading for anyone interested in one of the major stories of our time.

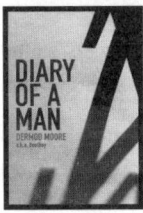

DIARY OF A MAN by Dermod Moore
Diary Of A Man is a wonderfully open, honest, finely written – and highly sexed – account of one person's journey through the myriad attractions and pitfalls of being a free agent in contemporary society. Written from a gay perspective, it is essential reading for anyone in search of the truth about themselves, exploring with passion and insight the needs that drive us, the choices we make and the search for fulfilment that is at the heart of our collective journey.

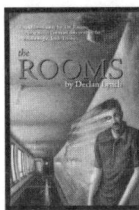

THE ROOMS
By Declan Lynch
The Rooms is an electrifying novel by one of the brightest stars of Irish fiction, Declan Lynch, that brings you inside the biggest secret organisation in the world. A love story that beguiles and challenges, it is at once powerful, moving and deeply revealing in its depiction of the world inside and outside of AA. In the doomy, wise-cracking Neil, it introduces a new kind of anti-hero to the pantheon of Irish fiction. One that you will never forget...